The Yale Ben Jonson

GENERAL EDITORS: ALVIN B. KERNAN AND RICHARD B. YOUNG

D0170051

A. Cokes

A Servant by his Master send abroad,
or with a Message, or some vsefull loade,
And stayes to gase on strangers differing
Sigtes parrells nowelties is a right Cokes,

Ben Jonson: Bartholomew Fair

EDITED BY EUGENE M. WAITH

NEW HAVEN AND LONDON:

YALE UNIVERSITY PRESS, 1963

Copyright © 1963 by Yale University.

All rights reserved. This book may not be
reproduced, in whole or in part, in any form
(except by reviewers for the public press),
without written permission from the publishers.

Library of Congress catalog card number: 63–13975

ISBN 0-300-09470-1

Contents

Preface of the General Editors

The Yale edition of the plays of Ben Jonson is intended to meet two fundamental requirements: first, the need of the modern reader for a readily intelligible text which will convey, as nearly as an edition can, the life and movement which invests the plays on the stage; second, the need of the critic and scholar for a readily available text which represents as accurately as possible, though it does not reproduce, the plays as Jonson printed them. These two requirements are not, we believe, incompatible, but the actual adjustment of one to the other has been determined by the judgment of the individual editors. In details of editorial practice, therefore, the individual volumes of the edition may vary, but in basic editorial principle they are consistent.

The texts are based primarily on the two folio volumes of Jonson's *Works*, the first published in 1616, the second in 1640. The 1616 volume was seen through the press by Jonson himself, and therefore represents to a degree unusual for dramatic texts of the period what the dramatist intended us to have. The 1640 volume presents more difficult textual problems; though Jonson himself began preparing individual plays for it as early as 1631, these were carelessly printed—a fact of which he was painfully aware—and the folio, under the editorship of the eccentric Sir Kenelm Digby, was not completed until after Jonson's death. The quarto editions have also been consulted, and where a quarto reading has been preferred by an editor the necessary information appears in the notes.

In editing Jonson for the modern reader, one of the central problems is that of annotation, a problem that is complicated rather than solved by providing a catalogue of Jonson's immense classical learning or of his contemporary lore. We have believed that annotation is most helpful not when it identifies or defines details but when it clarifies the context of the detail. Consequently, citation of sources, allusions, and analogues, whether classical or colloquial, has been controlled by and restricted to what is relevant in the judgment of the editors to a meaningful understanding of the dramatic and poetic values of the passage in question and of the play as a whole. For the same reason, all editorial apparatus—introductions, notes, and glosses—frequently and deliberately deal with critical and interpretative matters in order to reanimate the topical details and give substance to the imaginative world each play creates.

To provide a readable text it has been necessary to revise some of the printing conventions of the seventeenth-century editions. In order to identify himself with the classical tradition of comedy, Jonson used as a model for his *Works* the first printed editions of Plautus, Terence, and Aristophanes, heading each scene with a list of all characters appearing in it, without marking individual entrances and exits. The present edition follows the more familiar practice of listing only those characters on stage at the beginning of a scene and indicates all entrances and exits. Stage directions, kept to an absolute minimum, have also been added where understanding of the dialogue depends on an implied but not explicit action, or on an unspecified location. With the exception of the first speech ascription in each scene, which is usually omitted by Jonson, all such additions and all material not in the original text have been enclosed in square brackets.

Where Jonson printed all verse in the metrical unit of the line, whether or not it represents the speech of one or more than one character, this edition divides the parts of such lines according to the speaker, and indicates the metrical unit by echeloning the parts of the line.

The original punctuation has been followed where its rhetorical effect has a dramatic value, but modern pointing has been used wherever necessary to clarify syntactical obscurities and to eliminate obvious errors or mere eccentricity. Spelling has been modernized except where orthographical change affects either meaning or meter. For example, where Jonson prints *'d* to indicate an unstressed ending of a past participle, this edition prints *-ed*, and where Jonson printed *-ed* to indicate stress this edition prints *-èd*. Jonson's frequent elisions, e.g. *th'* or *i'*, are retained, and all unusual accents are marked.

In the original text the entrance of a new character usually, though not invariably, initiates a new scene, so that there are many more scenes than a fully modernized text would allow. This edition retains Jonson's act and scene divisions in the belief that in most cases they represent the linking effect, the *liason des scènes*, characteristic of the developing neoclassic drama; in all cases they represent Jonson's own conception of dramatic form; and the fact of form is part of the meaning of his plays.

Retaining the original act and scene divisions means that the act and scene numbers of the Yale Ben Jonson correspond to those of the standard edition of Jonson, edited by C. H. Herford and Percy Simpson (11 vols. Oxford, 1925–52). This enables the reader to consult with ease the notes of Herford and Simpson, who list all classical sources and analogues, and to refer without difficulty to the original text.

Introduction

Ben Jonson is at his best in *Bartholomew Fair*. His prose has its distinctive combination of grotesque exuberance and iron control. His perceptions are at their sharpest, as he records all the odd details which fasten the play to seventeenth-century London —customs, habits of speech, bits of local gossip, reference to recent events—and the eye which sees this surface so clearly also sees through it to what is archetypal. Without losing any of its particularity, the Fair presents us with the very patterns of folly. Jonson's characterization is as varied and lively as in any of his plays and his comic invention runs on to the end as if it could never tire.

When the play was first performed, in 1614 (see Appendix II), the other major comedies, *Volpone*, *Epicene*, and *The Alchemist*, had already made Jonson a great name in the theater. His reputation was enhanced by this new comedy, which struck audiences all the more favorably in contrast to Jonson's most recent play, *Catiline*, a tragedy which had been received very coldly. There is a tradition, recorded by William Oldys, an eighteenth-century scholar, that *Bartholomew Fair* inspired the famous exclamation, "O rare Ben Jonson," later inscribed on his tombstone. The first enthusiasm for the play did not last, however, and until quite recently it has been underrated. Undoubtedly, the coarse language of some of the characters is partly responsible. Ursula, Knockem, and their sleazy companions belong to a rough and ill-smelling world of which their conversation is a humorous, but for some tastes too accurate, reflection. And Humphrey Wasp, short-tempered and foul-mouthed, is hardly one's idea of a proper "governor" for a young man. But more than changing canons of decency in language is involved in these shifts of reputation. *Bartholomew Fair* has suffered by comparison to *Volpone*, *The Alchemist*, and *Epicene*.

It is not hard to guess at some of the reasons for this deprecia-tion, and they will serve as pointers to the special quality of the play. In the first place, no single character dominates it to provide the intense focus of interest found in the other three. Even Ursula, massive and brilliant creation that she is, does not control the action like Volpone or Subtle, whose machinations constantly fascinate at the same time that they repel. Nor is she, like Morose in *Epicene*, the chief "blocking character" (to use Northrop Frye's term) against whom the whole strategy of the plot is planned and most of the satiric barbs directed. Ursula's booth is indeed a central point from which most of the chicanery and corruption of the Fair radiate, but the active agents are her accomplices, Knockem and Whit, Edgworth and Nightingale, who are less dependent on her than are Dol and Face on Subtle in *The Alchemist*. Among these various imposers upon society in *Bartholomew Fair* interest is more diffused than it is in the preced-ing comedies.

Furthermore, the direction of the satirical thrust is less im-mediately clear. In *Epicene* Dauphine, who is being put upon by his misanthropic uncle, commands our sympathy in his plots with his friends Truewit and Clerimont. Here the tricksters, as is so often the case in Roman comedy, rescue the world of the play from the domination of a comic tyrant. In *Volpone* and *The Alchemist*, where neither the tricksters nor most of their dupes inspire sympathy, it is abundantly clear how the audience is expected to feel about the greed and self-deception of which most of the characters are guilty. In *Bartholomew Fair*, satirical exposure of the tricksters who impose on Bartholomew Cokes and, to a lesser extent, on Mistress Overdo and Mistress Littlewit, is balanced by ridicule of Justice Overdo and Rabbi Busy, the arch-enemies of the tricksters. In the conclusion the enemies of the Fair are exposed even more mercilessly than the swindlers within it, and the laughter is at the expense of knaves, gulls, and reformers alike. Not only is none of the main characters truly sympathetic, but the attitudes satirized seem, in a sense, to cancel each other out. One is obliged to make a more complex judgment on the folly of the play than scorn for a preposterous tyrant or the orthodox condemnation of greed. Both in the mechanics of its plot and in the satirical view which they support, *Bartholomew Fair* is a more complex comedy than those which preceded it.

Finally, it may be that the style of this play has seemed deficient when compared to the accepted examples of Jonson's best. Style, for anyone so conscious of literary decorum as Jonson, is so intimately related to setting that one can hardly be surprised if the prose of his Smithfield lacks the grace of the poetry he devised for the Venetian splendors of *Volpone*. Even the spurious glitter of Volpone's prayer to his gold or his courtship of Celia has an undeniable attraction. Similarly, the clever young men in *Epicene*, who inhabit higher strata of London society than anyone in *Bartholomew Fair*, converse with an Ovidian urbanity and a quickness of repartee beyond the reach of a Littlewit. Quarlous can be witty on occasion, but we have nothing here like the opening dialogue of *Epicene*. *The Alchemist* is closer to *Bartholomew Fair* in setting: there, too, characters from the London underworld are pitted against citizens, though there is one knight amongst them, Sir Epicure Mammon. It is not so much a difference of milieu as it is the choice of mode which distinguishes the styles of these two plays. Despite the many realistic touches in

3

The Alchemist, Jonson chooses to emphasize the fantastic element in the avaricious dreams of his characters, giving his comic over-reacher, Sir Epicure, poetry which is magnificently excessive, and constructing vast and crazy edifices out of Subtle's alchemical terms. In the prose of *Bartholomew Fair* it is appropriateness which is emphasized. Though there are a few splendid set pieces, such as Quarlous' diatribe against widows and Overdo's oration against tobacco,[1] Jonson goes further in the direction of realistic dialogue than in most of his other plays. The subtle modulations of this style constitute a major achievement, but one which is more apparent after a second or third reading than at the first.

The brief comparisons I have made suggest that the success of *Bartholomew Fair* is more dependent on the expert joining of many pieces than upon the shaping of any one of them; that its comic structure is complex—a delicate balance of forces; and that its style, marked by verisimilitude, is also less distinguished by single brilliant strokes than by the adjustments which make a unified verbal texture out of the clearly distinct voices of many characters. To this general impression of superbly ordered multiplicity one must add another, of outstanding vitality, for no comedy of Jonson's—perhaps none of any author's—exudes more of the "life force" which Bernard Shaw so admired. Old Ursula, sweating profusely in her pig-booth, "all fire and fat," is the perfect emblem of this force, but there is hardly a character who does not share in it. It is the nature of a fair to be all movement—to be popping with activities of every sort—and the vitality of the play, as well as its complexity, is therefore directly related to Jonson's choice of this milieu.

The cloth fair established in Smithfield in 1120 and held annually on St. Bartholomew's Day, August 24, had become a

---

1. See Jonas Barish, *Ben Jonson and the Language of Prose Comedy* (Cambridge, Mass., 1960), pp. 187–239.

major event by the early seventeenth century. Many other kinds of merchandise than cloth were sold by the vendors who set up their booths there, and as at all fairs, visitors were tempted by various kinds of food (Bartholomew-pig was the best known) and by entertainment, reputable and disreputable. Naturally, it attracted its share of criminals, from confidence men to thieves and pimps, and consequently had its session of the special court of Pie Powders, so called from the French, *pied poudreux*, or dusty foot, a term which needs no explaining to the visitor of any fair. For a writer of comedy, or still more for a satirist, a fair provides an ideal bringing-together of the most diverse types—any types he may choose to ridicule—in a situation which is itself an obvious symbol for the "vanity of human wishes." Since the Puritans had been quick to seize upon this last significance, and to decry fairs along with May Day celebrations, stage plays, luxurious clothes, and church ritual as manifestations of heathen immorality and idolatry, Jonson was provided by the history of his times with one natural source of conflict in his drama. He had only to include a Puritan family among the visitors.

From the opening of Act II to the end of the play the Fair holds the stage, its distinctive shapes always present in the structures discussed in Appendix II. There are the stocks, the booths of the gingerbread-woman and the hobbyhorse-man, and what Justice Overdo calls "the very womb and bed of enormity," the pig-woman's booth. There, too, in the last act, is the puppet booth which epitomizes the Fair as the Fair epitomizes the world. The comic truth about Jonson's characters emerges from the meetings which the Fair occasions, the encounters between the Fair-people, the suspicious justice, the Puritans, the men-about-town, the foolish Bartholomew Cokes, and his crotchety tutor. Thus the Fair, delightful in itself, is put to work by Jonson in a character-istic fashion as a device for producing a series of comic opposi-tions. It is to some of these that we must now turn.

A basic feature of the structure already referred to is the opposition of the predatory swindlers to their natural prey, on the one hand, and to representatives of the laws of God and man, on the other. The core of the first group is composed of the cutpurse with his co-worker, the ballad-man, the procurer and his rakish friend the horse-courser (seducers who do a little thieving on the side) and the pig-woman who makes her booth the reception center for stolen goods. Closely associated with these industrious workers are the vendors of gingerbread and hobbyhorses, who, if they don't exactly cheat (and each accuses the other of doing just that), dedicate themselves to getting as much money as possible for baubles of almost no intrinsic worth. In their way they are as great seducers and thieves as their friends. Lantern Leatherhead, the hobbyhorse-seller, has a further claim on our interest, since he is also a puppeteer. The two occupations have curious similarities. Along with hobbyhorses he sells dolls, toy drums, toy fiddles, toy dogs and birds—a miniature world designed to appeal to children or to the child in every adult. The puppets are dolls too, of course, as even their name tells us, and Cokes makes the connection explicit by associating each of the puppets with one of his toys. Both toys and puppets exemplify a reduction not only in size but in value—a debasement and parody of human worth. To notice this is to recognize Leatherhead as a worthy companion to Ursula, Edgworth, and the rest. All of them are shrewd exploiters of human weakness whom success has made cynical and contemptuous. Knockem's way of talking about people as horses is typical of the attitude they all have toward the human animal. Hence Ursula's booth is not only a practical convenience for them but an expression of this attitude, for in the back part of the booth, blackened by the fire which keeps her sweating, her customers come to eat and drink, to relieve themselves, and to pick up "birds o' the game." The predators act on the assumption that everyone can be reduced to the sum of his instincts. Yet in spite of such cynicism, this group is remarkably jolly and, on the surface, engaging. One is inclined, against one's better judgment to accept Knockem's words to Ursula, "There's no malice in these fat folks," and apply them to the rest as well. The very name of the ballad-man, Nightingale, almost disarms censure.

Censure is embodied in Rabbi Zeal-of-the-land Busy, Justice Adam Overdo, and Cokes' tutor, Humphrey Wasp. The Puritan claims to see the Fair as apocalyptic evil. He throws over a stand of gingerbread like an Old Testament prophet destroying heathen idols, and shouts "Down with Dagon" as he enters the puppet theater. His special animus against actors—even puppets! —is obviously a reflection in Jonson's distorting-mirror of the Puritan enmity to the stage, already active in 1583 when Sir Philip Sidney wrote his *Defence of Poesie*. In 1633 William Prynne wrote the most famous of the Puritan attacks, *Histriomastix*, which in certain passages sounds remarkably like an imitation of Jonson's rabbi. Yet in spite of his professed horror of worldly pleasure, Busy manages to rationalize his indulgence in Bartholomew-pig. Both excessive zeal and hypocrisy make his opposition to the Fair ludicrous and his character as deplorable as that of any of the swindlers. Overdo, though more laudable, can hardly be taken much more seriously. His awareness that there are "enormities" in the Fair is sound enough, but his ability to uncover them is ludicrously small, especially when it is compared with his complacent self-estimate. Nevertheless, he is far from being the absolutely self-assured bigot that Busy is: when the Puritan collapses like a pricked balloon, Overdo is able to accept himself as "but Adam, flesh and blood," and thus to retain some of his human dignity through humility.

Wasp has less grandiose ambitions than the other two. He aims only to protect his charge from the Fair either by keeping him away or preventing him from spending or losing his money. His prudence is as well justified as Overdo's suspicions, yet his tutorial rages are ridiculous and he is made still more absurd when he loses the license and then falls afoul of the law. The avowed enemies of the Fair do not prosper.

The third of the three elements in the basic structure is made up of the victims of the Fair. In the broadest view all the visitors to the Fair could be included here, even Busy and Overdo, but they are mainly victims of their own zeal and overdoing. It is Cokes who is the perfect gull to be practiced upon. His childlike delight in everything he sees opposes him to the clever and cynical rogues as it does to his "governor" and to the censorious justice and rabbi. He is foolish to a superlative degree and thoroughly in his element. The Fair, with its toys and puppets, is precisely his world—it is "his" Fair, as he reminds us by referring to his first name. Wasp indulges in the conceit that Cokes has the Fair so much on his brain that his head is full of drums, rattles, cockleshells, and various other sights which a traveler might well visit (I.5.87). Yet Jonson does not seem to imply that Cokes' childishness is unique. In a passage of *Discoveries* containing a verbal echo of Wasp, he compares adults to children: "*What* petty things they are, wee wonder at? like children, that esteeme every trifle; and preferre a *Fairing* before their Fathers: what difference is betweene us, and them? but that we are dearer Fooles, Cockscombes, at a higher rate? They are pleas'd with Cockleshels, Whistles, Hobby-horses, and such like: wee with Statues, marble Pillars, Pictures, guilded Roofes, where underneath is Lath, and Lyme; perhaps Lome" (*H & S,8,* 607). Certainly the Littlewits' enthusiasm for the Fair is hardly less than Cokes', and his sister, the Justice's wife, is almost as easily beguiled as he is. The typical visitor to the Fair, on whom the rogues practice all their wiles, is always something of a child.

Here another way of dividing the characters begins to emerge. We note that Littlewit is both a visitor (and hence in some sense a victim) and one of the Fair-people, providing Leatherhead with a puppet play. Also that Cokes has less in common with his tutor, a fellow victim, than with those who have taken advantage of him, for his sizable losses hardly cloud for more than a moment 'the pleasure of his visit. A basic difference, then, divides those who participate gladly in the Fair and those who disapprove; the distinction between exploiters and exploited comes to seem much less important. On one side of the dividing line is indulgence, on the other denial, but though the play often displays a Saturnalian mood, it does not finally countenance either alternative.

It is already obvious that Jonson arranges his characters in shifting patterns of relationship, highlighting a resemblance here, an opposition there, in accordance with the demands of plot or theme. One part of this counterpoint consists in an intricate system of reflectors, which serve to intensify certain traits of character. Cokes, for instance, admires the fatuous attempts at wit on which Littlewit prides himself, and the rapprochement of these two minds provides a frightening concentration of folly. More surprisingly, when Busy denounces the puppets and Cokes defends them, we see that Busy's attitude toward them is fully as naïve as Cokes': both of them treat the puppets like real people. But the best example of all is the multiplication of the images of quarrelsomeness. Busy, Overdo, and Wasp reflect each other, and their common trait is then expanded and, so to speak, rarified in the absurd game of "vapors" in Act IV, where the spirit of contradiction is shown to be without sense or substance. That Wasp, the most obviously angry man of the play, should become so involved in this game that he is robbed and then arrested is a commentary on him and on the trait he shares with the others. In this same scene Quarlous, who is also something of a brawler, is drawn into a fight against his will, and is thus distinguished from the other quarrelsome characters in a manner which has an important bearing on the ending of the play. There he appears not as an agent of discord but as a restorer of order. The reflections of hostility do not end in the game of vapors, however, The final reflectors are the puppets, screaming shrilly at each other and at the human beings. If stupid contradiction is blown up in one case, it is reduced to Lilliputian dimensions in the other, and with it the scale of the human quarrelers is also diminished: at the end we have the great Rabbi Busy not only arguing with a puppet but losing the argument.

Accentuated by these reflections, certain kinds of behavior assume the importance of thematic motifs. Foolish quarrelsomeness is one of them, but Busy's match with the puppet exemplifies another in a somewhat less obvious way. We are often reminded in the play that "hypocrite" was almost a cant term for a Puritan, for reasons which Busy's actions make clear. Its applicability is even wider when we recall that the root meaning of the word is "stage-actor." Hence the force of Grace's comment, "I know no fitter match than a puppet to commit with an hypocrite!" (V.5.43-4). Playing a part, usually with a view to practicing some deception, is an almost universal activity in *Bartholomew Fair*, sometimes a diversion, sometimes more nearly a profession. All the trickery of the play could be brought under this head, but there are particularly striking examples. Littlewit urges Winwife to act a little madder if he means to win Dame Purecraft, and Quarlous succeeds in this enterprise by disguising himself as a madman. Win assures her husband that she can be "hypocrite enough" (I.5.147-8) and proceeds to groan with her counterfeit longing. Her mother, "a most elect hypocrite" (I.5.150), turns out to be a hypocritical hypocrite, since she only pretends to be a Puritan for her own advantage. Her name, Purecraft, is as appropriate as her fate—to be taken in by another pretender. Justice Overdo disguises himself first as an old madman, then as a porter, and is thoroughly deceived by Edgworth's well-practiced role of the innocent young man. Win and Mistress Overdo are prevailed upon to disguise themselves as ladies. Since imposture is so important both as plot-mechanism and as a target for Jonson's humor, it is fitting that the puppet booth is the locus of the final action. It takes on a symbolic value comparable in importance with that of Ursula's pig-booth.

Pretending, since it is a concealment of the truth, brings about a certain distortion of value. Two verbal habits to be observed in the play add notably to this distortion; one is discontinuity and the other is amplification. By the first I refer to the way Cokes turns from one question to another which is totally unrelated, never much interested in answers and incapable of logic: "Dost thou know where I dwell, I pray thee? Nay, on with thy tune, I ha' no such haste for an answer. I'll practise with thee" (IV.2.26–7), he says to the ballad-man. When he hears about Wasp in the stocks, his attention is caught only momentarily: "For what, i' faith? I am glad o' that; remember to tell me on't anon; I have enough now! What manner of matter is this, Master Littlewit? What kind of actors ha' you? Are they good actors?" (V.3.45–8). And later in the puppet theater: "Come, sit down, Numps; I'll interpret to thee. Did you see Mistress Grace? It's no matter, neither, now I think on't, tell me anon" (V.4.108–10). The indiscriminate movement of this questioning mind from object to object levels all values with the thoroughness of a bulldozer. Though his childishness is more appealing than Knockem's cynicism, it is just as reductive in its way. His most personal problems are equated with the multifarious delights of the Fair, and one is reminded again of the resemblance Wasp sees between the Fair and Cokes' head. Both represent diversity without distinction.

Wasp's buzzing garrulity is only slightly more consistent in the direction it takes. He is quite capable of reversing himself in midflight, as when he shouts at Littlewit: "I know? I know nothing, I. What tell you me of knowing? Now I am in haste, sir, I do not know, and I will not know, and I scorn to know, and yet (now I think on't) I will and do know as well as another . . ." (I.4.18–21). Like Cokes, but for different reasons, his mind is in such endless motion that there is never time to establish a fixed center. Instead of embracing all the world he rejects it all, thereby showing no more discrimination than Cokes.

The repetitions of this speech of Wasp's reveal the other verbal characteristic which I have mentioned, amplification.[2] It is a disease found in the language of several of the characters, but takes a virulent form in the speeches of Busy and Overdo. When Busy says, "Very likely, exceeding likely, very exceeding likely" (I.6.96), neither the satire on his pulpit manner nor the emphasis on excess can be missed, but he outdoes even himself in the swelling rhetoric of his attack on the stage:

> I will remove Dagon there, I say, that idol, that heathenish idol, that
> remains, as I may say, a beam, a very beam, not a beam of the sun, nor
> a beam of the moon, nor a beam of a balance, neither a house-beam
> nor a weaver's beam, but a beam in the eye, in the eye of the brethren;
> a very great beam, an exceeding great beam; such as are your stage-
> players . . . . (V.5.4–9)

The amplification in Overdo's oration against tobacco is of a slightly different sort. Instead of piling up repeated nouns with their increment of accumulated modifiers ("a beam in the eye, in the eye of the brethren; a very great beam, an exceeding great beam"), he develops and enhances his theme by means of the illustrations, exhortations, apostrophes, verbal ornaments, and other devices recommended in Renaissance handbooks for the achieving of "copiousness":[3]

---

2. Barish discusses repetitiveness, pp. 198–204.
3. See Barish, pp. 204–13.

The creeping venom of which subtle serpent, as some late writers affirm, neither the cutting of the perilous plant, not the drying of it, nor the lighting or burning, can any way persway or assuage. . . . Hark, o you sons and daughters of Smithfield! and hear what malady it doth the mind: it causeth swearing, it causeth swaggering, it causeth snuffling, and snarling, and now and then a hurt. (II.6.33–6, 63–6)

These "brave words," as Cokes calls them, constitute a special case, because they are part of Overdo's disguise—an imitation of the style of "mad Arthur of Bradley." Nevertheless, we find him up to the same tricks when he speaks in his own person in the stocks: "I do not feel it, I do not think of it, it is a thing without me. Adam, thou art above these batt'ries, these contumelies" (IV.6.85–6); whereupon he quotes Horace and Persius. As in Busy's case, the greatest swellings in Overdo's prose appear in his last great speech. He is warming to the denunciation of the Fair:

Now to my enormities: look upon me, o London! and see me, o Smithfield! the example of justice and mirror of magistrates, the true top of formality and scourge of enormity. Hearken unto my labors and but observe my discoveries, and compare Hercules with me, if thou dar'st, of old; or Columbus, Magellan, or our countryman Drake of later times. (V.6.33–8)

All the tumid phrases of these speeches of Busy and Overdo are, of course, expressions of their overdoing—their overreaching. In the last one we hear with special clarity the note of self-congratulation which is present in them all. Wherever amplification occurs in the play it points to some example of complacency or bigotry, and such false valuations of self and of the world are major targets for Jonson's satire, along with quarrelsomeness, imposture, and indiscriminate acceptance or rejection.

To speak of "Jonson's satire" and "Jonson's comedy" is to approach topics with which he was much concerned—the relationship between the two genres and the proper tone for each.[4] Like his contemporaries, Jonson believed that both comedy and satire had a didactic purpose and that the exposure of folly was, in both cases, part of that purpose. It was generally thought that satire should deal more harshly than comedy with the fools it exposed and that it might often deal with worse than fools. A favorite image of the satirist (thanks to an etymological confusion) was that of a rough satyr wielding a scourge.[5] The titles of two seventeenth-century works immediately convey the tone of this sort of satire: George Wither's *Abuses Stript and Whipt* (1613) and William Prynne's *Histriomastix, The Player's Scourge . . .* (1633). Jonson, much as he believed in teaching and correcting, inclined to a more genial form of satire and to comedy that remained merry even though the author gave moral instruction. He found it necessary to explain in a dedicatory epistle why the most severe of his comedies, *Volpone*, did not end on a more cheerful note. Satire of the kind Jonson favored could well be combined with comedy, but if good humor was to prevail, bitterness had to be carefully avoided. In fact, scourging satirists are themselves the objects of satire in some of Jonson's early plays. It is for this reason that Jonson takes pains to disavow in the Induction to *Bartholomew Fair* any living models for his characters, for personal satire was closely associated with the scourging of which he disapproved. Another seventeenth-century title may suggest Jonson's ideal, though he would never have been guilty of the jingle: *No Whipping nor Tripping, but a kind friendly Snipping*. In *Bartholomew Fair* Jonson snips at almost

---

4. See O. J. Campbell, *Comicall Satyre and Shakespeare's Troilus and Cressida* (San Marino, Calif., 1938), pp. 1–14, 24–34; Alvin B. Kernan, *The Cankered Muse* (New Haven, 1959), pp. 20, 28–29, 150–91.

5. See Kernan, pp. 81–140, and E. M. Waith, *The Pattern of Tragicomedy in Beaumont and Fletcher* (New Haven, 1952), pp. 50–70.

all his characters, and not always kindly; yet the tone of the play is notoriously genial.

It has already been noted that the "disapprovers," Wasp, Overdo, and Busy, form a distinct group. It may now be clear that their attitude has something in common with that of the more severe kind of satirist, bent on exposing and punishing. This is especially true of Busy, who verbally scourges the Fair and most other amusements at every opportunity, echoing the standard arguments of the Puritans. Jonson not only expresses the dislike of Puritans which anyone in the theater was bound to have as a result of the continual Puritan attacks, but he makes his Zeal-of-the-land an example of how not to deal with iniquity. Busy's discomfiture in the argument with the puppet, one of the best scenes in the play, reveals the radically negative character of his outlook, which makes it in the final analysis ludicrous.

In dealing with various forms of human aberration in the play, Jonson himself is the antithesis of such scourgers of the flesh. The final treatment accorded to his characters shows a good deal about his attitude, though it does not wholly explain the tone of the play. The enemies of the Fair are treated the most severely— they are all put in the stocks briefly and all humiliated in various ways—but the emphasis in each case is not on punishment but on changing their patterns of behavior. In Jonson's earlier comedies, where his characters are distinguished by some "humor"—a mental or physical imbalance or sometimes a mere affectation— the dénouement consists in putting them out of their humors and thus restoring the balance. In a similar way, each of the three characters we are discussing is made to give up his customary ways, two of them abruptly and one more gradually. When Wasp finds that his punishment in the stocks is known to his pupil, he knows that his authority is at an end, and though he continues to be waspish, he gives no more orders. The collapse of Busy is so abrupt that it seems a flaw to some critics of the play. It is true that if Busy fully believed in the wickedness of men playing the parts of women on the stage—one of the oldest charges against actors—we could not expect him to be dissuaded by the revelation that puppets have no sex, but to reason in this way is to take the whole situation too seriously. It is initially absurd that he should agree to argue about the stage with a puppet; if we can accept this as a comic hypothesis, we can also accept his "conversion." The truth is that the entire conception of the character of the Puritan Rabbi is several degrees further removed from realism than that of Ursula, for instance, and the scene of the argument with the puppet approaches pure fantasy. It seems only proper to recognize such gradations in judging the outcome, and to grant that Busy's sudden deflation is no more preposterous than many other things he does.

The change that comes over Adam Overdo is better prepared and has still more to do with the tone of the play. We know from his comments in Act IV, Scene 1, that he has the willingness to correct his own faults when they are pointed out, for he there determines to make some recompense to Trouble-all, whom he has wronged, and sees that "compassion may become a justice." We also know that he plans to make a joke of his beating to amuse his family at table. We cannot be surprised, then, by his compliance with the suggestions of Quarlous: "remember you are but Adam, flesh and blood! You have your frailty; forget your other name of Overdo and invite us all to supper" (V.6.94–6). At the end Overdo performs a function similar to that of Justice Clement in *Every Man in his Humor*, assuring the proper comic tone in the midst of distributing rewards and punishments, but since Overdo is a more serious and slightly more complex character than the merry justice of the earlier play, the triumph of geniality in *Bartholomew Fair* provides a curiously moving finale.

The fate of the other characters has been partly implied by what has already been said. Since Overdo has been comically gullible for all his solemn pretensions to clairvoyance, he does not entirely succeed in revealing the "enormities" of the Fair, though thanks to the assistance of Quarlous, the various malefactors are eventually shown up. Exposure and the accompanying blow to their professional pride are the only punishment they receive, as humiliation is the worst penalty suffered by their victims. Again the comic tone is preserved.

Even more important in the achievement of this tone, however, is the extraordinary balance, certain aspects of which have already been mentioned. It is best seen in the dénouement of the play and in the treatment of three characters who have not been much discussed as yet. The last major event of this day at the Fair is the puppet show—Littlewit's appalling vulgarization of the stories of Hero and Leander and Damon and Pythias, which he has combined and, as he says, "made a little easy and modern for the times," that is, reduced to the level of the Stage-keeper in the Induction, who would doubtless relish Littlewit's "motion." Amusing as it undoubtedly is, after the fashion of the lowest of low comedy, it is an artistic nullity and a trenchant commentary on popular taste. The worst possible representative of the theater is therefore opposed to the worst possible representative of morality: the one is as debased as the other is narrow-minded. Between them there is little to choose, though naturally that little is in favor of the puppets. Overdo for once displays great insight when he pairs Busy with Leatherhead as equally undesirable extremes: "First, Rabbi Busy, thou super-lunatical hypocrite. Next, thou other extremity, thou profane professor of puppetry ..." (V.6.39–41). Had Jonson presented a more favorable example of the theater, the balance would have been destroyed, and the result would have been more like polemic than comedy.

Winwife, Quarlous, and Grace form a group somewhat

apart, as is suggested at times even by their position on stage, when they stand to one side, amusing each other by their observations on the other characters. They are too involved in the action to be called mere commentators—the two men make advantageous matches by their intrigues and Grace agrees to the trick by means of which she is stolen from her guardian and her fiancé—yet they are never totally involved. Grace is at the Fair against her will, sure that nobody "of any quality or fashion" goes there. The young gentlemen, who also consider themselves a cut above the fair-haunting public, are there for a lark. Even so, Winwife's zest for the adventure has to be recharged by his friend, and both of them are adept in getting out of the way when any trouble is brewing. The three of them are waders who have no intention of immersing themselves.

Though they are not ideal characters and can lay claim to no extraordinary wisdom, they strike a kind of balance between the characteristics of the others, and thus serve a normative function. While they have far more common sense and sharper perceptions than either the gulls or the self-appointed censors, their tricks are less criminal than those of the rogues. The quarrelsomeness of Quarlous is more high spirits than fixed hostility and helps to bring out what is truly deviant about the natures of the other quarrelers. His madness is a manner, an affectation, which is fundamentally more sane than the obsessions of some of the characters who are not outwardly mad. Grace is the one truly balanced, and hence truly self-possessed, character in the play. Sure of her own standards to the point of seeming prim in some scenes, she is made attractive by her clear-sightedness and wit. Her occasional comments are as neat as they are acid. In Grace, minor character that she is, we come closer to the point of view of the author than in any other character.

Perhaps it is Grace's detachment which chiefly reminds one of Jonson, for the impartiality of this comedy has already been noted. Jonson sees the world as a fair, as in the passage from *Discoveries*, and commits himself no more to his characters than does the visitor to a fair. This is the sort of detachment which is a hallmark of comedy. Yet for all that, Jonson's attitude is significantly different from Grace's. He looks on with not only amusement but relish, to which the warmth of the characterizations of Ursula, Knockem, Whit, and the rest testify. The balance of Jonson's point of view is not only a matter of impartiality but also of an emotional adjustment which makes disapproval and warm enjoyment possible at the same time.

Jonson's realism in giving substance to the characters in his fair has often been remarked on, but the word cannot be allowed to stand without some qualification, for the experience of reading or seeing the play is importantly affected by several non-realistic techniques. The use of an induction is the most conspicuous of these. Here the author, instead of keeping himself invisible, as the truly realistic author attempts to do, makes his presence felt powerfully, even if indirectly. He allows his play to be damned by the Stage-keeper, that representative of the commonest taste, and thus conveys negatively something of his own point of view. Through the Book-holder and Scrivener he makes his pact with the audience, in the course of which he deplores several critical attitudes such as arrogance or fickleness, stand-pat conservatism or infatuation with the latest style, ignorance, or super subtlety in identifying the models of the characters. The audience is directly addressed—cajoled and teased—while at a realistic play the actors must pretend to be unaware that the audience can see and hear them through the barrier of the invisible fourth wall of the stage. From the start, then, contact is established between the audience, the author, and the actors. The characters impersonated and the situations acted out achieve their reality within this framework, which is never wholly lost. In the body of the play the audience's awareness of theatrical contrivance is kept alive in other ways. Visual realism, never complete on the Elizabethan stage, is modified here by the use of conventions reminiscent of the medieval mystery plays (see Appendix II), and the illusion of Smithfield never obscures the reality of the stage as stage.

Another nonrealistic technique is the extreme ingenuity of the plot. We cannot be oblivious to the clever meshing of the intrigues of Littlewit, Edgworth, Knockem, Whit, Winwife, Quarlous, and Overdo, for instance, and the way in which the final resolutions of all of them are concentrated in the last act. The treatment of time in the play is both a contribution to realism and an exceedingly clever part of the plot contrivance. The entire action of the play occurs during one day, and once we are taken to the Fair, we have the sense of almost continuous action, though it is morning in Act II and late afternoon in Act V. This seeming brevity adds verisimilitude (as if the action of the story lasted scarcely longer than our stay in the theater), but, perhaps more importantly, it reinforces the impression of neatness given by the tying up of all strands of the plot. Both are evidences of Jonson's much-discussed classicism.

The degree of realism in characterization varies greatly, as I have already suggested, the portrayal of Busy in his scene with the puppet moving rather far from verisimilitude. The character of Wasp is so narrowly and rigidly defined that it is almost a "humor," and mad Trouble-all is hardly more than a few phrases with legs: "By what warrant?" "Quit ye and multiply ye!"[6] His rapid disappearances and reappearances throughout Act IV build up an atmosphere of absurd irrationality which has been adum-

---

6. See the excellent discussion of Trouble-all and the importance of warrants in Ray L. Heffner, Jr., "Unifying Symbols in the Comedy of Ben Jonson," in *Elizabethian Drama*, ed. Ralph J. Kaufman (New York, 1961), pp. 170-86.

brated by the madman disguise of Overdo and is perpetuated by Quarlous when he disguises himself in Trouble-all's cloak. Madness may be seen as the paradoxical means by which some semblance of a reasonable order is finally restored. In such treatment of character the working out of a theme clearly takes precedence over the accurate portrayal of the inhabitants of seventeenth-century London.

To notice these ways in which Jonson's realism is qualified is to return once more to a point made near the beginning of this introduction. The Fair is given a most convincing, concrete reality on the stage, but at every moment the art which brings it to life also transforms that life into a comprehensive comic vision. It is the extraordinary vitality of the vision which makes the most lasting impression.

In preparing this edition I have been greatly aided by the work of previous editors, such as Carroll S. Alden, C. H. Herford and Percy and Evelyn Simpson, Harry Levin, and E. A. Horsman. I am happy to acknowledge my indebtedness to the General Editors for their painstaking supervision and valuable suggestions, as well as to Professors F. P. Wilson and Carroll Camden for their prompt and full answers to my queries. Professor Helge Kökeritz was most generous in advising me on linguistic problems. The material of Appendix II appeared in a slightly different form as "The Staging of *Bartholomew Fair*" in *Studies in English Literature*, 2 (1962), 181–95; my thanks are due to the editor for permission to reprint. I am most grateful to Professor Alois M. Nagler of the Yale School of Drama and Professor Dunbar H. Ogden of the University of California for their painstaking criticism of the first draft of this appendix. The frontispiece, 'A Cokes,' from the anonymous mid-seventeenth-century pamphlet, *A Pack of Knaves*, is reproduced by kind permission of The Huntington Library, San Marino, California. Translations of Latin quotations are usually those in the Loeb Classical Library, with acknowledgement given to the translators.

The following abbreviations are used in the glosses:

F   The Workes of Benjamin Jonson. The Second Volume. London, 1640.

H & S   *Ben Jonson*, ed. C. H. Herford and Percy and Evelyn Simpson, 11 vols., Oxford, 1925–52.

Horsman   *Bartholomew Fair*, ed. E. A. Horsman, The Revels Plays, Cambridge, Mass., 1960.

OED   *The Oxford English Dictionary*, 13 vols., Oxford, 1961.

THE
PROLOGUE
TO
THE KING'S
MAJESTY

Your Majesty is welcome to a Fair;
Such place, such men, such language and such ware,
You must expect; with these the zealous noise
Of your land's faction, scandalized at toys,
As babies, hobbyhorses, puppet plays,   5
And such like rage, whereof the petulant ways
Yourself have known, and have been vexed with long.
These for your sport, without particular wrong,
Or just complaint of any private man
Who of himself or shall think well or can,   10
The maker doth present, and hopes tonight
To give you for a fairing true delight.

PROLOGUE *for the performance at court, November 1, 1614.*
4 FACTION *the Puritans.* TOYS *trifles, rubbish.*
5 BABIES *dolls.*
8 PARTICULAR WRONG *satirizing individuals* N. (*N. refers throughout to corresponding note at the end of text.*)
10 OR . . . OR *either . . . or.*
12 FAIRING *present given at a fair.*

23

The Persons of the Play

John Littlewit, a proctor
[Solomon, his man]
Win Littlewit, his wife
Dame Purecraft, her mother and a widow
Zeal-of-the-land Busy, her suitor, a Banbury man
Winwife, his rival, a gentleman
Quarlous, his companion, a gamester
Bartholomew Cokes, an esquire of Harrow
Humphrey Wasp, his man
Adam Overdo, a justice of peace
Dame Overdo, his wife
Grace Wellborn, his ward
Lantern Leatherhead, a hobbyhorse-seller
Joan Trash, a gingerbread-woman
Ezekiel Edgworth, a cutpurse
Nightingale, a ballad-singer
Ursula, a pig-woman
Mooncalf, her tapster
Jordan Knockem, a horse-courser and ranger o' Turnbull
Val Cutting, a roarer

PROCTOR *legal agent; see Induction, l. 3.*
BANBURY *famous for Puritans.*
GAMESTER *rake, joker.*
BARTHOLOMEW *pronounced Bartlemew or Bartlemy; the normal spelling in the Folio is Bartholmew.*
COKES *a cokes is a silly fellow, one easily taken in; see frontispiece.*
HOBBYHORSE-SELLER *also a seller of dolls, toys, etc.*
URSULA *pronounced Ursla and normally so spelled in the Folio.*
MOONCALF *deformed person, monster.*
HORSE-COURSER *dealer in "ridden" (broken-in) horses.*
RANGER *keeper of a park; also rake; "knock" was also slang for copulate.*
TURNBULL *Turnmill (or Turnbull) Street was notorious for prostitutes.*
VAL CUTTING *"Cutting Dick" was a famous highwayman.*
ROARER *bully, rowdy.*

Captain Whit, a bawd
Punk Alice, mistress o' the game
Trouble-all a madman
Watchmen, three [Haggis, Bristle, and Poacher, a beadle
Costermonger
[Passengers]
[Corncutter]
[Tinderbox-man]
Clothier [Northern]
Wrestler [Puppy]
Doorkeepers [Filcher and Sharkwell]
Puppets

> BAWD *pimp.*
> PUNK *prostitute.*
> MISTRESS O' THE GAME *prostitute.*
> POACHER *one who pushes or shoves, e.g. into another's business.*
> BEADLE *"one who delivers the messages or executes the mandates of an authority"* (OED).
> COSTERMONGER *peddler of fruit or vegetables.*
> [PASSENGERS] *passersby.*
> [TINDERBOX-MAN] *N.*
> DOORKEEPERS *hired men who collected admissions at the doors of the theater.*

[*Enter Stage-keeper.*]

[*Stage-keeper.*] Gentlemen, have a little patience, they are e'en upon coming, instantly. He that should begin the play, Master Littlewit, the proctor, has a stitch new fall'n in his black silk stocking; 'twill be drawn up ere you can tell twenty. He plays one o' the Arches, that dwells about the hospital, and he has a very 5 pretty part. But for the whole play, will you ha' the truth on't? (I am looking, lest the poet hear me, or his man, Master Brome, behind the arras) it is like to be a very conceited scurvy one, in plain English. When't comes to the Fair once, you were e'en as good go to Virginia, for anything there is of Smithfield. He has not hit the 10 humors, he does not know 'em; he has not conversed with the

INDUCTION *brief dramatic introduction to a full-length play* N
SD *for the form of the stage directions* see ^
SD [STAGE-KEEPER] *an atte*
jobs N.
5 ONE O' THE ARCHES *a proct*
Bow Church.
5 HOSPITAL *St. Bartholomew in*
7 BROME *Richard Brome, the*
servant.
8 ARRAS *hanging on the back wal*
8 CONCEITED *full of conceits, fan*
10 SMITHFIELD *site of the Fair.*
11 HUMORS *characteristic oddities o*

Barthol'mew-birds, as they say; he has ne'er a sword-and-buckler man in his Fair, nor a little Davy to take toll o' the bawds there, as in my time, nor a Kindheart, if anybody's teeth should chance to
15 ache in his play. Nor a juggler with a well-educated ape to come over the chain for the King of England and back again for the Prince, and sit still on his arse for the Pope and the King of Spain! None o' these fine sights! Nor has he the canvas-cut i' the night for a hobbyhorse-man to creep in to his she-neighbor and take
20 his leap there! Nothing! No, an' some writer (that I know) had had but the penning o' this matter, he would ha' made you such a jig-a-jog i' the booths, you should ha' thought an earthquake had been i' the Fair! But these master-poets, they will ha' their own absurd courses; they will be informed of nothing! He has,
25 sir-reverence, kicked me three or four times about the tiring-house, I thank him, for but offering to put in, with my experience. I'll be judged by you, gentlemen, now, but for one conceit of mine! Would not a fine pump upon the stage ha' done well for a property now? And a punk set under upon her head, with her
30 stern upward, and ha' been soused by my witty young masters o' the Inns o' Court? What think you o' this for a show, now? He will not hear o' this! I am an ass, I! And yet I kept the stage in

---

12 BARTHOL'MEW BIRDS *the characters who haunt the fair.*
12–3 SWORD-AND-BUCKLER MAN *ruffian who came to Smithfield to fight.*
13 LITTLE DAVY *a bully, who was expert at sword and buckler.*
14 KINDHEART *a famous itinerant toothdrawer.*
LEAP *a brothel was called a leaping-house.*
N' and, *meaning if; in this sense it is always printed an' in this edition.*
REVERENCE *with all respect.*
G-HOUSE *part of the public theater in back of the stage where the oms were.*
RT *buildings belonging to the four societies of law students; the " enthusiasts for the drama, were also known for their wild*

Master Tarlton's time, I thank my stars. Ho! an' that man had lived
to have played in *Barthol'mew Fair*, you should ha' seen him ha'
come in, and ha' been cozened i' the cloth-quarter, so finely! And   35
Adams, the rogue, ha' leaped and capered upon him, and ha' dealt
his vermin about as though they had cost him nothing. And then
a substantial watch to ha' stol'n in upon 'em, and taken 'em away
with mistaking words, as the fashion is in the stage-practice.

[*Enter Book-holder, Scrivener.*]

Book-holder. How now? What rare discourse are you fall'n upon,   40
ha? Ha' you found any familiars here, that you are so free? What's
the business?

Stage-keeper. Nothing, but the understanding gentlemen o'
the ground here asked my judgment.

Book-holder. Your judgment, rascal? For what? Sweeping the   45
stage? Or gathering up the broken apples for the bears within?
Away rogue, it's come to a fine degree in these spectacles when
such a youth as you pretend to a judgment. [*Exit Stage-keeper.*]
And yet he may, i' the most o' this matter i' faith; for the author
hath writ it just to his meridian, and the scale of the grounded   50
judgments here, his play-fellows in wit. Gentlemen, not for want

33 TARLTON *a clown, well known on the Elizabethan stage until his death in 1588.*

35 CLOTH-QUARTER *booths where the cloth fair was held; one of Tarlton's "jests"
was the story of his being cheated of his clothes there.*

36 ADAMS *fellow actor of Tarlton's.*

36-7 DEALT . . . ABOUT *i.e. shook off as he "leaped and capered."*

37 VERMIN *such as fleas from the padded hose which men wore.*

38 SUBSTANTIAL *burly, sturdy.*

39 MISTAKING WORDS *malapropisms like those of Dogberry and Verges in* Much
Ado about Nothing.

40 BOOK-HOLDER *prompter.*

43-4 UNDERSTANDING GENTLEMEN O' THE GROUND *spectators in the pit,
standing around the raised stage, the "groundlings."*

46 BEARS *the Hope Theater was also used for bear-baiting; see Appendix* II, *p. 205.*

50 TO HIS MERIDAN *to the height of his understanding.*

50-1 GROUNDED JUDGMENTS *another punning reference to the groundlings.*

of a prologue, but by way of a new one, I am sent out to you here with a scrivener and certain articles drawn out in haste between our author and you; which if you please to hear, and as they appear
55 reasonable, to approve of, the play will follow presently. Read, scribe; gi' me the counterpane.

Scrivener. Articles of Agreement indented between the spectators or hearers at the Hope on the Bankside, in the county of Surrey, on the one party, and the author of *Barthol'mew Fair* in
60 the said place and county, on the other party, the one and thirtieth day of October, 1614, and in the twelfth year of the reign of our Sovereign Lord, James, by the grace of God King of England, France, and Ireland, Defender of the Faith; and of Scotland the seven and fortieth.

65 INPRIMIS, It is covenanted and agreed by and between the parties above-said and the said spectators and hearers, as well the curious and envious as the favoring and judicious, as also the grounded judgments and under-standings do for themselves severally covenant and agree, to remain in the places their money or
70 friends have put them in, with patience, for the space of two hours and an half and somewhat more. In which time the author promiseth to present them, by us, with a new sufficient play called *Barthol'mew Fair*, merry, and as full of noise as sport, made to delight all, and to offend none; provided they have either the wit
75 or the honesty to think well of themselves.

It is further agreed that every person here have his or their free-will of censure, to like or dislike at their own charge, the author

56 COUNTERPANE *the other (duplicate) part of the indenture.*
58 BANKSIDE *section of London south of the Thames.*
65 INPRIMIS *first.*
67 CURIOUS *particular, difficult to satisfy.*
77 CENSURE *judgment, either favourable or adverse.*
77 CHARGE *expense.*

having now departed with his right: it shall be lawful for any man to judge his six pen'orth, his twelve pen'orth, so to his eighteen pence, two shillings, half a crown, to the value of his place; provided always his place get not above his wit. And if he pay for half a dozen, he may censure for all them too, so that he will undertake that they shall be silent. He shall put in for censures here as they do for lots at the lottery; marry, if he drop but sixpence at the door, and will censure a crown's worth, it is thought there is no conscience or justice in that.

It is also agreed that every man here exercise his own judgment, and not censure by contagion, or upon trust, from another's voice or face that sits by him, be he never so first in the commission of wit; as also, that he be fixed and settled in his censure, that what he approves or not approves today, he will do the same tomorrow, and if tomorrow, the next day, and so the next week (if need be), and not to be brought about by any that sits on the bench with him, though they indict and arraign plays daily. He that will swear *Jeronimo* or *Andronicus* are the best plays yet, shall pass unexcepted at here as a man whose judgment shows it is constant, and hath stood still these five and twenty, or thirty years. Though it be an ignorance, it is a virtuous and staid

78 DEPARTED *parted.*
79 SIX PEN'ORTH *sixpenny-worth; i.e. the value of a sixpenny seat N.*
80 HALF A CROWN *two shillings and sixpence.*
84 LOTTERY *a national lottery was opened in 1612 to raise money for the Virginia voyage and plantation.*
88 CONTAGION *infection of his neighbors' opinions.*
90 COMMISION OF WIT *as if a commission had been appointed to investigate or arraign the play.*
95 JERONIMO OR ANDRONICUS The Spanish Tragedy *by Thomas Kyd or* Titus Andronicus *by Shakespeare N.*
96 UNEXCEPTED AT *unchallenged.*
97 FIVE AND TWENTY, OR THIRTY YEARS *N.*

ignorance, and next to truth, a confirmed error does well; such a
100 one the author knows where to find him.

It is further covenanted, concluded, and agreed that how great
soever the expectation be, no person here is to expect more than
he knows, or better ware than a Fair will afford; neither to look back
to the sword-and-buckler age of Smithfield, but content himself
105 with the present. Instead of a little Davy to take toll o' the bawds,
the author doth promise a strutting horse-courser with a leer
drunkard, two or three to attend him in as good equipage as you
would wish. And then for Kindheart, the tooth-drawer, a fine
oily pig-woman with her tapster to bid you welcome, and a
110 consort of roarers for music. A wise justice of peace *meditant*,
instead of a juggler with an ape. A civil cutpurse *searchant*. A
sweet singer of new ballads *allurant;* and as fresh an hypocrite as
ever was broached *rampant*. If there be never a servant-monster i'
the Fair, who can help it? he says; nor a nest of antics? He is loth
115 to make nature afraid in his plays, like those that beget Tales,
Tempests, and such like drolleries, to mix his head with other
men's heels, let the concupiscence of jigs and dances reign as
strong as it will amongst you; yet if the puppets will please anybody, they shall be entreated to come in.
120 In consideration of which, it is finally agreed by the foresaid

106 LEER *a leer horse was one without rider or load, hence often a led horse.*
107 EQUIPAGE *equipment, dress.*
110–2 MEDITANT . . . SEARCHANT . . . ALLURANT *formed in imitation of
heraldic terms such as rampant and couchant.*
113 SERVANT-MONSTER *alluding to Caliban in* The Tempest.
114 NEST *group.*
114 ANTICS *people in grotesque or fantastic costume, often dancers.*
115–6 TALES, TEMPESTS *alluding, no doubt to* The Winter's Tale *and* The
Tempest, *recently performed; fantasy and romance as well as spectacular
production made these comedies decidedly unrealistic.*
116 DROLLERIES *entertainments.*
117 JIGS AND DANCES *N.*

hearers and spectators that they neither in themselves conceal, nor suffer by them to be concealed, any state-decipherer, or politic picklock of the scene, so solemnly ridiculous as to search out who was meant by the gingerbread-woman, who by the hobbyhorse-man, who by the costermonger, nay, who by their wares. Or that will pretend to affirm, on his own inspired ignorance, what mirror of magistrates is meant by the Justice, what great lady by the pig-woman, what concealed statesman by the seller of mousetraps, and so of the rest. But that such person or persons, so found, be left discovered to the mercy of the author, as a forfeiture to the stage and your laughter aforesaid. As also, such as shall so desperately or ambitiously play the fool by his place aforesaid, to challenge the author of scurrility because the language somewhere savors of Smithfield, the booth, and the pig-broth; or of profane-ness because a madman cries, "God quit you," or "bless you." In witness whereof, as you have preposterously put to your seals already (which is your money), you will now add the other part of suffrage, your hands. The play shall presently begin. And though the Fair be not kept in the same region that some here, perhaps, would have it, yet think that therein the author hath observed a

122 POLITIC *well-versed in affairs of state, as Sir Politic Wouldbe in* Volpone *thinks he is.*

123–4 WHO WAS MEANT *Jonson was frequently accused of satirizing individuals.*

126–7 MIRROR OF MAGISTRATES *N.*

130 DISCOVERED *revealed.*

133 CHALLENGE *accuse.*

135 QUIT *requite, reward; cf. Trouble-all's characteristic greetings.*

136 PREPOSTEROUSLY *literally, in reversed order; sealing would normally be done last.*

136 PUT TO *affixed.*

138 SUFFRAGE *assent.*

special decorum, the place being as dirty as Smithfield, and as stinking every whit.

Howsoever, he prays you to believe his ware is still the same; else you will make him justly suspect that he that is so loth to look
145 on a baby or an hobbyhorse here, would be glad to take up a commodity of them, at any laughter, or loss, in another place.

[*Exeunt.*]

141 DECORUM *appropriateness, as in suiting style to subject-matter; refers here to staging.*
141–2 DIRTY . . . STINKING *see l. 46 above.*
143 STILL THE SAME *always of the same (high) quality; i.e. worthy of your laughter.*
146 COMMODITY *quantity, job lot N.*

Act I Scene i

[*Enter Littlewit holding a licence.*]
Littlewit. A pretty conceit, and worth the finding! I ha' such
luck to spin out these fine things still, and like a silk-worm, out of
myself. Here's Master Barthol'mew Cokes, of Harrow o' th' Hill,
i' th' County of Middlesex, Esquire, takes forth his licence to
marry Mistress Grace Wellborn of the said place and county. And   5
when does he take it forth? Today! The four and twentieth of
August! Barthol'mew Day! Barthol'mew upon Barthol'mew!
There's the device! Who would have marked such a leap-frog
chance now? A very less than ames-ace on two dice! Well, go
thy ways, John Littlewit, Proctor John Littlewit—one o' the   10
pretty wits o' Paul's, the "Little-wit of London" (so thou art
called) and something beside. When a quirk or a quiblin does
'scape thee, and thou dost not watch, and apprehend it, and bring

8 DEVICE *conceit, motto.*
8–9 LEAP-FROG CHANCE *"long" chance.*
9 A VERY LESS *truly less.*
9 AMES-ACE *ambsace, double aces, the lowest throw at dice.*
11 PAUL'S *N.*
12 QUIRK *quip, witty turn.*
12 QUIBLIN *quibble, pun.*

it afore the constable of conceit (there now, I speak quib too),
15 let 'em carry thee out o' the archdeacon's court into his kitchen,
and make a Jack of thee, instead of a John. (There I am again, la!)
[*Enter Win.*]
Win, good morrow, Win. Aye marry, Win! Now you look finely
indeed, Win! This cap does convince! You'd not ha' worn it,
Win, nor ha' had it velvet, but a rough country beaver with a
20 copper band, like the coney-skin woman of Budge Row! Sweet
Win, let me kiss it! And her fine high shoes, like the Spanish
lady! Good Win, go a little; I would fain see thee pace, pretty
Win! By this fine cap, I could never leave kissing on't.
    Win. Come, indeed la, you are such a fool, still!
25   *Littlewit.* No, but half a one, Win; you are the tother half: man
and wife make one fool, Win. (Good!) Is there the proctor, or
doctor indeed, i' the diocese, that ever had the fortune to win him
such a Win! (There I am again!) I do feel conceits coming upon
me, more than I am able to turn tongue to. A pox o' these
30 pretenders to wit! your Three Cranes, Mitre, and Mermaid men!
Not a corn of true salt nor a grain of right mustard amongst them

14 QUIB *in a punning or quipping style.*
15 ARCHDEACON'S COURT *the Court of Arches was an ecclesiastical court.*
16 JACK *knave or servant.*
18 DOES CONVINCE *is stunning (literally "overpowers").*
20 COPPER BAND *metal hat-bands were common; copper was naturally less elegant than gold or silver.*
20 CONEY *rabbit.*
20 BUDGE ROW *a street where skin dealers lived. Budge is a kind of fur.*
21–2 SPANISH LADY *N.*
22 GO *walk.*
24 INDEED LA *characteristic Puritan expression.*
30 THREE CRANES, MITRE, AND MERMAID *London taverns. Jonson and his friends frequented the Mermaid.*
31 CORN *grain.*
31 SALT, MUSTARD *suggesting the pungency of wit.*

all. They may stand for places or so, again the next witfall, and pay twopence in a quart more for their canary than other men. But gi' me the man can start up a justice of wit out of six-shillings beer, and give the law to all the poets and poet-suckers i' town, 35 because they are the players' gossips! 'Slid, other men have wives as fine as the players, and as well dressed. Come hither, Win.

[*He kisses her.*]

32 PLACES *in the crowded tavern.*
32 AGAIN *against, in anticipation of.*
33 CANARY *light, sweet wine.*
34-5 SIX-SHILLING BEER *beer at six shillings a barrel.*
35 POET-SUCKERS *sucking (i.e. young) poets.*
36 BECAUSE . . . GOSSIPS *N.*
36 GOSSIPS *friends.*
36 'SLID *by God's (eye) lid.*

Act I Scene ii

[*Enter Winwife.*]

Winwife. Why, how now, Master Littlewit? Measuring of lips or moulding of kisses? Which is it?

Littlewit. Troth, I am a little taken with my Win's dressing here! Does't not fine, Master Winwife? How do you apprehend, sir? She would not ha' worn this habit. I challenge all Cheapside 5 to show such another—Moorfields, Pimlico path, or the Exchange, in a summer evening—with a lace to boot, as this has. Dear Win, let Master Winwife kiss you. He comes a-wooing to

4 APPREHEND *think.*
5 CHEAPSIDE *part of London known for its cloth merchants.*
6 MOORFIELDS *a park just outside the city.*
6 PIMLICO *a tavern near London famous for cakes and ale.*
6-7 EXCHANGE *probably the New Exchange, a fashionable shopping center.*

our mother, Win, and may be our father perhaps, Win. There's
10 no harm in him, Win.

    Winwife. None i' the earth, Master Littlewit.   [*He kisses her.*]

    Littlewit. I envy no man my delicates, sir.

    Winwife. Alas, you ha' the garden where they grow still! A
wife here with a strawberry-breath, cherry-lips, apricot-cheeks,
15 and a soft velvet head, like a melicotton.

    Littlewit. Good i' faith! Now dullness upon me, that I had not
that before him, that I should not light on't as well as he! Velvet
head!

    Winwife. But my taste, Master Littlewit, tends to fruit of a later
20 kind: the sober matron, your wife's mother.

    Littlewit. Aye! we know you are a suitor, sir. Win and I both
wish you well; by this licence here, would you had her, that your
two names were as fast in it, as here are a couple. Win would fain
have a fine young father i' law with a feather, that her mother
25 might hood it and chain it with Mistress Overdo. But you do not
take the right course, Master Winwife.

    Winwife. No, Master Littlewit? Why?

    Littlewit. You are not mad enough.

    Winwife. How? Is madness a right course?

30   *Littlewit.* I say nothing, but I wink upon Win. You have a friend,
one Master Quarlous, comes here sometimes?

    Winwife. Why? he makes no love to her, does he?

    Littlewit. Not a tokenworth that ever I saw, I assure you, but—

    Winwife. What?

35   *Littlewit.* He is the more madcap o' the two. You do not
apprehend me.

    Win. You have a hot coal i' your mouth now, you cannot hold.

---

15 MELICOTTON *a cross between a peach and a quince.*
25 HOOD . . . CHAIN *both signs of rank.*
33 TOKENWORTH *a token was a halfpenny or farthing coin.*

Littlewit. Let me out with it, dear Win.

Win. I'll tell him myself.

Littlewit. Do, and take all the thanks, and much good do thy   40
pretty heart, Win.

Win. Sir, my mother has had her nativity-water cast lately by
the cunning men in Cow-lane, and they ha' told her her fortune,
and do ensure her she shall never have happy hour, unless she
marry within this sen'night, and when it is, it must be a madman,   45
they say.

Littlewit. Aye, but it must be a gentleman madman.

Win. Yes, so the tother man of Moorfields says.

Winwife. But does she believe 'em?

Littlewit. Yes, and has been at Bedlam twice since, every day, to   50
inquire if any gentleman be there, or to come there, mad!

Winwife. Why, this is a confederacy, a mere piece of practice
upon her, by these imposters!

Littlewit. I tell her so; or else say I that they mean some young
madcap-gentleman (for the devil can equivocate as well as a shop-   55
keeper) and therefore would I advise you to be a little madder
than Master Quarlous, hereafter.

Winwife. Where is she? Stirring yet?

Littlewit. Stirring! Yes, and studying an old elder, come from
Banbury, a suitor that puts in here at meal-tide, to praise the   60
painful brethren, or pray that the sweet singers may be restored;

42 NATIVITY-WATER CAST *to cast water was to diagnose disease by inspection of*
  the urine; to cast a nativity was to predict the future by means of a horoscope;
  Purecraft may have had both services performed.
43 CUNNING MEN *fortune-tellers.*
45 SEN'NIGHT *week.*
50 BEDLAM *the hospital of St. Mary of Bethlehem, an insane asylum. Visiting the*
  madmen was a common amusement.
52 CONFEDERACY *conspiracy.*
61 PAINFUL *hard-working.*
61 PAINFUL BRETHREN . . . SWEET SINGERS *Puritans.*

says a grace as long as his breath lasts him! Sometime the
spirit is so strong with him, it gets quite out of him, and then my
mother, or Win, are fain to fetch it again with malmsey, or *aqua*
65 *coelestis.*

Win. Yes indeed, we have such a tedious life with him for his
diet, and his clothes too; he breaks his buttons and cracks seams at
every saying he sobs out.

Littlewit. He cannot abide my vocation, he says.

70 *Win.* No, he told my mother a proctor was a claw of the
Beast, and that she had little less than committed abomination in
marrying me so as she has done.

Littlewit. Every line, he says, that a proctor writes, when it comes
to be read in the Bishop's court, is a long black hair, kembed out
75 of the tail of Antichrist.

Winwife. When came this proselyte?

Littlewit. Some three days since.

62 GRACE AS LONG *a Puritan grace was notoriously long.*

64 MALMSEY *rich, sweet wine.*

64–5 AQUA COELESTIS *a cordial.*

71 BEAST *cf. Revelation 13.*

74 KEMBED *combed.*

Act I Scene iii

[*Enter Quarlous.*]

Quarlous. O sir, ha' you ta'en soil here? It's well a man may
reach you after three hours running, yet! What an unmerciful
companion art thou, to quit thy lodging at such ungentlemanly

1 TA'EN SOIL *taken refuge; "a hunting term for a stag taking to water when hard
pressed" (H & S).*

hours! None but a scattered covey of fiddlers, or one of these rag-rakers in dunghills, or some marrow-bone man at most, would have been up when thou wert gone abroad, by all description. I pray thee what ailest thou, thou canst not sleep? Hast thou thorns i' thy eyelids, or thistles i' thy bed?

Winwife. I cannot tell. It seems you had neither i' your feet, that took this pain to find me.

Quarlous. No, an' I had, all the lyam-hounds o' the City should have drawn after you by the scent rather. Master John Littlewit! God save you, sir. 'Twas a hot night with some of us, last night, John. Shall we pluck a hair o' the same wolf today, Proctor John?

Littlewit. Do you remember, Master Quarlous, what we discoursed on last night?

Quarlous. Not I, John. Nothing that I either discourse or do; at those times I forfeit all to forgetfulness.

Littlewit. No? not concerning Win? Look you, there she is, and dressed as I told you she should be. Hark you, sir, had you forgot?
                                                    [*Whispers to Quarlous.*]

Quarlous. By this head, I'll beware how I keep you company, John, when I am drunk, an' you have this dangerous memory! That's certain.

Littlewit. Why sir?

Quarlous. Why? [*Turning to Winwife.*] We were all a little stained last night, sprinkled with a cup or two, and I agreed with Proctor John here to come and do somewhat with Win (I know not what 'twas) today; and he puts me in mind on't, now; he says he was coming to fetch me.——Before truth, if you have

5

10

15

20

25

30

---

5 MARROW-BONE MAN *praying man (who knelt on his "marrow-bones"), bound for morning prayer.*
11 LYAM-HOUNDS *blood-hounds, held by a lyam, or leather strap.*
14 HAIR O' THE SAME WOLF *cf. "hair of the dog that bit you."*

that fearful quality, John, to remember, when you are sober, John, what you promise drunk, John, I shall take heed of you, John. For this once, I am content to wink at you. Where's your wife? Come hither, Win.   *He kisseth her.*

35 *Win.* Why, John! do you see this, John? Look you! help me, John.

Littlewit. O Win, fie, what do you mean, Win? Be womanly, Win? make an outcry to your mother, Win? Master Quarlous is an honest gentleman, and our worshipful good friend, Win;

40 and he is Master Winwife's friend, too. And Master Winwife comes a suitor to your mother, Win, as I told you before, Win, and may perhaps be our father, Win. They'll do you no harm, Win; they are both our worshipful good friends. Master Quarlous! You must know Master Quarlous, Win; you must

45 not quarrel with Master Quarlous, Win.

Quarlous. No, we'll kiss again and fall in.

Littlewit. Yes, do, good Win.

Win. I' faith you are a fool, John.

Littlewit. A fool-John she calls me, do you mark that, gentle-

50 men? Pretty littlewit of velvet! A fool-John!

Quarlous. She may call you an apple-John, if you use this.

Winwife. Pray thee forbear, for my respect somewhat.

Quarlous. Hoy-day! How respective you are become o' the sudden! I fear this family will turn you reformed too; pray you

55 come about again. Because she is in possibility to be your

---

33 WINK AT YOU *overlook your fault.*

46 FALL IN *become reconciled.*

51 APPLE-JOHN *an apple which becomes very shriveled when kept; may also allude to "apple-squire," a pander.*

51 USE THIS *behave in this way usually.*

53 RESPECTIVE *concerned with respectability.*

55 COME ABOUT *"come round to a person's side or opinion" (OED).*

daughter-in-law, and may ask you blessing hereafter, when she
courts it to Tottenham to eat cream—well, I will forbear, sir; but
i' faith, would thou wouldst leave thy exercise of widow-
hunting once, this drawing after an old reverend smock by the
splay-foot! There cannot be an ancient tripe or trillibub i' the   60
town, but thou art straight nosing it; and 'tis a fine occupation
thou'lt confine thyself to, when thou hast got one—-scrubbing a
piece of buff, as if thou hadst the perpetuity of Pannyer Alley to
stink in; or perhaps, worse, currying a carcass that thou hast bound
thyself to alive. I'll be sworn, some of them, that thou art or hast   65
been a suitor to, are so old as no chaste or married pleasure can ever
become 'em. The honest instrument of procreation has, forty
years since, left to belong to 'em. Thou must visit 'em, as thou
wouldst do a tomb, with a torch, or three handfuls of link,
flaming hot, and so thou mayst hap to make 'em feel thee, and   70
after, come to inherit according to thy inches. A sweet course for
a man to waste the brand of life for, to be still raking himself a
fortune in an old woman's embers; we shall ha' thee, after thou
hast been but a month married to one of 'em, look like the
quartan ague and the black jaundice met in a face, and walk as if   75
thou hadst borrowed legs of a spinner, and voice of a cricket. I
would endure to hear fifteen sermons a week for her, and such

57 TOTTENHAM *Tottenham Court, known for cakes and cream, etc.*
59 DRAWING AFTER *hunting term: tracking by the scent.*
59 SMOCK *derogatory term for a woman.*
60 TRIPE OR TRILLIBUB *literally, entrails; applied contemptuously to a person.*
63 PERPETUITY *perpetual tenure.*
63 PANNYER ALLEY *associated with buff leather.*
69 LINK *tow and pitch for torches.*
71 INHERIT . . . INCHES *N.*
72 BRAND *torch.*
75 QUARTAN AGUE *fever in which paroxysms recur every fourth day.*
76 SPINNER *spider.*
77 FOR *instead of.*

coarse and loud ones as some of 'em must be; I would e'en desire
of Fate I might dwell in a drum, and take in my sustenance with
80 an old broken tobacco-pipe and a straw. Dost thou ever think to
bring thine ears or stomach to the patience of a dry grace as long as
thy tablecloth, and droned out by thy son here, that might be thy
father, till all the meat o' thy board has forgot it was that day i' the
kitchen? Or to brook the noise made in a question of predestina-
85 tion, by the good laborers and painful eaters assembled together,
put to 'em by the matron, your spouse, who moderates with a cup
of wine, ever and anon, and a sentence out of Knox between? Or
the perpetual spitting, before and after a sober drawn exhortation
of six hours, whose better part was the hum-ha-hum? Or to hear
90 prayers groaned out over thy iron-chests, as if they were charms to
break 'em? And all this, for the hope of two apostle-spoons, to
suffer! And a cup to eat a caudle in! For that will be thy legacy.
She'll ha' conveyed her state, safe enough from thee, an' she be a
right widow.

95   *Winwife.* Alas, I am quite off that scent now.

   Quarlous. How so?

   Winwife. Put off by a brother of Banbury, one that, they say, is
come here and governs all, already.

   Quarlous. What do you call him? I knew divers of those Ban-
100 burians when I was in Oxford.

   Winwife. Master Littlewit can tell us.

   Littlewit. Sir! Good Win, go in, and if Master Barthol'mew
Cokes his man come for the licence (the little old fellow), let him

81 PATIENCE *suffering.*
86 MODERATES *presides, arbitrates.*
87 SENTENCE *pithy saying* (L. sententia).
88 DRAWN *long drawn out.*
90 IRON-CHESTS *iron or iron-bound coffers in which valuables were kept.*
91 APOSTLE-SPOONS *spoons ornamented with figures of the apostles.*
93 CONVEYED HER STATE *willed her estate to someone else.*

speak with me. What say you, gentlemen?   [*Exit Win.*]

   Winwife. What call you the reverend elder you told me of 105
—your Banbury man?

   Littlewit. Rabbi Busy, sir. He is more than an elder, he is a
prophet, sir.

   Quarlous. O, I know him! A baker, is he not?

   Littlewit. He was a baker, sir, but he does dream now, and see 110
visions; he has given over his trade.

   Quarlous. I remember that too—out of a scruple he took, that
(in spiced conscience) those cakes he made were served to bridals,
maypoles, morrises, and such profane feasts and meetings. His
Christian name is Zeal-of-the-land.   115

   Littlewit. Yes, sir, Zeal-of-the-land Busy.

   Winwife. How, what a name's there!

   Littlewit. O, they have all such names, sir. He was witness for
Win here (they will not be called godfathers), and named her Win-
the-fight. You thought her name had been Winifred, did you 120
not?

   Winwife. I did indeed.

   Littlewit. He would ha' thought himself a stark reprobate, if it
had.

   Quarlous. Aye, for there was a blue-starch-woman o' the name, 125
at the same time. A notable hypocritical vermin it is; I know him.
One that stands upon his face more than his faith, at all times; ever
in seditious motion, and reproving for vain-glory; of a most

113 SPICED *over-scrupulous.*
113 BRIDALS *wedding feasts.*
114 MORRISES *morris-dances, performed at May-day games and other rustic
    festivals, condemned by the Puritans as pagan rites.*
125 BLUE-STARCH-WOMAN *woman who sold blue starch, which was used for ruffs;
    starch was associated with luxurious dress and hence pride.*
127 STANDS UPON *relies on.*
128 SEDITIOUS MOTION *i.e. looking for trouble and stirring discontent.*

lunatic conscience and spleen, and affects the violence of singu-
130 larity in all he does; (he has undone a grocer here, in Newgate-
market, that broke with him, trusted him with currants, as
arrant a zeal as he, that's by the way). By his profession he will
ever be i' the state of innocence, though, and childhood; derides
all antiquity; defies any other learning than inspiration; and what
135 discretion soever years should afford him, it is all prevented in his
original ignorance. Ha' not to do with him; for he is a fellow of a
most arrogant and invincible dullness, I assure you. Who is this?

130-2 (HE HAS UNDONE . . . WAY) *N.*
132 BY HIS PROFESSION *ostensibly, according to his profession (of faith).*
135 PREVENTED *forestalled.*

Act I Scene iv

[*Enter Wasp, Win.*]

Wasp. By your leave, gentlemen, with all my heart to you, and
God you good morrow. Master Littlewit, my business is to you.
Is this licence ready?

Littlewit. Here, I ha' it for you in my hand, Master Humphrey.
5 *Wasp.* That's well. Nay, never open or read it to me; it's labor
in vain, you know. I am no clerk, I scorn to be saved by my book,
i' faith I'll hang first. Fold it up o' your word and gi' it me. What
must you ha' for't?

Littlewit. We'll talk of that anon, Master Humphrey.
10 *Wasp.* Now, or not at all, good Master Proctor; I am for no
anons, I assure you.

2 GOD YOU *God give you.*
6 SAVED . . . BOOK *N.*

Littlewit. Sweet Win, bid Solomon send me the little black box within, in my study.

Wasp. Aye, quickly, good mistress, I pray you; for I have both eggs o' the spit, and iron i' the fire. Say what you must have, good Master Littlewit. [*Exit Win.*]

Littlewit. Why, you know the price, Master Numps.

Wasp. I know? I know nothing, I. What tell you me of knowing? Now I am in haste, sir, I do not know, and I will not know, and I scorn to know, and yet (now I think on't) I will and do know as well as another; you must have a mark for your thing here, and eightpence for the box. I could ha' saved twopence i' that, an' I had bought it myself, but here's fourteen shillings for you. Good Lord, how long your little wife stays! Pray God, Solomon, your clerk, be not looking i' the wrong box, Master Proctor.

Littlewit. Good i' faith! No. I warrant you, Solomon is wiser than so, sir.

Wasp. Fie, fie, fie, by your leave, Master Littlewit, this is scurvy, idle, foolish, and abominable; with all my heart, I do not like it.

Winwife. Do you hear, Jack Littlewit? What business does thy pretty head think this fellow may have, that he keeps such a coil with?

Quarlous. More than buying of gingerbread i' the Cloister, here (for that we allow him), or a gilt pouch i' the Fair?

Littlewit. Master Quarlous, do not mistake him. He is his master's both-hands, I assure you.

Quarlous. What? to pull on his boots, a-mornings, or his stockings, does he?

Littlewit. Sir, if you have a mind to mock him, mock him softly, and look tother way; for if he apprehend you flout him

21 MARK *thirteen shillings and fourpence.*
31 KEEPS SUCH A COIL *makes such a fuss.*
33 CLOISTER *N.*

once, he will fly at you presently. A terrible testy old fellow, and his name is Wasp too.

Quarlous. Pretty insect! make much on him.

Wasp. A plague o' this box, and the pox too, and on him that
45 made it, and her that went for't, and all that should ha' sought it, sent it, or brought it! Do you see, sir?

Littlewit. Nay, good Master Wasp.

Wasp. Good Master Hornet, turd i' your teeth, hold you your tongue! Do not I know you? Your father was a 'pothecary, and
50 sold glisters, more than he gave, I wusse. And turd i' your little wife's teeth too—here she comes—'twill make her spit, as fine as she is, for all her velvet-custard on her head, sir.

[*Re-enter Win.*]

Littlewit. O! be civil, Master Numps.

Wasp. Why, say I have a humor not to be civil; how then? Who
55 shall compel me? You?

Littlewit. Here is the box now.

Wasp. Why a pox o' your box, once again. Let your little wife stale in it, an' she will. Sir, I would have you to understand, and these gentlemen too, if they please—

60 *Winwife.* With all our hearts, sir.

Wasp. That I have a charge, gentlemen.

Littlewit. They do apprehend, sir.

Wasp. Pardon me, sir, neither they nor you can apprehend me yet. (You are an ass.) I have a young master, he is now upon his
65 making and marring; the whole care of his well-doing is now mine. His foolish schoolmasters have done nothing but run up

50 GLISTERS *enemas.*

50 I WUSSE *certainly (variant of iwis).*

52 VELVET-CUSTARD *velvet hat, shaped like a custard (a kind of pie).*

58 STALE *urinate (usually of animals).*

and down the country with him to beg puddings and cake-bread of his tenants, and almost spoiled him; he has learned nothing but to sing catches and repeat *Rattle bladder rattle* and *O Madge*. I dare not let him walk alone for fear of learning of vile 70 tunes, which he will sing at supper and in the sermon-times! If he meet but a carman i' the street, and I find him not talk to keep him off on him, he will whistle him and all his tunes over at night in his sleep! He has a head full of bees! I am fain now, for this little time I am absent, to leave him in charge with a gentlewoman. 75 'Tis true, she is a justice of peace his wife, and a gentlewoman o' the hood, and his natural sister; but what may happen under a woman's government, there's the doubt. Gentlemen, you do not know him. He is another manner of piece than you think for — but nineteen year old, and yet he is taller than either of you, by the 80 head, God bless him.

Quarlous. [*To Winwife.*] Well, methinks this is a fine fellow!

Winwife. He has made his master a finer by this description, I should think.

Quarlous. 'Faith, much about one; it's cross and pile whether, 85 for a new farthing.

Wasp. I'll tell you, gentlemen—

Littlewit. Will't please you drink, Master Wasp?

Wasp. Why, I ha' not talked so long to be dry, sir. You see no dust or cobwebs come out o' my mouth, do you? You'd ha' me 90 gone, would you?

---

67 PUDDINGS *sausages.*
67–8 CAKE-BREAD *bread of fine quality.*
72 CARMAN *carter, carrier; carmen were proverbially whistlers.*
73 ON *from.*
74 HAS A HEAD . . . BEES *is full of eccentric whims.*
74 FAIN *obliged.*
85 CROSS AND PILE *the two sides of a coin; hence, head or tails.*
85 WHETHER *which (of the two).*

Littlewit. No, but you were in haste e'en now, Master Numps.

Wasp. What an' I were? So I am still, and yet I will stay too. Meddle you with your match, your Win, there; she has as little wit
95 as her husband it seems. I have others to talk to.

Littlewit. She's my match indeed, and as little wit as I, good!

Wasp. We ha' been but a day and a half in town, gentlemen, 'tis true; and yesterday i' the afternoon we walked London to show the city to the gentlewoman he shall marry, Mistress Grace;
100 but afore I will endure such another half day with him I'll be drawn with a good gib-cat through the great pond at home, as his uncle Hodge was! Why, we could not meet that heathen thing all day, but stayed him. He would name you all the signs over, as he went, aloud; and where he spied a parrot or a monkey, there he
105 was pitched with all the little long-coats about him, male and female; no getting him away! I thought he would ha' run mad o' the black boy in Bucklersbury that takes the scurvy, roguy tobacco there.

Littlewit. You say true, Master Numps; there's such a one
110 indeed.

Wasp. It's no matter whether there be or no. What's that to you? *Quarlous.* He will not allow of John's reading at any hand.

101 DRAWN . . . POND *N.*
101 GIB-CAT *tomcat; Gib is short for Gilbert.*
103 STAYED *waited for.*
105 PITCHED *planted.*
105 LITTLE LONG-COATS *children.*
107 BUCKLERSBURY *name of a street.*
112 READING *comment.*
112 AT ANY HAND *on any condition.*

Act I Scene v

[Enter Cokes, Mistress Overdo, Grace.]

Cokes. O Numps! are you here, Numps? Look where I am, Numps! And Mistress Grace, too! Nay, do not look angerly, Numps. My sister is here, and all. I do not come without her.

Wasp. What the mischief, do you come with her? Or she with you? 5

Cokes. We came all to seek you, Numps.

Wasp. To seek me? Why, did you all think I was lost? Or run away with your fourteen shillings worth of small ware here? Or that I had changed it i' the Fair for hobbyhorses? 'Sprecious—to seek me! 10

Mistress Overdo. Nay, good Master Numps, do you show discretion, though he be exorbitant, as Master Overdo says, an't be but for conservation of the peace.

Wasp. Marry gip, goody she-justice, Mistress French-hood! Turd i' your teeth; and turd i' your French-hood's teeth, too, to 15 do you service, do you see? Must you quote your Adam to me? You think you are Madam Regent still, Mistress Overdo, when I am in place? No such matter, I assure you; your reign is out when I am in, dame.

Mistress Overdo. I am content to be in abeyance, sir, and be 20

---

9 'SPRECIOUS *by God's precious blood.*

11 DO YOU SHOW *not a question, but a polite command.*

12 AN'T *if it.*

14 MARRY GIP *get along with you; "gip" (like gee-up, addressed to a horse) was confused with "by Mary Gipcy" (by St. Mary of Egypt).*

14 FRENCH-HOOD *a fashionable hood, especially among citizens' wives.*

governed by you; so should he too, if he did well; but 'twill be
expected you should also govern your passions.

   Wasp. Will't so forsooth? Good Lord! How sharp you are!
With being at Bedlam yesterday? Whetstone has set an edge upon
25 you, has he?

   Mistress Overdo. Nay, if you know not what belongs to your
dignity, I do, yet, to mine.

   Wasp. Very well, then.

   Cokes. Is this the licence, Numps? For love's sake, let me see't. I
30 never saw a licence.

   Wasp. Did you not so? Why, you shall not see't, then.

   Cokes. An' you love me, good Numps.

   Wasp. Sir, I love you, and yet I do not love you, i' these
fooleries; set your heart at rest; there's nothing in't but hard
35 words; and what would you see't for?

   Cokes. I would see the length and the breadth on't, that's all;
and I will see't now, so I will.

   Wasp. You sha' not see it here.

   Cokes. Then I'll see't at home, and I'll look upo' the case here.
40   *Wasp.* Why, do so; [*Holds up the box.*] a man must give way to
him a little in trifles, gentlemen: these are errors, diseases of youth,
which he will mend when he comes to judgment and knowledge
of matters. I pray you conceive so, and I thank you. And I pray
you pardon him, and I thank you again.
45   *Quarlous.* Well, this dry nurse, I say still, is a delicate man.

   Winwife. And I am for the cosset, his charge! Did you ever see a
fellow's face more accuse him for an ass?

   Quarlous. Accuse him? It confesses him one without accusing.
What pity 'tis yonder wench should marry such a cokes!
50   *Winwife.* 'Tis true.

   24 WHETSTONE "*Probably the name of a keeper at the Bethlehem Hospital*"
   (*H &S*), *in any case punning on the stone for sharpening knives.*
   46 COSSET *spoilt child.*

Quarlous. She seems to be discreet, and as sober as she is handsome.

Winwife. Aye, and if you mark her, what a restrained scorn she casts upon all his behavior and speeches!

Cokes. Well, Numps, I am now for another piece of business   55
more, the Fair, Numps, and then—

Wasp. Bless me! deliver me, help, hold me! the Fair!

Cokes. Nay, never fidge up and down, Numps, and vex itself. I am resolute Barthol'mew, in this; I'll make no suit on't to you; 'twas all the end of my journey, indeed, to show Mistress Grace   60
my Fair. I call't my Fair because of Barthol'mew: you know my name is Barthol'mew, and Barthol'mew Fair.

Littlewit. That was mine afore, gentlemen—this morning. I had that i' faith, upon his licence; believe me, there he comes after me.   65

Quarlous. Come, John, this ambitious wit of yours, I am afraid, will do you no good i' the end.

Littlewit. No? Why sir?

Quarlous. You grow so insolent with it, and overdoing, John, that if you look not to it, and tie it up, it will bring you to some   70
obscure place in time, and there 'twill leave you.

Winwife. Do not trust it too much, John; be more sparing, and use it but now and then. A wit is a dangerous thing in this age; do not overbuy it.

Littlewit. Think you so, gentlemen? I'll take heed on't hereafter.   75

Win. Yes, do, John.

Cokes. A pretty little soul, this same Mistress Littlewit! Would I might marry her.

Grace. [*Aside.*] So would I, or anybody else, so I might 'scape you.   80

58 FIDGE *move restlessly.*
58 ITSELF *humorous or contemptuous variant of yourself.*
74 OVERBUY *buy too much of (?) or pay too much for.*

Cokes. Numps, I will see it, Numps, 'tis decreed. Never be melancholy for the matter.

Wasp. Why, see it, sir, do see it! Who hinders you? Why do you not go see it? 'Slid, see it.

85 *Cokes.* The Fair, Numps, the Fair.

Wasp. Would the Fair and all the drums and rattles in't were i' your belly for me! They are already i' your brain; he that had the means to travel your head, now, should meet finer sights than any are i' the Fair, and make a finer voyage on't, to see it all hung with
90 cockle-shells, pebbles, fine wheat-straws, and here and there a chicken's feather and a cobweb.

Quarlous. Good faith, he looks, methinks, an' you mark him, like one that were made to catch flies, with his Sir Cranion legs.

Winwife. And his Numps to flap 'em away.

95 *Wasp.* God be w'you, sir. There's your bee in a box, and much good do't you.   [*Gives him the box and starts to leave.*]

Cokes. Why, your friend, and Barthol'mew, an' you be so contumacious.

Quarlous. What mean you, Numps?

100 *Wasp.* I'll not be guilty, I, gentlemen.

Mistress Overdo. You will not let him go, brother, and lose him?

Cokes. Who can hold that will away? I had rather lose him than the Fair, I wusse.

Wasp. You do not know the inconvenience, gentlemen, you
105 persuade to; nor what trouble I have with him in these humors. If he go to the Fair, he will buy of everything to a baby there; and household-stuff for that too. If a leg or an arm on him did not grow on, he would lose it i' the press. Pray heaven I bring him off with one stone! And then he is such a ravener after fruit!

93 SIR CRANION *crane-fly, which has long legs.*
95 GOD BE W'YOU *God be with you, good bye.*
109 STONE *testicle.*

You will not believe what a coil I had t'other day to compound a 110
business between a Cather'ne-pear-woman and him about snatch-
ing! 'Tis intolerable, gentlemen.

Winwife. O! but you must not leave him now to these hazards,
Numps.

Wasp. Nay, he knows too well I will not leave him, and that 115
makes him presume. Well, sir, will you go now? If you have
such an itch i' your feet to foot it to the Fair, why do you stop?
Am I your tarriers? Go, will you go, sir? Why do you not go?

Cokes. O Numps! have I brought you about? Come, Mistress
Grace, and sister, I am resolute Bat, i'faith, still. 120

Grace. Truly, I have no such fancy to the Fair, nor ambition to
see it; there's none goes thither of any quality or fashion.

Cokes. O Lord, sir! You shall pardon me, Mistress Grace, we
are enow of ourselves to make it a fashion; and for qualities, let
Numps alone, he'll find qualities. 125

　　　　　[Exeunt Cokes, Wasp, Grace, Mistress Overdo.]

Quarlous. What a rogue in apprehension is this, to understand
her language no better!

Winwife. Aye, and offer to marry to her! Well, I will leave the
chase of my widow for today, and directly to the Fair. These flies
cannot, this hot season, but engender us excellent creeping sport. 130

Quarlous. A man that has but a spoonful of brain would think
so. Farewell, John.　　　　　*[Exeunt Quarlous, Winwife.]*

Littlewit. Win, you see 'tis in fashion to go to the Fair, Win. We
must to the Fair too, you and I, Win. I have an affair i' the Fair,

---

111 CATHER'NE PEAR *Catherine pear; cf. IV.2.43.*
118 TARRIERS *hinderers, delayers.*
124 QUALITIES *characteristics, moral attributes (Grace used "quality" in the
　　sense of social position).*
124–5 LET . . . ALONE *leave it to, trust.*
126 APPREHENSION *understanding.*

135 Win, a puppet play of mine own making—say nothing—that I
writ for the motion-man, which you must see, Win.

Win. I would I might, John, but my mother will never consent
to such a "profane motion," she will call it.

Littlewit. Tut, we'll have a device, a dainty one; (now, Wit, help
140 at a pinch, good Wit come, come, good Wit, an't be thy will). I
have it, Win, I have it i' faith, and 'tis a fine one. Win, long to
eat of a pig, sweet Win, i' the Fair; do you see? I' the heart o' the
Fair; not at Pie-corner. Your mother will do anything, Win, to
satisfy your longing, you know; pray thee long, presently, and be
145 sick o' the sudden, good Win. I'll go in and tell her. Cut thy lace
i' the meantime, and play the hypocrite, sweet Win.

Win. No, I'll not make me unready for it. I can be hypocrite
enough, though I were never so strait-laced.

Littlewit. You say true. You have been bred i' the family, and
150 brought up to't. Our mother is a most elect hypocrite, and has
maintained us all this seven year with it, like gentlefolks.

Win. Aye, let her alone, John; she is not a wise wilful widow
for nothing, nor a sanctified sister for a song. And let me alone too;
I ha' somewhat o' the mother in me, you shall see. Fetch her, fetch
155 her. Ah ah!   [*Exit Littlewit.*]

136 MOTION-MAN *puppet-master.*
143 PIE-CORNER *on the edge of Smithfield.*
145 LACE *i.e. of her bodice.*
147 MAKE ME UNREADY *undress.*
148 STRAIT-LACED *both literally (with bodice tightly laced) and figuratively
(strict in morality).*
150 ELECT *referring to the Puritan belief that some are chosen for salvation at
birth.*
151 SEVEN YEAR *see* V.2.49–50.
154 MOTHER *punning on the figurative meaning: hysteria, thought to originate in
the womb.*

Act I Scene vi

[*Enter Purecraft, Littlewit.*]

Purecraft. Now the blaze of the beauteous discipline fright away this evil from our house! How now, Win-the-fight, child, how do you? Sweet child, speak to me.

Win. Yes, forsooth.

Purecraft. Look up, sweet Win-the-fight, and suffer not the enemy to enter you at this door; remember that your education has been with the purest. What polluted one was it that named first the unclean beast, pig, to you, child?   5

Win. Uh, uh!

Littlewit. Not I, o' my sincerity, mother. She longed above three hours ere she would let me know it. Who was it, Win?   10

Win. A profane black thing with a beard, John.

Purecraft. O! resist it, Win-the-fight, it is the Tempter, the wicked Tempter; you may know it by the fleshly motion of pig. Be strong against it, and its foul temptations, in these assaults, whereby it broacheth flesh and blood, as it were, on the weaker side; and pray against its carnal provocations, good child, sweet child, pray.   15

Littlewit. Good mother, I pray you that she may eat some pig, and her belly full, too; and do not you cast away your own child, and perhaps one of mine, with your tale of the Tempter. How do you, Win? Are you not sick?   20

Win. Yes, a great deal, John. Uh, uh!

Purecraft. What shall we do? Call our zealous brother Busy

1   BEAUTEOUS DISCIPLINE *cant phrase for Puritan doctrine.*
14   MOTION *urging.*
16   BROACHETH *breaks into.*

hither, for his faithful fortification in this charge of the adversary;
25 child, my dear child, you shall eat pig, be comforted, my sweet
child. [*Exit Littlewit.*]

Win. Aye, but i' the Fair, mother.

Purecraft. I mean i' the Fair, if it can be anyway made or found
lawful. Where is our brother Busy? Will he not come? Look up,
30 child.

[*Re-enter Littlewit.*]

Littlewit. Presently, mother, as soon as he has cleansed his
beard. I found him fast by the teeth i' the cold turkey-pie i' the
cupboard, with a great white loaf on his left hand, and a glass of
malmsey on his right.

35 *Purecraft.* Slander not the brethren, wicked one.

Littlewit. Here he is now, purified, mother.

[*Enter Busy.*]

Purecraft. O Brother Busy! your help here to edify and raise us
up in a scruple. My daughter Win-the-fight is visited with a
natural disease of woman, called "A longing to eat pig."

40 *Littlewit.* Aye sir, a Barthol'mew-pig, and in the Fair.

Purecraft. And I would be satisfied from you, religiously-wise,
whether a widow of the sanctified assembly, or a widow's
daughter, may commit the act without offence to the weaker
sisters.

45 *Busy.* Verily, for the disease of longing, it is a disease, a carnal
disease, or appetite, incident to woman; and as it is carnal, and
incident, it is natural, very natural. Now pig, it is a meat, and a
meat that is nourishing, and may be longed for, and so consequently eaten; it may be eaten; very exceeding well eaten. But
50 in the Fair, and as a Barthol'mew-pig, it cannot be eaten, for the
very calling it a Barthol'mew-pig, and to eat it so, is a spice of

51 SPICE *kind.*

idolatry, and you make the Fair no better than one of the high places. This, I take it, is the state of the question. A high place.

Littlewit. Aye, but in state of necessity, place should give place, Master Busy. (I have a conceit left, yet.)   55

Purecraft. Good Brother Zeal-of-the-land, think to make it as lawful as you can.

Littlewit. Yes sir, and as soon as you can; for it must be, sir; you see the danger my little wife is in, sir.

Purecraft. Truly, I do love my child dearly, and I would not   60
have her miscarry, or hazard her first fruits, if it might be otherwise.

Busy. Surely it may be otherwise, but it is subject to construction—subject, and hath a face of offence with the weak, a great face, a foul face, but that face may have a veil put over it, and be   65
shadowed, as it were. It may be eaten, and in the Fair, I take it, in a booth, the tents of the wicked. The place is not much, not very much; we may be religious in midst of the profane, so it be eaten with a reformed mouth, with sobriety, and humbleness; not gorged in with gluttony or greediness; there's the fear: for,   70
should she go there, as taking pride in the place, or delight in the unclean dressing, to feed the vanity of the eye or the lust of the palate, it were not well, it were not fit, it were abominable, and not good.

Littlewit. Nay, I knew that afore, and told her on't; but courage,   75
Win, we'll be humble enough; we'll seek out the homeliest booth i' the Fair, that's certain. Rather than fail, we'll eat it o' the ground.

Purecraft. Aye, and I'll go with you myself, Win-the-fight, and my brother, Zeal-of-the-land, shall go with us too, for our better   80
consolation.

---

52 IDOLATRY *because of the use of a saint's name.*
52-3 HIGH PLACES *associated in the Bible with the worship of idols; cf.* III.6.85–6.

Win. Uh, uh!

Littlewit. Aye, and Solomon, too, Win; the more the merrier.

Win; [*Aside to Win.*] we'll leave Rabbi Busy in a booth.—
85 Solomon, my cloak.

[*Enter Solomon.*]

Solomon. Here, sir.

Busy. In the way of comfort to the weak, I will go and eat. I
will eat exceedingly and prophesy; there may be a good use made
of it, too, now I think on't: by the public eating of swine's flesh,
90 to profess our hate and loathing of Judaism, whereof the brethren
stand taxed. I will therefore eat, yea, I will eat exceedingly.

Littlewit. Good, i' faith, I will eat heartily too, because I will be
no Jew; I could never away with that stiffnecked generation. And
truly, I hope my little one will be like me, that cries for pig so, i'
95 the mother's belly.

Busy. Very likely, exceeding likely, very exceeding likely.

[*Exeunt.*]

---

91 STAND TAXED *because of their emphasis on the Old Testament, which also
explains the semi-humorous reference to him as Rabbi Busy.*

93 AWAY *agree.*

Act II Scene i

[*Enter Justice Overdo, disguised as mad Arthur of Bradley. During his soliloquy Leatherhead and Trash enter and set up their stands.*]

Overdo. Well, in justice' name, and the King's, and for the commonwealth! defy all the world, Adam Overdo, for a disguise, and all story; for thou hast fitted thyself, I swear. Fain would I meet the Lynceus now, that eagle's eye, that piercing Epidaurian serpent (as my Quintus Horace calls him), that could 5 discover a justice of peace (and lately of the quorum) under this covering. They may have seen many a fool in the habit of a justice; but never till now a justice in the habit of a fool. Thus must we do, though, that wake for the public good; and thus hath the wise magistrate done in all ages. There is a doing of right out of wrong, 10

SD *see Appendix* II, *p. 211, and* II.2.N.
MAD ARTHUR OF BRADLEY *see* II.2.117–8.
2 COMMONWEALTH *common weal, general good.*
3 FITTED *furnished.*
4 LYNCEUS *an Argonaut with extraordinarily keen sight.*
5 EPIDAURIAN SERPENT *serpents, which were supposed to have keen sight, were sacred to Aesculapius, whose chief temple was at Epidaurus.*
6 QUORUM *"originally certain justices of the peace, usually of eminent learning or ability, whose presence was necessary to constitute a bench"* (OED).
9 WAKE *stay awake, watch out.*

Act II Scene i

if the way be found. Never shall I enough commend a worthy
worshipful man, sometime a capital member of this city, for his
high wisdom in this point, who would take you, now the habit
of a porter, now of a carman, now of the dog-killer, in this month
15 of August; and in the winter of a seller of tinder-boxes. And what
would he do in all these shapes? Marry, go you into every ale-
house, and down into every cellar; measure the length of puddings,
take the gauge of black pots and cans, aye, and custards, with a
stick; and their circumference, with a thread; weigh the loaves of
20 bread on his middle-finger; then would he send for 'em, home;
give the puddings to the poor, the bread to the hungry, the
custards to his children; break the pots and burn the cans himself;
he would not trust his corrupt officers; he would do't himself.
Would all men in authority would follow this worthy precedent!
25 For alas, as we are public persons, what do we know? Nay, what
can we know? We hear with other men's ears; we see with other
men's eyes. A foolish constable or a sleepy watchman is all our
information; he slanders a gentleman by the virtue of his place,
as he calls it, and we, by the vice of ours, must believe him. As, a
30 while gone, they made me, yea me, to mistake an honest zealous
pursuivant for a seminary, and a proper young Bachelor of Music
for a bawd. This we are subject to, that live in high place; all our
intelligence is idle, and most of our intelligencers knaves; and, by
your leave, ourselves thought little better, if not arrant fools, for
35 believing 'em. I, Adam Overdo, am resolved therefore to spare

11–2 A WORTHY . . . MAN N.

12 CAPITAL *leading.*

31 PURSUIVANT *civil servant employed to summon Catholics or Puritans before
the ecclesiastical courts.*

31 SEMINARY *priest trained abroad in a Catholic seminary.*

33 INTELLIGENCE *information.*

33 IDLE *baseless.*

33 INTELLIGENCERS *informers.*

spy-money hereafter, and make mine own discoveries. Many are the yearly enormities of this Fair, in whose courts of Pie-powders I have had the honor during the three days sometimes to sit as judge. But this is the special day for detection of those foresaid enormities. Here is my black book for the purpose; this the cloud that hides me; under this covert I shall see and not be seen. On, Junius Brutus! And as I began so I'll end: in justice' name, and the King's; and for the commonwealth!

40

37 PIE-POWDERS "*a summary court formerly held at fairs and markets to administer justice among itinerant dealers and others temporarily present*" (OED), *see Intro., p. 5.*
40 CLOUD *possibly, as Alden suggests, an allusion to the cloud which hid Aeneas and his followers as they entered Carthage* (Aeneid, I, *412*).
41 COVERT *cover.*
42 JUNIUS BRUTUS *Roman hero of the time of the Tarquins, known for disguising himself as an idiot to escape execution and for his inflexibility as a judge.*

Act II Scene ii

Leatherhead. The Fair's pest'lence dead, methinks; people come not abroad today, whatever the matter is. Do you hear, Sister Trash, Lady o' the Basket? Sit farther with your gingerbread-progeny there, and hinder not the prospect of my shop, or I'll ha' it proclaimed i' the Fair what stuff they are made on.

5

Trash. Why, what stuff are they made on, Brother Leatherhead? Nothing but what's wholesome, I assure you.

Leatherhead. Yes, stale bread, rotten eggs, musty ginger, and dead honey, you know.

ACT II SCENE II *N.*
1 PEST'LENCE DEAD *as deserted as if the plague were rampant.*

10   *Overdo.* [*Aside.*] Aye! have I met with enormity so soon?

      Leatherhead. I shall mar your market, old Joan.

      Trash. Mar my market, thou too-proud pedlar? Do thy worst; I defy thee, I, and thy stable of hobbyhorses. I pay for my ground as well as thou dost; an' thou wrong'st me, for all thou

15 art parcel-poet and an inginer, I'll find a friend shall right me and make a ballad of thee and thy cattel all over. Are you puffed up with the pride of your wares? Your arsedine?

      Leatherhead. Go to, old Joan, I'll talk with you anon; and take you down too afore Justice Overdo; he is the man must charm

20 you. I'll ha' you i' the Pie-powders.

      Trash. Charm me? I'll meet thee face to face afore his worship when thou dar'st; and though I be a little crooked o' my body, I'll be found as upright in my dealing as any woman in Smithfield, I. Charm me?

25   *Overdo.* [*Aside.*] I am glad to hear my name is their terror, yet; this is doing of justice.

               [*Enter Passengers.*]

      Leatherhead. What do you lack? What is't you buy? What do you lack? Rattles, drums, halberts, horses, babies o' the best? Fiddles o' th' finest?

        Enter Costermonger [*followed by Nightingale*].

30   *Costermonger.* Buy any pears, pears, fine, very fine pears!

      Trash. Buy any gingerbread, gilt gingerbread!

---

15 PARCEL-POET *part poet, with the implication of poetaster.*

15 INGINER *inventor, contriver (of puppet shows, etc.)*

16 CATTEL *property.*

17 ARSEDINE *imitation gold leaf used to decorate toys.*

18–9 TAKE . . . DOWN *humble.*

19 CHARM *overcome or subdue.*

27 WHAT DO YOU LACK? *the stock phrase of the Elizabethan storekeeper or peddler.*

28 DRUMS, HALBERTS *toy drums and halberts.*

31 GILT *"Gold leaf was used to decorate gingerbread"* (Horsman).

Nightingale.   *Hey, now the Fair's a filling!*
                   O, for a tune to startle
                   The birds o' the booths here billing
                   Yearly with old Saint Bartle!   35
                   The drunkards they are wading,
                   The punks and chapmen trading;
                   Who'd see the Fair without his lading?

Buy any ballads; new ballads? [*Exeunt Passengers, Costermonger.*]
[*Enter Ursula from the back part of her booth.*]

Ursula. Fie upon't! Who would wear out their youth and prime   40
thus in roasting of pigs, that had any cooler vocation? Hell's a kind
of cold cellar to't, a very fine vault, o' my conscience! What,
Mooncalf!

Mooncalf. [*Within.*] Here, Mistress.

Nightingale. How now, Urs'la? In a heat, in a heat?   45

Ursula. [*To Mooncalf.*] My chair, you false faucet you; and my
morning's draught, quickly, a bottle of ale to quench me, rascal.
—I am all fire and fat, Nightingale; I shall e'en melt away to the
first woman, a rib again, I am afraid. I do water the ground in knots
as I go, like a great garden-pot; you may follow me by the S's I   50
make.

Nightingale. Alas, good Urs; was 'Zekiel here this morning?

Ursula. 'Zekiel? what 'Zekiel?

Nightingale. 'Zekiel Edgworth, the civil cutpurse; you know

36 WADING *i.e. staggering.*
37 CHAPMEN *merchants.*
38 LADING *load (of purchases).*
42 WHAT *a customary word for summoning a servant.*
46 FAUCET *tap for a barrel. Appropriate to Mooncalf's occupation and to his
    slightness.*
49 KNOTS *lines criss-crossing each other.*
50 GARDEN-POT *sprinkling can.*

55 him well enough—he that talks bawdy to you still. I call him my
secretary.

Ursula. He promised to be here this morning, I remember.

Nightingale. When he comes, bid him stay. I'll be back again
presently.

60   *Ursula.* Best take your morning's dew in your belly, Nightingale. (*Mooncalf brings in the chair.*) Come, sir, set it here. Did not
I bid you should get this chair let out o' the sides for me, that my
hips might play? You'll never think of anything till your dame
be rump-galled. 'Tis well, changeling; because it can take in your
65 grasshopper's thighs you care for no more. Now you look as
you had been i' the corner o' the booth, fleaing your breech with
a candle's end, and set fire o' the Fair. Fill, stote, fill.

Overdo. [*Aside.*] This pig-woman do I know, and I will put her
in for my second enormity; she hath been before me, punk,
70 pinnace, and bawd, any time these two and twenty years, upon
record i' the Pie-powders.

Ursula. Fill again, you unlucky vermin.

Mooncalf. Pray you be not angry, mistress; I'll ha' it widened
anon.

75   *Ursula.* No, no, I shall e'en dwindle away to't, ere the Fair be
done you think, now you ha' heated me! A poor vexed thing I
am. I feel myself dropping already, as fast as I can; two stone o'
suet a day is my proportion. I can but hold life and soul together

---

56 SECRETARY *literally, a confidant.*

64 CHANGELING *"a child (usually stupid or ugly) supposed to have been left by
fairies in exchange for one stolen"* (OED).

66–7 FLEAING YOUR BREECH . . . END *using a candle flame to get the fleas out of the
seams in your breeches.*

67 STOTE *weasel; another allusion to Mooncalf's slightness; cf.* II.5.57.

70 PINNACE *prostitute or go-between.*

77 TWO STONE *twenty-eight pounds.*

with this (here's to you, Nightingale) and a whiff of tobacco, at most. Where's my pipe now? Not filled? Thou arrant incubee!   80

Nightingale. Nay, Urs'la, thou'lt gall between the tongue and the teeth with fretting, now.

Ursula. How can I hope that ever he'll discharge his place of trust—tapster, a man of reckoning under me—that remembers nothing I say to him? [*Exit Nightingale.*] But look to't, sirrah, you   85
were best; threepence a pipeful I will ha' made of all my whole half-pound of tobacco, and a quarter of a pound of coltsfoot mixed with it too, to itch it out. I that have dealt so long in the fire will not be to seek in smoke, now. Then, six and twenty shillings a barrel I will advance o' my beer, and fifty shillings a   90
hundred o' my bottle-ale; I ha' told you the ways how to raise it. Froth your cans well i' the filling, at length, rogue, and jog your bottles o' the buttock, sirrah, then skink out the first glass, ever, and drink with all companies, though you be sure to be drunk; you'll misreckon the better, and be less ashamed on't. But your   95
true trick, rascal, must be to be ever busy, and mis-take away the bottles and cans in haste before they be half drunk off, and never hear anybody call (if they should chance to mark you) till you ha' brought fresh, and be able to forswear 'em. Give me a drink of ale.   100

Overdo. [*Aside.*] This is the very womb and bed of enormity,

---

80 INCUBEE *incubus, evil spirit.*
84 MAN OF RECKONING *both man of distinction (Horsman) and one who keeps accounts for the drinks.*
87 COLTSFOOT *an herb used as an adulterant in tobacco.*
88 ITCH ... OUT *variant form of eke ... out: supplement.*
89 TO SEEK *at a loss.*
90 ADVANCE *raise the price.*
93 SKINK *pour.*

gross as herself! This must all down for enormity, all, every whit
on't.   *One knocks.*

 Ursula. Look who's there, sirrah! Five shillings a pig is my price,
105 at least; if it be a sow-pig, sixpence more; if she be a great-bellied
wife, and long for't, sixpence more for that.

 Overdo. [*Aside.*] *O tempora! O mores!* I would not ha' lost my discovery of this one grievance for my place and worship o' the
bench. How is the poor subject abused here! Well, I will fall in
110 with her, and with her Mooncalf, and win out wonders of
enormity. [*To Ursula.*] By thy leave, goodly woman, and the fat-
ness of the Fair, oily as the King's constable's lamp, and shining
as his shoeing-horn! Hath thy ale virtue, or thy beer strength?
that the tongue of man may be tickled? and his palate pleased in
115 the morning? Let thy pretty nephew here go search and see.

 Ursula. What new roarer is this?

 Mooncalf. O Lord! do you not know him, mistress? 'Tis mad
Arthur of Bradley, that makes the orations. Brave master, old
Arthur of Bradley, how do you? Welcome to the Fair! When
120 shall we hear you again, to handle your matters? With your back
again a booth, ha? I ha' been one o' your little disciples i' my
days!

 Overdo. Let me drink, boy, with my love, thy aunt, here, that
I may be eloquent; but of thy best, lest it be bitter in my mouth,
125 and my words fall foul on the Fair.

103 SD ONE KNOCKS *Overdo N.*
107 O TEMPORA! O MORSE! *Cicero,* Against Catiline, *I, i, 2: "What an age!
What manners!"*
108 WORSHIP *respect.*
115 NEPHEW *not meant literally; used loosely of a close relationship.*
118 ARTHUR OF BRADLEY *the name is taken from an old ballad; the imaginary
personage referred to is described in the text.*
120 HANDLE YOUR MATTERS *treat your various topics.*
121 AGAIN *against.*
123 AUNT *not meant literally; cf.* NEPHEW *above.*

Ursula. Why dost thou not fetch him drink? And offer him to sit?

Mooncalf. Is't ale or beer, Master Arthur?

Overdo. Thy best, pretty stripling, thy best; the same thy dove drinketh and thou drawest on holy days.   130

Ursula. Bring him a sixpenny bottle of ale; they say a fool's handsel is lucky.

Overdo. Bring both, child. Ale for Arthur and beer for Bradley. Ale for thy aunt, boy. [*Exit Mooncalf.*] [*Aside.*] My disguise takes to the very wish and reach of it. I shall, by the benefit of this,   135 discover enough and more, and yet get off with the reputation of what I would be: a certain middling thing between a fool and a madman.

132 HANDSEL *"the first money taken by a trader in the morning, a luck-penny"* (OED).
134 TAKES *works.*

Act II Scene iii

[*Enter Knockem.*]

Knockem. What! my little lean Urs'la! my she-bear! art thou alive yet, with thy litter of pigs, to grunt out another Barthol'mew Fair, ha?

Ursula. Yes, and to amble afoot, when the Fair is done, to hear you groan out of a cart, up the heavy hill.   5

Knockem. Of Holborn, Urs'la, meanst thou so? For what? For what, pretty Urs?

1 SHE-BEAR *literal translation of Latin* ursa, *of which her name is a diminutive.*
5 HEAVY HILL *Holborn Hill, on the way to the gallows at Tyburn, where condemned criminals were taken by cart.*

    Ursula. For cutting halfpenny purses, or stealing little penny dogs out o' the Fair.

10   *Knockem.* O! good words, good words, Urs.

    Overdo. [*Aside.*] Another special enormity. A cutpurse of the sword, the boot, and the feather! Those are his marks.

                  [*Re-enter Mooncalf.*]

    Ursula. You are one of those horse-leeches that gave out I was dead in Turnbull Street of a surfeit of bottle-ale and tripes?

15   *Knockem.* No, 'twas better meat, Urs: cow's udders, cow's udders!

    Ursula. Well, I shall be meet with your mumbling mouth one day.

    Knockem. What? Thou'lt poison me with a newt in a bottle of
20 ale, wilt thou? Or a spider in a tobacco-pipe, Urs? Come, there's no malice in these fat folks. I never fear thee, an' I can 'scape thy lean Mooncalf here. Let's drink it out, good Urs, and no vapors!

                  [*Exit Ursula.*]

    Overdo. Dost thou hear, boy? (There's for thy ale, and the remnant for thee.) Speak in thy faith of a faucet, now; is this
25 goodly person before us here, this vapors, a knight of the knife?

    Mooncalf. What mean you by that, Master Arthur?

    Overdo. I mean a child of the horn-thumb, a babe of booty, boy; a cutpurse.

    Mooncalf. O Lord, sir! far from it. This is Master Dan

---

13 HORSE-LEECHES *veterinarians; figuratively, insatiable predators.*

17 MEET *even.*

19–20 NEWT . . . ALE *see* II.6.12.

22 VAPORS *here, as in* IV.4, *senseless quarreling* N.

27 CHILD *with perhaps a pun on the archaic meaning, a noble youth, as in* Childe Harold; *cf. "a knight of the knife" just before.*

27 HORN-THUMB *a sort of thimble worn by a cutpurse to protect his thumb from the edge of the knife.*

Knockem—Jordan, the ranger of Turnbull. He is a horse- 30
courser, sir.

Overdo. Thy dainty dame, though, called him cutpurse.

Mooncalf. Like enough, sir. She'll do forty such things in an
hour (an' you listen to her) for her recreation, if the toy take her i'
the greasy kerchief. It makes her fat, you see. She battens with it. 35

Overdo. [*Aside.*] Here might I ha' been deceived, now, and ha'
put a fool's blot upon myself, if I had not played an after-game o'
discretion.

Ursula comes in again dropping.

Knockem. Alas, poor Urs, this's an ill season for thee.

Ursula. Hang yourself, hackney-man. 40

Knockem. How, how, Urs? vapors? motion breed vapors?

Ursula. Vapors? Never tusk nor twirl your dibble, good
Jordan. I know what you'll take to a very drop. Though you be
captain o' the roarers, and fight well at the case of piss-pots, you
shall not fright me with your lion-chap, sir, nor your tusks. You 45
angry? You are hungry. Come, a pig's head will stop your mouth
and stay your stomach at all times.

Knockem. Thou art such another mad merry Urs still! Troth, I
do make conscience of vexing thee now i' the dog-days, this hot

---

30 JORDAN *Knockem's nickname — literally, chamber-pot; frequently used as a term
of abuse.*

34 TOY *whim.*

35 GREASY KERCHIEF *on Ursula's head.*

37 AFTER-GAME *"a second game played in order to reverse or improve the issues of
the first"* (*OED*).

42 TUSK *"form into a tuft"* (*Horsman*).

42 DIBBLE *small pointed instrument used by gardeners; hence probably, a spade
beard.*

45 CHAP *jaw.*

45 TUSKS *mustache.*

50 weather, for fear of found'ring thee i' the body, and melting down
a pillar of the Fair. Pray thee take thy chair again, and keep state;
and let's have a fresh bottle of ale and a pipe of tobacco; and no
vapors. I'll ha' this belly o' thine taken up and thy grass scoured,
wench. Look! here's Ezekiel Edgworth, a fine boy of his inches
55 as any is i' the Fair! Has still money in his purse, and will pay
all with a kind heart; and good vapors.

[*Motions to Edgworth to sit down.*]

50 FOUND'RING *as applied to a horse, making seriously ill by allowing it to drink
too much when it is hot N.*

51 KEEP STATE *hold forth in a regal manner; chairs, being rare, were usually
reserved for the most important persons present; others sat on stools or benches.*

53 TAKEN UP *reduced.*

53 GRASS SCOURED *more exactly, belly scoured by purging it of grass; another
veterinary term.*

54 HERE'S EZEKIEL EDGWORTH *N.*

Act II Scene iv

[*Enter Edgworth, Nightingale, Corncutter,
Tinderbox-man, Passengers.*]

Edgworth. That I will, indeed, willingly, Master Knockem; [*To
Mooncalf.*] fetch some ale and tobacco.   [*Exit Mooncalf.*]

Leatherhead. What do you lack, gentlemen? Maid, see a fine
hobbyhorse for your young master; cost you but a token a week
5 his provender.

Corncutter. Ha' you any corns i' your feet and toes?

Tinderbox-man. Buy a mousetrap, a mousetrap, or a tormentor
for a flea.

SD TINDERBOX-MAN *see note under "The Persons of the Play".*

7 TORMENTOR *trap.*

Trash. Buy some gingerbread.

Nightingale. Ballads, ballads! fine new ballads: 10
        Hear for your love and buy for your money!
        A delicate ballad o' "The Ferret and the Coney."
        "A Preservative again the Punks' Evil."
        Another of "Goose-green Starch and the Devil."
        "A Dozen of Divine Points" and "The Godly   15
          Garters."
        "The Fairing of Good Counsel," of an ell and three
          quarters.

What is't you buy?
        "The Windmill blown down by the witch's fart!"
        Or "Saint George, that O! did break the dragon's
          heart!"
        [*Re-enter Mooncalf.*]

Edgworth. Master Nightingale, come hither, leave your mart a   20
little.
      [*Exeunt Passengers, Corncutter, Tinderbox-man.*]

Nightingale. O my secretary! What says my secretary?

Overdo. Child o' the bottles, what's he? what's he?

Mooncalf. A civil young gentleman, Master Arthur, that keeps
company with the roarers and disburses all, still. He has ever   25
money in his purse; he pays for them, and they roar for him: one
does good offices for another. They call him the secretary, but he
serves nobody. A great friend of the ballad-man's—they are
never asunder.

Overdo. What pity 'tis so civil a young man should haunt this   30

---

11 HEAR ... MONEY *proverbial.*
12 FERRET, CONEY *thieves' slang for swindler and dupe.*
14 GOOSE-GREEN *yellowish green, a fashionable color, inelegantly called goose-turd green.*
20 MART *market; i.e. selling.*
26 ROAR *act noisily, riotously, in the manner of a rowdy.*

debauched company! Here's the bane of the youth of our time apparent. A proper penman, I see't in his countenance; he has a good clerk's look with him, and I warrant him a quick hand.

    Mooncalf. A very quick hand, sir.   [*Exit.*]

35   *Edgworth.* [*To Nightingale.*] All the purses   *This*
and purchase I give you today by conveyance,   *they*
bring hither to Urs'la's presently. Here we will   *whisper,*
meet at night in her lodge, and share. Look you   *that*
choose good places for your standing i' the   *Overdo*
40 Fair when you sing, Nightingale.   *hears*

    Ursula. Aye, near the fullest passages; and   *it*
shift 'em often.   *not.*

    Edgworth. And i' your singing you must use your hawk's eye nimbly, and fly the purse to a mark still—where 'tis worn and o'
45 which side—that you may gi' me the sign with your beak, or hang your head that way i' the tune.

    Ursula. Enough, talk no more on't. Your friendship, masters, is not now to begin. Drink your draught of indenture, your sup of covenant, and away. The Fair fills apace, company begins to
50 come in, and I ha' ne'er a pig ready yet.

    Knockem. Well said! Fill the cups and light the tobacco. Let's give fire i' th' works and noble vapors.

    Edgworth. And shall we ha' smocks, Urs'la and good whimsies, ha?
55   *Ursula.* Come, you are i' your bawdy vein! The best the Fair will afford, 'Zekiel, if bawd Whit keep his word.

                  [*Re-enter Mooncalf.*]

    36 PURCHASE *booty.*
    36 CONVEYANCE *transference, stealing; also sleight of hand.*
    44 FLY . . . TO A MARK *hawking term referring to the way a goshawk shows the falconer where the prey is hidden.*
    48 NOT NOW TO BEGIN *i.e. well established.*
    53 WHIMSIES *women.*

How do the pigs, Mooncalf?

Mooncalf. Very passionate, mistress; one on 'em has wept out an eye. Master Arthur o' Bradley is melancholy, here; nobody talks to him. Will you any tobacco, Master Arthur?　　60

Overdo. No, boy, let my meditations alone.

Mooncalf. He's studying for an oration, now.

Overdo. [*Aside.*] If I can, with this day's travail, and all my policy, but rescue this youth here out of the hands of the lewd man and the strange woman, I will sit down at night and say with　65 my friend Ovid, *Iamque opus exegi, quod nec Iovis ira, nec ignis, etc.*

Knockem. Here 'Zekiel; here's a health to Urs'la, and a kind vapor. Thou hast money i' thy purse still; and store! How dost thou come by it? Pray thee vapor thy friends some in a courteous vapor.　　　　　　　　　　　　　　　　[*Exit Ursula.*]　70

Edgworth. Half I have, Master Dan Knockem, is always at your service.

Overdo. [*Aside.*] Ha, sweet nature! What goshawk would prey upon such a lamb?

Knockem. Let's see what 'tis, 'Zekiel! Count it, come, fill him　75 to pledge me.　　　　　　　[*Edgworth starts counting his money.*]

58 PASSIONATE *sorrowful.*

64 POLICY *contrivance.*

65 STRANGE WOMAN *scriptural phrase for harlot.*

66 IAMQUE . . . IGNIS, ETC. *Ovid*, Metamorphoses, XV, *871–2: "And now my work is done, which neither the wrath of Jove, nor fire, nor sword, nor the gnawing tooth of time shall ever be able to undo" (F. J. Miller).*

68 STORE *plenty.*

Act II Scene v

[*Enter Winwife, Quarlous.*]

Winwife. We are here before 'em, methinks.

Quarlous. All the better; we shall see 'em come in now.

Leatherhead. What do you lack, gentlemen, what is't you lack?
A fine horse? A lion? A bull? A bear? A dog, or a cat? An
5 excellent fine Barthol'mew-bird? Or an instrument? What is't
you lack?

Quarlous. 'Slid! here's Orpheus among the beasts, with his fiddle
and all!

Trash. Will you buy any comfortable bread, gentlemen?

10 *Quarlous.* And Ceres selling her daughter's picture in ginger-
work!

Winwife. That these people should be so ignorant to think us
chapmen for 'em! Do we look as if we would buy ginger bread? Or
hobbyhorses?

15 *Quarlous.* Why, they know no better ware than they have, nor
better customers than come. And our very being here makes us
fit to be demanded, as well as others. Would Cokes would come!
There were a true customer for 'em.

Knockem. [*To Edgworth.*] How much is't? Thirty shillings?
20 Who's yonder? Ned Winwife? and Tom Quarlous, I think! Yes.
(Gi' me it all, gi' me it all.) Master Winwife! Master Quarlous!
Will you take a pipe of tobacco with us? (Do not discredit me now,
'Zekiel.)

---

9 COMFORTABLE *sustaining, refreshing.*
10 CERES *mother of Proserpina.*
13 CHAPMEN *customers.*

Winwife. Do not see him! He is the roaring horse-courser. Pray thee let's avoid him; turn down this way.   25

Quarlous. 'Slood, I'll see him, and roar with him too, an' he roared as loud as Neptune; pray thee go with me.

Winwife. You may draw me to as likely an inconvenience, when you please, as this.

Quarlous. Go to then, come along. We ha' nothing to do, man,   30
but to see sights now.

Knockem. Welcome, Master Quarlous and Master Winwife! Will you take any froth and smoke with us?

Quarlous. Yes, sir, but you'll pardon us if we knew not of so much familiarity between us afore.   35

Knockem. As what, sir?

Quarlous. To be so lightly invited to smoke and froth.

Knockem. A good vapor! Will you sit down, sir? This is old Urs'la's mansion. How like you her bower? Here you may ha' your punk and your pig in state, sir, both piping hot.   40

Quarlous. I had rather ha' my punk cold, sir.

Overdo [Aside.] There's for me; punk! and pig!

Ursula. (She calls within.) What, Mooncalf? You rogue.

Mooncalf. By and by; the bottle is almost off, mistress. Here, Master Arthur.   45

Ursula. [Within.] I'll part you and your play-fellow there i' the guarded coat, an' you sunder not the sooner.

---

24 ROARING *see* ROAR, II.4.26.

26 'SLOOD (*or* 'Sblood) *by God's blood.*

28–9 YOU MAY . . . THIS *i.e.* "*If you want to embarrass me, this is a good way to do it.*"

39 MANSION *ironically elegant term; Jonson may also allude to stage "mansions";*
   see Appendix II, *p. 212.*

39 BOWER *also ironic, but the booth is shaded by boughs* (III.2.53).

44 OFF *emptied.*

47 GUARDED *trimmed with braid, velvet, etc.*

Knockem. Master Winwife, you are proud, methinks; you do not talk nor drink; are you proud?

50 *Winwife.* Not of the company I am in, sir, nor the place, I assure you.

Knockem. You do not except at the company, do you? Are you in vapors, sir?

Mooncalf. Nay, good Master Dan Knockem, respect my
55 mistress' bower, as you call it; for the honor of our booth, none o' your vapors here.

Ursula. (She comes out with a firebrand.) Why, you thin lean polecat you, an' they have a mind to be i' their vapors, must you hinder 'em? What did you know, vermin, if they would ha' lost a cloak,
60 or such a trifle? Must you be drawing the air of pacification here, while I am tormented, within, i' the fire, you weasel?

Mooncalf. Good mistress, 'twas in the behalf of your booth's credit that I spoke.

Ursula. Why? Would my booth ha' broke if they had fall'n out
65 in't, sir? Or would their heat ha' fired it? In, you rogue, and wipe the pigs, and mend the fire, that they fall not, or I'll both baste and roast you till your eyes drop out like 'em. (Leave the bottle behind you, and be curst awhile.) *[Exit Mooncalf.]*

Quarlous. Body o' the Fair! what's this? Mother o' the bawds?
70 *Knockem.* No, she's mother o' the pigs, sir, mother o' the pigs!

Winwife. Mother o' the Furies, I think, by her firebrand.

Quarlous. Nay, she is too fat to be a Fury, sure some walking sow of tallow!

Winwife. An inspired vessel of kitchen-stuff!

She drinks this while.

52 EXCEPT AT *take exception to.*
64 HA' BROKE *gone bankrupt or, literally, fallen apart.*
66 BASTE *in addition to its culinary meanings can mean "beat."*
74 INSPIRED *"animated by divine or supernatural influence" (OED).*
74 VESSEL *often used metaphorically of a person, especially by the Puritans.*

Quarlous. She'll make excellent gear for the coach-makers here   75
in Smithfield to anoint wheels and axle-trees with.

Ursula. Aye, aye, gamesters, mock a plain plump soft wench o'
the suburbs, do, because she's juicy and wholesome. You must ha'
your thin pinched ware, pent up i' the compass of a dog-collar (or
'twill not do), that looks like a long laced conger, set upright, and   80
a green feather, like fennel, i' the jowl on't.

Knockem. Well said, Urs, my good Urs; to 'em, Urs.

Quarlous. Is she your quagmire, Dan Knockem? Is this your bog?

Nightingale. We shall have a quarrel presently.

Knockem. How? Bog? Quagmire? Foul vapors! Hum'h!   85

Quarlous. Yes, he that would venture for't, I assure him, might
sink into her and be drowned a week ere any friend he had could
find where he were.

Winwife. And then he would be a fortnight weighing up again.

Quarlous. 'Twere like falling into a whole shire of butter. They   90
had need be a team of Dutchmen, should draw him out.

Knockem. Answer 'em, Urs; where's thy Barthol'mew-wit,
now, Urs? thy Barthol'mew-wit?

Ursula. Hang 'em, rotten, roguy cheaters, I hope to see 'em
plagued one day (poxed they are already, I am sure) with lean   95
playhouse poultry, that has the bony rump sticking out like the
ace of spades or the point of a partizan, that every rib of 'em is like

75 GEAR *matter, material.*

78 SUBURBS *noted for their prostitutes.*

80 LACED *striped, streaked.*

81 JOWL *fish head.*

83 QUAGMIRE, BOG *horse dealers had a corner of their yard where unsound horses
could stand up to their knees in wet clay; the sexual hints here are obvious.*

89 WEIGHING UP *being raised up (like a sunken ship).*

91 DUTCHMEN *popularly represented as gross butter-eaters.*

95 POXED *sick with the "great pox," syphilis.*

96 PLAYHOUSE POULTRY *available women who frequented the playhouses.*

97 PARTIZAN *long-handled spear with one or more projecting blades.*

the tooth of a saw; and will so grate 'em with their hips and shoulders, as (take 'em altogether) they were as good lie with a
100 hurdle.

Quarlous. Out upon her, how she drips! She's able to give a man the sweating sickness with looking on her.

Ursula. Marry look off, with a patch o' your face and a dozen i' your breech, though they be o' scarlet, sir. I ha' seen as fine outsides
105 as either o' yours bring lousy linings to the brokers ere now, twice a week!

Quarlous. Do you think there may be a fine new cucking-stool i' the Fair to be purchased? One large enough, I mean. I know there is a pond of capacity for her.

110 *Ursula.* For your mother, you rascal! Out, you rogue, you hedge-bird, you pimp, you pannier-man's bastard, you!

Quarlous. Ha, ha, ha.

Ursula. Do you sneer, you dog's-head, you trendle-tail! You look as you were begotten atop of a cart in harvest-time, when the
115 whelp was hot and eager. Go, snuff after your brother's bitch, Mistress Commodity. That's the livery you wear; 'twill be out at the elbows shortly. It's time you went to't, for the tother remnant.

Knockem. Peace, Urs, peace, Urs. [*Aside.*] They'll kill the poor
120 whale and make oil of her.—Pray thee go in.

---

102 SWEATING SICKNESS *a form of the plague.*

103–4 PATCH . . . BREECH *patches were used for the pox.*

105 BROKERS *second-hand dealers.*

107 CUCKING-STOOL "*a chair in which scolds were fastened and then conveyed to a pond and ducked*" (H & S).

111 HEDGE-BIRD *bandit.*

111 PANNIER-MAN'S *peddler's.*

113 TRENDLE-TAIL *low-bred dog.*

116 COMMODITY *self-interest, gain.*

Ursula. I'll see 'em poxed first, and piled, and double piled.

Winwife. Let's away; her language grows greasier than her pigs.

Ursula. Does't so, snotty nose? Good Lord! are you snivelling? You were engendered on a she-beggar in a barn when the bald 125 thrasher, your sire, was scarce warm.

Winwife. Pray thee, let's go.

Quarlous. No, faith; I'll stay the end of her, now; I know she cannot last long; I find by her similes she wanes apace.

Ursula. Does she so? I'll set you gone.Gi' me my pig-pan hither 130 a little. I'll scald you hence, an' you will not go.   [*Exit.*]

Knockem. Gentlemen, these are very strange vapors! And very idle vapors, I assure you!

Quarlous. You are a very serious ass, we assure you.

Knockem. Hum'h! Ass? And serious? Nay, then pardon me my 135 vapor. I have a foolish vapor, gentlemen: any man that does vapor me the ass, Master Quarlous—

Quarlous. What then, Master Jordan?

Knockem. I do vapor him the lie.

Quarlous. Faith, and to any man that vapors me the lie, I do 140 vapor that.   [*Strikes him.*]

Knockem. Nay, then, vapors upon vapors.

Edgworth. Nightingale. 'Ware the pan, the pan, the pan; she comes with the pan, gentlemen. (*Ursula comes in with the scalding-pan. They fight. She falls with it.*) God bless the woman.   145

Ursula. Oh!   [*Exeunt Quarlous, Winwife.*]

Trash. [*Running to Ursula's booth.*] What's the matter?

Overdo. Goodly woman!

Mooncalf. Mistress!

---

121 PILED *stripped of hair (by the pox) or afflicted with piles.*
121 DOUBLE PILED *used of cloth with pile or nap of double closeness.*
130 SET YOU GONE *set you going.*

150   *Ursula.* Curse of hell, that ever I saw these fiends! Oh! I ha'
scalded my leg, my leg, my leg, my leg! I ha' lost a limb in the
service! Run for some cream and salad oil, quickly! [*To Mooncalf.*]
Are you under-peering, you baboon? Rip off my hose, an' you
be men, men, men!

155   *Mooncalf.* Run you for some cream, good mother Joan. I'll look
to your basket.   [*Exit Trash.*]

   Leatherhead. Best sit up i' your chair, Urs'la. Help, gentlemen.
                                      [*They lift her up.*]

   Knockem. Be of good cheer, Urs; thou hast hindered me the
currying of a couple of stallions here, that abused the good race-
160 bawd o' Smithfield; 'twas time for 'em to go.

   Nightingale. I'faith, when the pan came, they had made you run
else. [*To Edgworth.*] This had been a fine time for purchase, if you
had ventured.

   Edgworth. Not a whit; these fellows were too fine to carry
165 money.

   Knockem. Nightingale, get some help to carry her leg out o' the
air; take off her shoes; body o' me, she has the mallanders, the
scratches, the crown scab, and the quitter bone i' the tother leg.

   Ursula. Oh! the pox, why do you put me in mind o' my leg
170 thus, to make it prick and shoot? Would you ha' me i' the
Hospital afore my time?

   Knockem. Patience, Urs. Take a good heart; 'tis but a blister as
big as a windgall. I'll take it away with the white of an egg, a little
honey, and hog's grease; ha' thy pasterns well rolled, and thou

159 CURRYING " '*dressing down,' beating*" (*Horsman*).

159–60 RACE-BAWD *as if she were for breeding bawds—the mother of them all.*

162 PURCHASE *acquisition (by robbery).*

164 FINE *both high-class and clever.*

166–7 MALLANDERS . . . QUITTER BONE *veterinary terms; diseases of a horse's legs
    and feet.*

173 WINDGALL *tumor on a horse's leg.*

shalt pace again by tomorrow. I'll tend thy booth and look to thy   175
affairs the while; thou shalt sit i' thy chair and give directions, and
shine Ursa major.
[*Knockem, Leatherhead, and Mooncalf carry Ursula in her chair into the*
back part of her booth. During the next scene Leatherhead returns and
goes back to his booth. Later Trash comes out of Ursula's with her basket
and returns to her place.]

177 URSA MAJOR *the constellation of the Great Bear.*

Act II Scene vi

[*Enter Cokes, Wasp, Mistress Overdo, Grace.*]
Overdo. These are the fruits of bottle-ale and tobacco! the foam
of the one and the fumes of the other! Stay, young man, and
despise not the wisdom of these few hairs that are grown grey
in care of thee.

Edgworth. Nightingale, stay a little. Indeed I'll hear some o' this!   5

Cokes. Come, Numps, come, where are you? Welcome into the
Fair, Mistress Grace.

Edgworth. [*To Nightingale.*] 'Slight, he will call company, you
shall see, and put us into doings presently.

Overdo. Thirst not after that frothy liquor, ale; for who knows,   10
when he openeth the stopple, what may be in the bottle? Hath
not a snail, a spider, yea, a newt been found there? Thirst not after
it, youth; thirst not after it.

Cokes. This is a brave fellow, Numps; let's hear him.

8 'SLIGHT *by God's light.*
14 BRAVE *fine.*

15 *Wasp.* 'Sblood, how brave is he? In a guarded coat? You were best truck with him; e'en strip and truck presently; it will become you. Why will you hear him? Because he is an ass, and may be akin to the Cokeses?

Cokes. O, good Numps!

20 *Overdo.* Neither do thou lust after that tawny weed, tobacco.

Cokes. Brave words!

Overdo. Whose complexion is like the Indian's that vents it!

Cokes. Are they not brave words, sister?

Overdo. And who can tell if, before the gathering and making
25 up thereof, the alligarta hath not pissed thereon?

Wasp. 'Heart, let 'em be brave words, as brave as they will! An' they were all the brave words in a country, how then? Will you away yet? Ha' you enough on him? Mistress Grace, come you away, I pray you, be not you accessory. If you do lose your
30 licence, or somewhat else, sir, with list'ning to his fables, say Numps is a witch, with all my heart, do, say so.

Cokes. Avoid, i' your satin doublet, Numps.

Overdo. The creeping venom of which subtle serpent, as some late writers affirm, neither the cutting of the perilous plant, nor the
35 drying of it, nor the lighting or burning, can any way persway or assuage.

Cokes. Good, i' faith! is't not, sister?

Overdo. Hence it is that the lungs of the tobacconist are rotted, the liver spotted, the brain smoked like the backside of the pig-
40 woman's booth, here, and the whole body within, black as her pan you saw e'en now, without.

16 TRUCK *deal.*
25 ALLIGARTA *alligator (Sp.* el lagarto) N.
32 AVOID *go away; with a play on "Avoid, Satan!" a pious interjection.*
33–4 SOME LATE WRITERS *among whom was King James* I.
35 PERSWAY *lessen.*
38 TOBACCONIST *smoker.*

Cokes. A fine similitude, that, sir! Did you see the pan?

Edgworth. Yes, sir.

Overdo. Nay, the hole in the nose here, of some tobacco-takers, or the third nostril (if I may so call it), which makes that they can 45 vent the tobacco out like the ace of clubs, or rather the flower-de-lys, is caused from the tobacco, the mere tobacco! when the poor innocent pox, having nothing to do there, is miserably, and most unconscionably slandered.

Cokes. Who would ha' missed this, sister? 50

Mistress Overdo. Not anybody but Numps.

Cokes. He does not understand.

Edgworth. Nor you feel.   *He picketh his purse.*

Cokes. What would you have, sister, of a fellow that knows nothing but a basket-hilt and an old fox in't? The best music i' the 55 Fair will not move a log.

Edgworth. [*Slipping the purse to Nightingale.*] In to Urs'la, Nightingale, and carry her comfort; see it told. This fellow was sent to us by fortune for our first fairing.   [*Exit Nightingale.*]

Overdo. But what speak I of the diseases of the body, children 60 of the Fair?

Cokes. That's to us, sister. Brave i' faith!

Overdo. Hark, o you sons and daughters of Smithfield! and hear what malady it doth the mind: it causeth swearing, it causeth swaggering, it causeth snuffling, and snarling, and now and then a 65 hurt.

Mistress Overdo. He hath something of Master Overdo, methinks, brother.

Cokes. So methought, sister, very much of my brother Overdo; and 'tis when he speaks. 70

44 HOLE IN THE NOSE *N.*
55 BASKET-HILT *hilt curved into the shape of a basket.*
55 FOX *sword.*
58 TOLD *counted.*

Overdo. Look into any angle o' the town—the Straits, or the Bermudas—where the quarrelling lesson is read, and how do they entertain the time but with bottle-ale and tobacco? The lecturer is o' one side, and his pupils o' the other; but the seconds are still
75 bottle-ale and tobacco, for which the lecturer reads and the novices pay. Thirty pound a week in bottle-ale! forty in tobacco! and ten more in ale again. Then for a suit to drink in, so much, and (that being slavered) so much for another suit, and then a third suit, and a fourth suit! and still the bottle-ale slavereth, and the tobacco
80 stinketh!

Wasp. Heart of a madman! are you rooted here? Will you never away? What can any man find out in this bawling fellow to grow here for? He is a full handful higher sin' he heard him. Will you fix here? And set up a booth, sir?

85 *Overdo.* I will conclude briefly—

Wasp. Hold your peace, you roaring rascal! I'll run my head i' your chaps else. [*To Cokes.*] You were best build a booth and entertain him; make your will, an' you say the word, and him your heir! Heart, I never knew one taken with a mouth of a peck, afore.
90 By this light, I'll carry you away o' my back, an' you will not come.   *He gets him up on pick-pack.*

Cokes. Stay, Numps, stay, set me down. I ha' lost my purse, Numps, O my purse! One o' my fine purses is gone.

Mistress Overdo. Is't indeed, brother?

95 *Cokes.* Aye, as I am an honest man, would I were an arrant rogue, else! A plague of all roguy, damned cutpurses for me.

Wasp. Bless 'em with all my heart, with all my heart, do you see! Now, as I am no infidel, that I know of, I am glad on't. Aye

---

71–2 STRAITS . . . BERMUDAS *referring to a disreputable section of London.*
74 SECONDS *things which assist or support.*
89 PECK *peck's capacity (eight quarts).*
96 ELSE *if you don't believe me.*

I am; here's my witness! do you see, sir? I did not tell you of his
fables, I? No, no, I am a dull malt-horse, I, I know nothing. Are   100
you not justly served i' your conscience now? Speak i' your conscience. Much good do you with all my heart, and his good heart
that has it, with all my heart again.

    Edgworth. [*Aside.*] This fellow is very charitable; would he had
a purse too! But I must not be too bold all at a time.   105

    Cokes. Nay, Numps, it is not my best purse.

    Wasp. Not your best! Death! why should it be your worst?
Why should it be any, indeed, at all? Answer me to that. Gi' me
a reason from you, why it should be any.

    Cokes. Nor my gold, Numps; I ha' that yet; look here else,   110
sister.   [*Holds up his purse.*]

    Wasp. Why so, there's all the feeling he has!

    Mistress Overdo. I pray you, have a better care of that, brother.

    Cokes. Nay, so I will, I warrant you; let him catch this, that
catch can. I would fain see him get this, look you here.   115

    Wasp. So, so, so, so, so, so, so, so! Very good.

    Cokes. I would ha' him come again, and but offer at it. Sister,
will you take notice of a good jest? I will put it just where th' other
was, and if we ha' good luck, you shall see a delicate fine trap to
catch the cutpurse nibbling.   120

    Edgworth. [*Aside.*] Faith, and he'll try ere you be out o' the Fair.

    Cokes. Come, Mistress Grace, prithee be not melancholy for my
mischance; sorrow wi' not keep it, sweetheart.

    Grace. I do not think on't, sir.

    Cokes. 'Twas but a little scurvy white money, hang it; it may   125
hang the cutpurse one day. I ha' gold left to gi' thee a fairing, yet,
as hard as the world goes. Nothing angers me but that nobody
here looked like a cutpurse, unless 'twere Numps.

100 MALT-HORSE *draft horse.*
125 WHITE MONEY *silver.*

Wasp. How? I? I look like a cutpurse? Death! your sister's a cut-
130 purse! and your mother and father and all your kin were cutpurses! And here is a rogue is the bawd o' the cutpurses, whom I
will beat to begin with.

They speak all together; and Wasp beats the Justice.

Cokes. Numps, Numps!

Mistress Overdo. Good
135 Master Humphrey.   .

Wasp. You are the Patrico,
are you? the patriarch of the
cutpurses? You share, sir, they
say; let them share this with
140 you. Are you i' your hot fit of
preaching again? I'll cool you.

Overdo. Murder, murder,
murder!

Overdo. Hold thy hand, child
of wrath and heir of anger.
Make it not Childermass day
in thy fury, or the feast of the
French Barthol'mew, parent of
the Massacre.

[*Exeunt all except Leatherhead
and Trash.*]

---

135 CHILDERMASS DAY *Feast of Holy Innocents, commemorating the slaughter of
the innocents.*

136 PATRICO *vagabond's cant for priest or parson.*

138 MASSACRE *massacre of Protestant leaders in Paris on St. Bartholomew's day,
1572.*

Act III Scene i

[*Enter Whit, Haggis, Bristle.*]

Whit. Nay, 'tish all gone, now! Dish 'tish, phen tou vilt not be phitin call, Master Offisher! Phat ish a man te better to lishen out noishes for tee an' tou art in an oder 'orld—being very shuffishient noishes and gallantsh too, one o' their brabblesh would have fed ush all dish fortnight; but tou art so bushy about beggersh still,   5 tou hast no leshure to intend shentlemen, an't be.

Haggis. Why, I told you, Davy Bristle..

Bristle. Come, come, you told me a pudding, Toby Haggis; a matter of nothing; I am sure it came to nothing! You said, "Let's go to Urs'la's," indeed; but then you met the man with the   10 monsters, and I could not get you from him. An old fool, not leave seeing yet?

Haggis. Why, who would ha' thought anybody would ha'

1–6 *Elizabethan stage-Irish N.*

2–3 PHAT . . . TEE *N.*

4 BRABBLESH (*brabbles*), *brawls.*

6 INTEND *attend to.*

6 AN'T BE *if it be; perhaps; a phrase of rather vague significance which Whit works hard.*

8 A PUDDING *slang for nothing; also a pun on Haggis, a kind of pudding.*

11 MONSTERS *freaks.*

quarrelled so early? Or that the ale o' the Fair would ha' been up
15 so soon?

Whit. Phy, phat o' clock tost tou tink it ish, man?

Haggis. I cannot tell.

Whit. Tou art a vishe vatchman, i' te mean teeme.

Haggis. Why, should the watch go by the clock, or the clock by
20 the watch, I pray?

Bristle. One should go by another, if they did well.

Whit. Tou art right now! Phen didst tou ever know or hear of
a shuffishient vatchman but he did tell the clock, phat bushiness
soever he had?

25 *Bristle.* Nay, that's most true, a sufficient watchman knows what
o'clock it is.

Whit. Shleeping or vaking! ash well as te clock himshelf, or te
jack dat shtrikes him!

Bristle. Let's inquire of Master Leatherhead, or Joan Trash here.
30 Master Leatherhead, do you hear, Master Leatherhead?

Whit. If it be a Ledderhead, tish a very tick Ledderhead, tat sho
mush noish vill not piersh him.

Leatherhead. I have a little business now, good friends; do not
trouble me.

35 *Whit.* Phat? Because o' ty wrought neet-cap and ty phelvet
sherkin, man? Phy? I have sheen tee in ty ledder sherkin ere now,
mashter o' de hobbyhorses, as bushy and as stately as tou
sheem'st to be.

Trash. Why, what an' you have, Captain Whit? He has his
40 choice of jerkins, you may see by that, and his caps too, I assure
you, when he pleases to be either sick or employed.

Leatherhead. God a mercy, Joan, answer for me.

23 TELL THE CLOCK *one meaning here is* "count the hours."
28 JACK *mechanical figure which strikes the bell.*
35 WROUGHT *embroidered.*
35 NEET-CAP *nightcap.*

Whit. Away, be not sheen i' my company; here be shentlemen, and men of vorship.   [*Exeunt Haggis, Bristle.*]

Act III Scene ii

[*Enter Quarlous, Winwife.*]

Quarlous. We had wonderful ill luck to miss this prologue o' the purse, but the best is we shall have five acts of him ere night. He'll be spectacle enough! I'll answer for't.

Whit. O Creesh! Duke Quarlous, how dosht tou? Tou dosht not know me, I fear? I am te vishesht man, but Justish Overdo, in   5 all Barthol'mew Fair, now. Gi' me twelvepence from tee, I vill help tee to a vife vorth forty marks for't, an't be.

Quarlous. Away, rogue, pimp, away.

Whit. And she shall show tee as fine cut 'ork for't in her shmock too, as tou cansht vish i' faith. Vilt tou have her, vorship-   10 ful Vinvife? I vill help tee to her, here, be an't be, in te pig-quarter, gi' me ty twel'pence from tee.

Winwife. Why, there's twel'pence; pray thee, wilt thou be gone?

Whit. Tou art a vorthy man, and a vorshipful man still.

Quarlous. Get you gone, rascal.   15

Whit. I do mean it, man. Prinsh Quarlous, if tou hasht need on me, tou shalt find me here at Urs'la's. I vill see phat ale and punk ish i' te pigshty for tee, bless ty good vorship.   [*Exit.*]

Quarlous. Look! who comes here! John Littlewit!

Winwife. And his wife and my widow, her mother: the whole   20 family.

[*Enter Busy, Purecraft, Littlewit, Win.*]

4 CREESH *Christ.*
9 CUT 'ORK (*cut-work*), *lace.*

Quarlous. 'Slight, you must gi' em all fairings, now!

Winwife. Not I, I'll not see 'em.

Quarlous. They are going a-feasting. What school-master's that
25 is with 'em?

Winwife. That's my rival, I believe, the baker!

Busy. So, walk on in the middle way, fore-right; turn neither
to the right hand nor to the left. Let not your eyes be drawn aside
with vanity, nor your ear with noises.

30 *Quarlous.* O, I know him by that start!

Leatherhead. What do you lack? What do you buy, pretty Mistress? a fine hobbyhorse, to make your son a tilter? a drum to make
a soldier? a fiddle to make him a reveller? What is't you lack?
Little dogs for your daughters? or babies, male or female?

35 *Busy.* Look not toward them, hearken not! The place is Smithfield, or the field of smiths, the grove of hobbyhorses and
trinkets. The wares are the wares of devils; and the whole Fair is
the shop of Satan! They are hooks and baits, very baits, that are
hung out on every side to catch you, and to hold you as it were,
40 by the gills and by the nostrils, as the fisher doth; therefore, you
must not look, nor turn toward them. The heathen man could
stop his ears with wax against the harlot o' the sea; do you the
like, with your fingers, against the bells of the Beast.

Winwife. What flashes comes from him!

45 *Quarlous.* O, he has those of his oven! A notable hot baker
'twas, when he plied the peel. He is leading his flock into the Fair,
now.

---

27 FORE-RIGHT *straight ahead.*

32 TILTER *jouster.*

41 HEATHEN MAN *Ulysses, who resisted the call of the sirens by having himself
lashed to the mast and having wax put in the ears of the crew.*

44 COMES *a plural form sometimes found in Elizabethan English.*

46 PEEL *long-handled shovel used by bakers in handling loaves.*

Winwife. Rather driving 'em to the pens; for he will let 'em look upon nothing.

[*Enter Knockem, Whit, from back part of Ursula's booth.*]

Knockem. Gentlewomen, the weather's hot!   *Littlewit is*   50
Whither walk you? Have a care o' your fine   *gazing at the*
velvet caps; the Fair is dusty. Take a sweet deli-   *sign; which is*
cate booth with boughs, here, i' the way, and   *the pig's head*
cool yourselves i' the shade, you and your   *with a large*
friends. The best pig and bottle-ale i' the Fair,   *writing under it.*   55
sir. Old Urs'la is cook, there you may read: the   pig's head
speaks it. Poor soul, she has had a stringhalt, the maryhinchco;
but she's prettily amended.

Whit. A delicate show-pig, little mistress, with shweet sauce,
and crackling like de bay leaf i' de fire, la! Tou shalt ha' de clean   60
side o' de table-clot and dy glass vashed with phatersh of Dame
Annessh Cleare.

Littlewit. This's fine, verily: "Here be the best pigs, and she does
roast 'em as well as ever she did," the pig's head says.

Knockem. Excellent, excellent, mistress, with fire o' juniper and   65
rosemary branches! The oracle of the pig's head, that, sir.

Purecraft. Son, were you not warned of the vanity of the eye?
Have you forgot the wholesome admonition so soon?

Littlewit. Good mother, how shall we find a pig if we do not look
about for't? Will it run off o' the spit into our mouths, think you?   70
as in Lubberland? and cry, "We, we"?

Busy. No, but your mother, religiously wise, conceiveth it may
offer itself by other means to the sense, as by way of steam, which

---

52-3 DELICATE *delightful.*

57 STRINGHALT, THE MARYHINCHCO *two names for a disease of a horse's legs.*

61-2 DAME ANNESSH CLEARE *a spring named for a London widow, Annis Clare.*

65 JUNIPER *N.*

71 LUBBERLAND "*where the pigs run about ready roasted and cry 'Come eat me*'"
     (*Robert Nares*, Glossary).

I think it doth here in this place. (Huh, huh) yes, it doth. (*Busy*
75 *scents after it like a hound.*) And it were a sin of obstinacy, great
obstinacy, high and horrible obstinacy, to decline or resist the good
titillation of the famelic sense, which is the smell. Therefore be
bold (huh, huh, huh); follow the scent. Enter the tents of the unclean for once, and satisfy your wife's frailty. Let your frail wife be
80 satisfied; your zealous mother and my suffering self will also be
satisfied.

    Littlewit. Come, Win, as good winny here as go farther and see
nothing.

    Busy. We 'scape so much of the other vanities by our early ent'-
85 ring.

    Purecraft. It is an edifying consideration.

    Win. This is scurvy, that we must come into the Fair and not
look on't.

    Littlewit. Win, have patience, Win, I'll tell you more anon.

90   *Knockem.* Mooncalf, entertain within there; the best pig i' the
booth, a pork-like pig. These are Banbury-bloods, o' the sincere
stud, come a pig-hunting. Whit, wait, Whit, look to your
charge. [*Exeunt Purecraft, Win, Littlewit, Whit into back part of booth.*]

    Busy. A pig prepare presently; let a pig be prepared to us.

[*He follows the others, immediately after which enter Mooncalf, Ursula.*]
95   *Mooncalf.* 'Slight, who be these?

    Ursula. Is this the good service, Jordan, you'd do me?

    Knockem. Why, Urs? Why, Urs? Thou'lt ha' vapors i' thy leg
again presently; pray thee go in; 't may turn to the scratches else.

---

77 FAMELIC *pertaining to hunger.*
82 WINNY *stay.*
91 SINCERE *genuine.*
92 STUD *breed.*
92 WAIT *wait on* (*Win Littlewit*) N.
SD HE FOLLOWS . . . URSULA N.

Ursula. Hang your vapors, they are stale, and stink like you. Are these the guests o' the game you promised to fill my pit 100 withal, today?

Knockem. Aye, what ail they, Urs?

Ursula. Ail they? They are all sippers, sippers o' the city. They look as they would not drink off two pen'orth of bottle-ale amongst 'em. 105

Mooncalf. A body may read that i' their small printed ruffs.

Knockem. Away, thou art a fool, Urs, and thy Mooncalf too, i' your ignorant vapors, now! hence! Good guests, I say, right hypocrites, good gluttons. In, and set a couple o' pigs o' the board, and half a dozen of the biggest bottles afore 'em, and call 110 Whit. I do not love to hear innocents abused. Fine ambling hypocrites! and a stone-puritan with a sorrel head and beard— good mouthed gluttons, two to a pig. Away!   [*Exit Mooncalf.*]

Ursula. Are you sure they are such?

Knockem. O' the right breed; thou shalt try 'em by the teeth, 115 Urs. Where's this Whit?

[*Re-enter Whit.*]

Whit. Behold, man, and see, what a worthy man am ee!
    With the fury of my sword, and the shaking of my beard,
    I will make ten thousand men afeared.

Knockem. Well said, brave Whit; in, and fear the ale out o' the 120 bottles into the bellies of the brethren and the sisters; drink to the cause, and pure vapors.   [*Exeunt Knockem, Whit, Ursula.*]

Quarlous. My roarer is turned tapster, methinks. Now were a

---

102 WHAT AIL THEY *What's the matter with them? (i.e. Why do you object to them?).*

106 SMALL PRINTED RUFFS *Puritans wore small ruffs, neatly folded—"in print," as it was called.*

112 STONE-PURITAN *male Puritan (like "stone-horse" for stallion).*

120 FEAR *catching up the last word of Whit's rhyme.*

122 CAUSE *Puritanism.*

fine time for thee, Winwife, to lay aboard thy widow; thou'lt
125 never be master of a better season or place; she that will venture
herself into the Fair and a pig-box will admit any assault, be
assured of that.

Winwife. I love not enterprises of that suddenness, though.

Quarlous. I'll warrant thee, then, no wife out o' the widow's
130 hundred. If I had but as much title to her as to have breathed once
on that strait stomacher of hers, I would now assure myself to carry
her yet, ere she went out of Smithfield. Or she should carry me,
which were the fitter sight, I confess. But you are a modest undertaker, by circumstances and degrees; come, 'tis disease in thee, not
135 judgment; I should offer at all together. Look, here's the poor
fool again that was stung by the wasp, erewhile.

124 LAY ABOARD *a nautical term for placing one ship alongside another in order to
attack.*
130 HUNDRED *formerly a subdivision of a county; here used figuratively to refer to
widows as a subdivision of society.*
131 STOMACHER *stiff embroidered front worn over the chest and abdomen.*
133–4 UNDERTAKER *one who undertakes a task.*
134 CIRCUMSTANCES *ceremonious actions.*
135 OFFER AT *make a try for.*

Act III Scene iii

[*Enter Overdo.*]

Overdo. I will make no more orations shall draw on these
tragical conclusions. And I begin now to think that, by a spice of
collateral justice, Adam Overdo deserved this beating; for I, the

1 SHALL *i.e. which shall.*
3 COLLATERAL *concomitant, indirect.*

said Adam, was one cause (a by-cause) why the purse was lost; and
my wife's brother's purse too, which they know not of yet. But I 5
shall make very good mirth with it at supper (that will be the
sport), and put my little friend Master Humphrey Wasp's choler
quite out of countenance. When, sitting at the upper end o' my
table, as I use, and drinking to my brother Cokes and Mistress Alice
Overdo, as I will, my wife, for their good affection to old Bradley, I 10
deliver to 'em it was I that was cudgelled, and show 'em the marks.
To see what bad events may peep out o' the tail of good purposes!
The care I had of that civil young man I took fancy to this
morning (and have not left it yet) drew me to that exhortation,
which drew the company, indeed, which drew the cutpurse; 15
which drew the money; which drew my brother Cokes his
loss; which drew on Wasp's anger; which drew on my beating:
a pretty gradation! And they shall ha' it i' their dish, i' faith, at
night for fruit; I love to be merry at my table, I had thought once, at
one special blow he ga' me, to have revealed myself; but then (I 20
thank thee, fortitude) I remembered that a wise man (and who is
ever so great a part o' the commonwealth in himself) for no particular disaster ought to abandon a public good design. The
husbandman ought not, for one unthankful year, to forsake the
plough; the shepherd ought not, for one scabbed sheep, to throw 25
by his tar-box; the pilot ought not, for one leak i' the poop, to
quit the helm; nor the alderman ought not, for one custard more
at a meal, to give up his cloak; the constable ought not to break
his staff and forswear the watch, for one roaring night; nor the
piper o' the parish (*ut parvis componere magna solebam*) to put up his 30

---

4 BY-CAUSE *secondary cause.*
25 SCABBED *afflicted with the mange.*
26 TAR-BOX *for treating the sores with tar.*
30 UT PARVIS . . . SOLEBAM *a slight misquotation of Virgil,* Eclogues, I, *23:*"[as]
       I used to compare great things with small" (H. R. Fairclough).

pipes, for one rainy Sunday. These are certain knocking conclusions; out of which I am resolved, come what come can—come
beating, come imprisonment, come infamy, come banishment,
nay, come the rack, come the hurdle, welcome all—I will not
35 discover who I am till my due time; and yet still all shall be, as I
said ever, in justice' name, and the King's and for the commonwealth!

Winwife. What does he talk to himself, and act so seriously?
Poor fool! [*Exit Overdo.*]
40 *Quarlous.* No matter what. Here's fresher argument, intend that.

34 HURDLE *a form of punishment.*
40 ARGUMENT *matter for thought.*

Act III Scene iv

[*Enter Cokes, Mistress Overdo, Grace, followed by Wasp,
loaded with toys, etc.*]

Cokes. Come, Mistress Grace, come sister, here's more fine
sights yet, i' faith. God's lid, where's Numps?

Leatherhead. What do you lack, gentlemen? What is't you buy?
Fine rattles? drums? babies? little dogs? and birds for ladies?
5 What do you lack?

Cokes. Good honest Numps, keep afore. I am so afraid thou'lt
lose somewhat; my heart was at my mouth when I m issed thee.

Wasp. You were best buy a whip i' your hand to drive me.

Cokes. Nay, do not mistake, Numps, thou art so apt to mistake;
10 I would but watch the goods. Look you now, the treble fiddle was
e'en almost like to be lost.

Wasp. Pray you take heed you lose not yourself. Your best way were e'en get up and ride for more surety. Buy a token's worth of great pins to fasten yourself to my shoulder.

Leatherhead. What do you lack, gentlemen? Fine purses, 15 pouches, pincases, pipes? What is't you lack? A pair o' smiths to wake you i' the morning? or a fine whistling bird?

Cokes. Numps, here be finer things than any we ha' bought, by odds! And more delicate horses, a great deal! Good Numps, stay, and come hither. 20

Wasp. Will you scourse with him? You are in Smithfield; you may fit yourself with a fine easy-going street-nag for your saddle again Michaelmas term, do. Has he ne'er a little odd cart for you, to make a caroche on, i' the country, with four pied hobbyhorses? Why the measles should you stand here with your train, 25 cheaping of dogs, birds, and babies? You ha' no children to bestow 'em on, ha' you?

Cokes. No, but again I ha' children, Numps, that's all one.

Wasp. Do, do, do, do. How many shall you have, think you? An' I were as you, I'd buy for all my tenants, too. They are a kind 30 o' civil savages that will part with their children for rattles, pipes, and knives. You were best buy a hatchet or two and truck with 'em.

Cokes. Good Numps, hold that little tongue o' thine, and save it a labor. I am resolute Bat, thou know'st. 35

Wasp. A resolute fool you are, I know, and a very sufficient coxcomb, with all my heart; nay, you have it, sir, an' you be angry, turd i' your teeth, twice (if I said it not once afore); and much good do you.

---

16 PAIR O' SMITHS *possibly toy figures run by clockwork.*

21 SCOURSE *deal, swap.*

23 AGAIN *against, in anticipation of.*

23 MICHAELMAS TERM *period following Michaelmas (September 29).*

24 CAROCHE *elegant carriage.*

26 CHEAPING OF *bargaining for.*

40   *Winwife*. Was there ever such a self-affliction? And so imperti-
nent?

    Quarlous. Alas! his care will go near to crack him; let's in and
comfort him.

    Wasp. Would I had been set i' the ground, all but the head on
45 me, and had my brains bowled at, or threshed out, when first I
underwent this plague of a charge!

    Quarlous. How now, Numps! Almost tired i' your protector-
ship? Overparted? Overparted?

    Wasp. Why, I cannot tell, sir; it may be I am; does't grieve
50 you?

    Quarlous. No, I swear does't not, Numps, to satisfy you.

    Wasp. Numps? 'Sblood, you are fine and familiar! How long
ha' we been acquainted, I pray you?

    Quarlous. I think it may be remembered, Numps, that? 'Twas
55 since morning sure.

    Wasp. Why, I hope I know't well enough, sir; I did not ask to
be told.

    Quarlous. No? Why then?

    Wasp. It's no matter why; you see with your eyes, now, what I
60 said to you today? You'll believe me another time?

    Quarlous. Are you removing the Fair, Numps?

    Wasp. A pretty question! and a very civil one! Yes faith, I ha'
my lading you see, or shall have anon; you may know whose beast
I am by my burthen. If the pannier-man's jack were ever better
55 known by his loins of mutton, I'll be flayed and feed dogs for him,
when his time comes.

42 CRACK *craze*.

48 OVERPARTED "*having too difficult a part . . . to play*" (OED).

52 FINE AND *cf. good and; very*.

64 PANNIER-MAN *an officer in the Inns of Court who brought provisions from the
market*.

64 JACK *servant*.

Winwife. How melancholy Mistress Grace is yonder! Pray thee let's go enter ourselves in grace with her.

Cokes. Those six horses, friend, I'll have—

Wasp. How!   70

Cokes. And the three Jew's trumps; and a half dozen o' birds, and that drum (I have one drum already) and your smiths (I like that device o' your smiths very pretty well) and four halberts— and (le'me see) that fine painted great lady, and her three women for state, I'll have.   75

Wasp. No, the shop; buy the whole shop, it will be best, the shop, the shop!

Leatherhead. If his worship please.

Wasp. Yes, and keep it during the Fair, bobchin.

Cokes. Peace, Numps. Friend, do not meddle with him, an' you   80
be wise, and would show your head above board. He will sting thorough your wrought nightcap, believe me. A set of these violins I would buy too, for a delicate young noise I have i' the country, that are every one a size less than another, just like your fiddles. I would fain have a fine young masque at my marriage,   85
now I think on't; but I do want such a number o' things. And Numps will not help me now, and I dare not speak to him.

Trash. Will your worship buy any gingerbread, very good bread, comfortable bread?

Cokes. Gingerbread! Yes, let's see.   *He runs to her shop.*   90

71 JEW'S TRUMPS *Jew's harps.*
75 STATE *ceremonious display.*
79 BOBCHIN *derisive epithet; exact meaning uncertain.*
81 ABOVE BOARD *in sight.*
82 THOROUGH *through.*
83 NOISE *band of musicians.*
85 MASQUE *group of masquers N.*

Wasp. There's the tother springe!

Leatherhead. Is this well, goody Joan? to interrupt my market? in the midst? and call away my customers? Can you answer this at the Pie-powders?

95 *Trash.* Why, if his mastership have a mind to buy, I hope my ware lies as open as another's; I may show my ware as well as you yours.

Cokes. Hold your peace; I'll content you both: I'll buy up his shop and thy basket.

100 *Wasp.* Will you i' faith?

Leatherhead. Why should you put him from it, friend?

Wasp. Cry you mercy! you'd be sold too, would you? What's the price on you? Jerkin and all, as you stand? Ha' you any qualities?

105 *Trash.* Yes, goodman angry-man, you shall find he has qualities, if you cheapen him.

Wasp. Godso, you ha' the selling of him! What are they? Will they be bought for love or money?

Trash. No indeed, sir.

110 *Wasp.* For what then? Victuals?

Trash. He scorns victuals, sir; he has bread and butter at home, thanks be to God! And yet he will do more for a good meal, if the toy take him i' the belly; marry then they must not set him at lower end; if they do, he'll go away, though he fast. But put him
115 atop o' the table, where his place is, and he'll do you forty fine

---

91 SPRINGE *snare (for birds or small game).*

92 GOODY *courtesy title for a woman of relatively low station (from goodwife).*

104 QUALITIES *accomplishments.*

105 GOODMAN *corresponds to goody for a woman.*

106 CHEAPEN *bargain for.*

107 GODSO *euphemistic alteration of catso, common exclamation (from Italian* cazzo, *penis).*

114 LOWER END *the end of the table for less important guests.*

things. He has not been sent for, and sought out, for nothing, at your great city-suppers, to put down Coriat and Cokely, and been laughed at for his labor. He'll play you all the puppets i' the town over, and the players, every company, and his own company too; he spares nobody!   120

Cokes. I' faith?

Trash. He was the first, sir, that ever baited the fellow i' the bear's skin, an't like your worship. No dog ever came near him since. And for fine motions!

Cokes. Is he good at those too? Can he set out a masque, trow?   125

Trash. O Lord, master! sought to, far and near, for his inventions; and he engrosses all, he makes all the puppets i' the Fair.

Cokes. Dost thou, in troth, old velvet jerkin? Give me thy hand.

Trash. Nay, sir, you shall see him in his velvet jerkin, and a scarf too, at night, when you hear him interpret Master Littlewit's   130 motion.

Cokes. Speak no more, but shut up shop presently, friend. I'll buy both it and thee too, to carry down with me, and her hamper beside. Thy shop shall furnish out the masque, and hers the banquet. I cannot go less, to set out anything with credit. What's   135 the price, at a word, o' thy whole shop, case and all as it stands?

117 CORIAT *Thomas Coryate, a court jester, whose story of his travels,* Coryats Crudities (*1611*), *was well known. Jonson contributed mock-commendatory verses.*

117 COKELY *a jester.*

118–9 PLAY . . . OVER *mimic.*

122–3 BAITED . . . SKIN *contemporary verses tell of an actor, dressed in a bear's skin, who was baited by men playing the parts of dogs.*

124 MOTIONS *puppet shows.*

125 TROW *I wonder.*

126–7 INVENTIONS *devices, works of imagination, such as plays or masques.*

127 ENGROSSES ALL *has a monopoly.*

130 INTERPRET *speak for the puppets.*

135 BANQUET *dessert.*

Leatherhead. Sir, it stands me in six and twenty shillings sevenpence halfpenny, besides three shillings for my ground.

Cokes. Well, thirty shillings will do all, then! And what comes
140 yours to?

Trash. Four shillings and elevenpence, sir, ground and all, an't like your worship.

Cokes. Yes, it does like my worship very well, poor woman; that's five shillings more. What a masque shall I furnish out for
145 forty shillings (twenty pound Scotch)! And a banquet of gingerbread! There's a stately thing! Numps! Sister! And my wedding gloves too! (That I never thought on afore.) All my wedding gloves gingerbread! O me! what a device will there be to make 'em eat their fingers' ends! And delicate brooches for the
150 bridemen and all! And then I'll ha' this posy put to 'em: "For the best grace," meaning Mistress Grace, my wedding posy.

Grace. I am beholden to you, sir, and to your Barthol'mew-wit.

Wasp. You do not mean this, do you? Is this your first pur-
155 chase?

Cokes. Yes, faith, and I do not think, Numps, but thou'lt say, it was the wisest act that ever I did in my wardship.

Wasp. Like enough! I shall say anything, I!

137 STANDS . . . IN *costs.*
145 POUND SCOTCH *worth one twelfth of a pound Sterling at the accession of James I in 1603.*
150 POSY *motto.*

Act III Scene v

[*Enter Overdo, Edgworth, Nightingale.*]

Overdo. [*Aside.*] I cannot beget a project, with all my political brain, yet; my project is how to fetch off this proper young man from his debauched company. I have followed him all the Fair over, and still I find him with this songster; and I begin shrewdly to suspect their familiarity; and the young man of a terrible   5
taint, poetry! with which idle disease if he be infected, there's no hope of him in a state-course. *Actum est* of him for a commonwealth's-man if he go to't in rhyme once.

Edgworth. [*To Nightingale.*] Yonder he is buying o' gingerbread. Set in quickly, before he part with too much on his   10
money.

Nightingale. My masters and friends and good people, draw near, etc.

Cokes. Ballads! hark, hark! Pray thee, fellow, stay a little; good Numps, look to the goods. What ballads hast thou? Let me see, let me see myself.   *He runs to the ballad-man.*   15

Wasp. Why so! He's flown to another lime-bush; there he will flutter as long more, till he ha' ne'er a feather left. Is there a vexation like this, gentlemen? Will you believe me now? Hereafter shall I have credit with you?

Quarlous. Yes faith, shalt thou, Numps, an' thou art worthy on't,   20

---

1 POLITICAL *scheming, shrewd.*
7 STATE-COURSE *possibly a course of life devoted to public affairs* (Horsman).
7 ACTUM EST OF HIM *he's done for.*
7–8 COMMONWEALTH'S-MAN *good citizen.*
16 LIME-BUSH *a bush smeared with birdlime to snare birds.*

for thou sweatest for't. I never saw a young pimp errant and his squire better matched.

Winwife. Faith, the sister comes after 'em well, too.

Grace. Nay, if you saw the justice her husband, my guardian,
25 you were fitted for the mess; he is such a wise one his way—

Winwife. I wonder we see him not here.

Grace. O! he is too serious for this place, and yet better sport than the other three, I assure you, gentlemen, where'er he is, though't be o' the bench.

30 *Cokes.* How dost thou call it? *A Caveat Against Cutpurses!* A good jest, i' faith; I would fain see that demon, your cutpurse, you talk of, that delicate-handed devil; they say he walks hereabout. I would see him walk, now. Look you, sister, here, here, let him come, sister, and welcome. (*He shows his purse boastingly.*) Ballad-
35 man, does any cutpurses haunt hereabout? Pray thee raise me one or two; begin and show me one.

Nightingale. Sir, this is a spell against 'em, spick and span new; and 'tis made as 'twere in mine own person, and I sing it in mine own defence. But 'twill cost a penny alone, if you buy it.

40 *Cokes.* No matter for the price; thou dost not know me, I see; I am an odd Barthol'mew.

Mistress Overdo. Has't a fine picture, brother?

Cokes. O sister, do you remember the ballads over the nursery-chimney at home o' my own pasting up? There be brave pictures!
45 Other manner of pictures than these, friend.

Wasp. Yet these will serve to pick the pictures out o' your pockets, you shall see.

Cokes. So I heard 'em say. Pray thee mind him not, fellow; he'll have an oar in everything.

50 *Nightingale.* It was intended, sir, as if a purse should chance to be

25 MESS *group of people who eat together.*
46 PICTURES *i.e. coins (with the king's picture).*

cut in my presence, now, I may be blameless, though; as by the
sequel will more plainly appear.

Cokes. We shall find that i' the matter. Pray thee begin.

Nightingale. To the tune of *Paggington's Pound*, sir.

Cokes. Fa, la la la, la la la, fa la la la. Nay, I'll put thee in tune, 55
and all! Mine own country dance! Pray thee begin.

Nightingale. It is a gentle admonition, you must know, sir, both
to the purse-cutter and the purse-bearer.

Cokes. Not a word more, out o' the tune, an' thou lov'st me.
Fa, la la la, la la la, fa la la la. Come, when? 60

Nightingale. *My masters and friends and good*
    people draw near,
    And look to your purses, for that I do say;

Cokes. Ha, ha, this chimes! Good counsel at first dash.

Nightingale. *And though little money in them*
    you do bear,
    It cost more to get than to lose in a day.   *Cokes.* Good! 65
    You oft have been told,
    Both the young and the old,
    And bidden beware of the cutpurse so bold;   *Cokes.* Well
    Then if you take heed not, free me from the   said! He were
    curse,   to blame that
    Who both give you warning for and the cut-   would not,
    purse.   i' faith. 70
    Youth, youth, thou hadst better been starved
    by thy nurse,
    Than live to be hangèd for cutting a purse.

Cokes. Good i' faith, how say you, Numps?
Is there any harm i' this?

54 PAGGINGTON'S POUND *an old dance tune.*
60 WHEN? *often addressed to negligent servants; more a command than a question.*
63 CHIMES *accords harmoniously, hence pleases.*
70 FOR AND *and moreover.*

75 Nightingale. *It hath been upbraided to men of*
my trade
That oftentimes we are the cause of this crime.
Alack and for pity, why should it be said?
As if they regarded or places or time.
Examples have been

80 *Of some that were seen*
In Westminster Hall, yea the pleaders be-
tween;
Then why should the judges be free from this
curse,
More than my poor self, for cutting the purse?
Youth, youth, thou hadst better been starved
by thy nurse,

85 *Than live to be hangèd for cutting a purse.*

Cokes. The
more coxcombs
they that did
it, I wusse.

Cokes. God a
mercy for that!
Why should
they be more
free indeed?
He sings the
burden with him.

Cokes. That again, good ballad-man, that again. O rare!
I would fain rub mine elbow now, but I dare not pull out my
hand. On, I pray thee; he that made this ballad shall be poet to
my masque.

90 Nightingale. *At Worcester 'tis known well, and*
even i' the jail,
A knight of good worship did there show his
face,
Against the foul sinners, in zeal for to rail,
And lost (ipso facto) his purse in the place.
Nay, once from the seat

95 *Of judgment so great*
A judge there did lose a fair pouch of velvet.
O Lord for thy mercy, how wicked or worse

Cokes. Is it
possible?

Cokes. I' faith?

---

81 WESTMINSTER HALL *where sessions of certain important law courts were held.*
87 RUB MINE ELBOW *as an indication of pleasure, like hugging oneself.*

Are those that so venture their necks for a
purse!
Youth, youth, etc.

Cokes. *Youth, youth, etc.* [*Sings with him again.*] Pray thee stay 100
a little, friend; Yet o' thy conscience, Numps, speak, is there any
harm i' this?

Wasp. To tell you true, 'tis too good for you, 'less you had
grace to follow it.

Overdo. [*Aside.*] It doth discover enormity, I'll mark it more; I 105
ha' not liked a paltry piece of poetry so well, a good while.

Cokes. Youth, youth, etc. Where's this youth, now? A man must
call upon him, for his own good, and yet he will not appear. Look
here, here's for him; handy-dandy, which hand will he have? (*He
shows his purse.*) On, I pray thee, with the rest; I do hear of him, but 110
I cannot see him, this Master Youth, the cutpurse.

Nightingale. *At plays and at sermons, and at the*
   sessions,
   'Tis daily their practice such booty to make:
   Yea, under the gallows, at executions,
   They stick not the stare-abouts' purses to take. 115

Nay, one without grace,	Cokes. That was
At a better place,	a fine fellow!
At court, and in Christmas, before the King's	I would have
face.	him, now.

   Alack then for pity, must I bear the curse
   That only belongs to the cunning cutpurse? 120

Cokes. But where's their cunning now, when they should use it?
They are all chained now, I warrant you. *Youth, youth, thou hadst*

___

109 HANDY-DANDY *children's game of guessing in which hand an object is concealed.*

better, etc. The rat-catchers' charm are all fools and asses to this! A
pox on 'em, that they will not come! that a man should have such a
125 desire to a thing and want it!

    Quarlous. 'Fore God, I'd give half the Fair, an' 'twere mine, for a
cutpurse for him, to save his longing.

    Cokes. Look you, sister, here, here, where is't now? which
pocket is't in, for a wager?   *He shows his purse again.*
130   *Wasp.* I beseech you leave your wagers and let him end his
matter, an't may be.

    Cokes. O, are you edified, Numps?

    Overdo. [*Aside.*] Indeed he does interrupt him too much; there
Numps spoke to purpose.

135   *Cokes.* Sister, I am an ass, I cannot keep my purse. On, on, I
pray thee, friend.   [*He shows it*] *again.*
[*During the song*] *Edgworth gets up to him and tickles him in the ear*
with a straw twice to draw his hand out of his pocket.

Nightingale. *But O, you vile nation of cutpurses*	*Winwife.* Will
all,	you see sport?
Relent and repent, and amend and be sound,	Look, there's a
And know that you ought not, by honest men's	fellow gathers
fall,	up to him,
Advance your own fortunes, to die above	mark.
140 *ground;*	*Quarlous.* Good,
And though you go gay	i' faith! O, he
In silks as you may,	has lighted on
It is not the highway to heaven (as they say).	the wrong
Repent then, repent you, for better, for worse:	pocket.
145 *And kiss not the gallows for cutting a purse.*	*Winwife.* He has

123 RAT-CATCHERS' CHARM *satirical rhyme by which it was supposed that rats in*
    Ireland were destroyed or driven away.
123 ARE ALL . . . THIS *syntactically confused or elliptical: the charm is nothing to*
    this song of Nightingale's; the ratcatchers are mere fools and asses in comparison.
125 WANT *lack.*

Youth, youth, thou hadst better been starved it, 'fore God he is
by thy nurse, a brave fellow;
Than live to be hangèd for cutting a purse. pity he should
be detected.

All. An excellent ballad! an excellent ballad!

Edgworth. Friend, let me ha' the first, let me ha' the first, I pray 150
you.

Cokes. Pardon me, sir. First come, first served; and I'll buy the
whole bundle too. [*Edgworth slips the purse to Nightingale.*]

Winwife. That conveyance was better than all, did you see't?
He has given the purse to the ballad-singer. 155

Quarlous. Has he?

Edgworth. Sir, I cry you mercy; I'll not hinder the poor man's
profit; pray you, mistake me not.

Cokes. Sir, I take you for an honest gentleman, if that be mistaking; I met you today afore. Ha! humh! O God! my purse is 160
gone, my purse, my purse, etc.

Wasp. Come, do not make a stir and cry yourself an ass
thorough the Fair afore your time.

Cokes. Why, hast thou it, Numps? Good Numps, how came you
by it? I mar'l! 165

Wasp. I pray you seek some other gamester to play the fool
with. You may lose it time enough, for all your Fair-wit.

Cokes. By this good hand, glove and all, I ha' lost it already, if
thou hast it not; feel else, and Mistress Grace's handkercher, too,
out o' the tother pocket. 170

Wasp. Why, 'tis well; very well, exceeding pretty, and well.

Edgworth. Are you sure you ha' lost it, sir?

Cokes. O God! yes; as I am an honest man, I had it but e'en now,
at *Youth, youth.*

163 THOROUGH *through.*
165 MAR'L *marvel.*
169 HANDKERCHER *a dialectical and vulgar form.*

175 *Nightingale.* I hope you suspect not me, sir.

  Edgworth. Thee? That were a jest indeed! Dost thou think the gentleman is foolish? Where hadst thou hands, I pray thee? [*To Nightingale.*] Away, ass, away.

       [*Exit Nightingale into back part of Ursula's booth.*]

  Overdo. [*Aside.*] I shall be beaten again if I be spied.

180 *Edgworth.* Sir, I suspect an odd fellow, yonder, is stealing away.

  Mistress Overdo. Brother, it is the preaching fellow! You shall suspect him. He was at your tother purse, you know! Nay, stay, sir, and view the work you ha' done; an' you be beneficed at the gallows and preach there, thank your own handiwork.

185 *Cokes.* Sir, you shall take no pride in your preferment; you shall be silenced quickly.

  Overdo. What do you mean, sweet buds of gentility?

  Cokes. To ha' my pennyworths out on you, bud. No less than two purses a day serve you? I thought you a simple fellow when

190 my man Numps beat you i' the morning, and pitied you—

  Mistress Overdo. So did I, I'll be sworn, brother; but now I see he is a lewd and pernicious enormity (as Master Overdo calls him).

  Overdo. [*Aside.*] Mine own words turned upon me like swords.

  Cokes. Cannot a man's purse be at quiet for you i' the master's

195 pocket, but you must entice it forth and debauch it?

  Wasp. Sir, sir, keep your debauch and your fine Barthol'mew-terms to yourself, and make as much on 'em as you please. But gi' me this from you i' the meantime; I beseech you, see if I can look to this.   [*Tries to take the box.*]

200 *Cokes.* Why, Numps?

  Wasp. Why? Because you are an ass, sir; there's a reason the shortest way, an' you will needs ha' it. Now you ha' got the trick of losing, you'd lose your breech, an't 'twere loose. I know you sir;

---

180 IS STEALING *who is stealing.*
183 BENEFICED *given a church preferment.*

come, deliver. (*Wasp takes the licence from him.*) You'll go and crack the vermin you breed now, will you? 'Tis very fine, will you ha' the truth on't? They are such retchless flies as you are, that blow cutpurses abroad in every corner; your foolish having of money makes 'em. An' there were no wiser than I, sir, the trade should lie open for you, sir; it should i' faith, sir. I would teach your wit to come to your head, sir, as well as your land to come into your hand, I assure you, sir.   210

Winwife. Alack, good Numps.

Wasp. Nay, gentlemen, never pity me; I am not worth it. Lord send me at home once, to Harrow o' the Hill again; if I travel any more, call me Coriat, with all my heart.   215

[*Exeunt Wasp, Cokes, and Mistress Overdo with Overdo.*]

Quarlous. Stay, sir, I must have a word with you in private. Do you hear?

Edgworth. With me, sir? What's your pleasure, good sir?

Quarlous. Do not deny it. You are a cutpurse, sir; this gentleman here, and I, saw you, nor do we mean to detect you (though we can sufficiently inform ourselves toward the danger of concealing you), but you must do us a piece of service.   220

Edgworth. Good gentlemen, do not undo me; I am a civil young man, and but a beginner, indeed.

Quarlous. Sir, your beginning shall bring on your ending, for us. We are no catchpoles nor constables. That you are to undertake is this; you saw the old fellow with the black box here?   225

204–5 CRACK . . . BREED *punish the criminals your carelessness breeds.*
206 RETCHLESS *heedless.*
206–7 BLOW CUTPURSES *as a fly deposits flyblow, or eggs.*
208 AN' THERE . . . I *i.e. if I had my way.*
208–9 THE TRADE . . . YOU *you would be taught some trade.*
220 DETECT *inform on.*
226 CATCHPOLES *petty officers empowered to make arrests.*

Edgworth. The little old governor, sir?

Quarlous. That same. I see you have flown him to a mark already.
230 I would ha' you get away that box from him, and bring it us.

Edgworth. Would you ha' the box and all, sir? or only that that
is in't? I'll get you that, and leave him the box to play with still
(which will be the harder o' the two), because I would gain your
worships' good opinion of me.

235 *Winwife.* He says well; 'tis the greater mastery, and 'twill make
the more sport when 'tis missed.

Edgworth. Aye, and 'twill be the longer a-missing, to draw on the
sport.

Quarlous. But look you do it now, sirrah, and keep your word,
240 or—

Edgworth. Sir, if ever I break my word with a gentleman, may I
never read word at my need. Where shall I find you?

Quarlous. Somewhere i' the Fair, hereabouts. Dispatch it
quickly. I would fain see the careful fool deluded! Of all beasts I
245 love the serious ass—he that takes pains to be one, and plays the
fool with the greatest diligence that can be.

Grace. Then you would not choose, sir, but love my guardian,
Justice Overdo, who is answerable to that description in every hair
of him.

250 *Quarlous.* So I have heard. But how came you, Mistress Wellborn, to be his ward, or have relation to him, at first?

Grace. Faith, through a common calamity; he bought me, sir;
and now he will marry me to his wife's brother, this wise gentleman that you see, or else I must pay value o' my land.

228 GOVERNOR *tutor.*

229 FLOWN . . . MARK *spotted; see* II.4.44.

242 READ WORD *see* I.4.6. N.

252 BOUGHT "*from the king, who had the right to sell the guardianship and
marriage of royal wards (minors who were heirs to tenants holding land from
him)*" (Horsman).

Quarlous. 'Slid, is there no device of disparagement, or so? Talk 255
with some crafty fellow, some picklock o' the law! Would I had
studied a year longer i' the Inns of Court, an't had been but i' your
case.

Winwife. [*Aside.*] Aye, Master Quarlous, are you proffering?

Grace. You'd bring but little aid, sir. 260

Winwife. [*Aside.*] I'll look to you i' faith, gamester.—An
unfortunate foolish tribe you are fall'n into, lady; I wonder you can
endure 'em.

Grace. Sir, they that cannot work their fetters off must wear
'em. 265

Winwife. You see what care they have on you, to leave you thus.

Grace. Faith, the same they have of themselves, sir. I cannot
greatly complain if this were all the plea I had against 'em.

Winwife. 'Tis true! but will you please to withdraw with us a
little, and make them think they have lost you? I hope our 270
manners ha' been such hitherto, and our language, as will give you
no cause to doubt yourself in our company.

Grace. Sir, I will give myself no cause; I am so secure of mine
own manners as I suspect not yours.

Quarlous. Look where John Littlewit comes. 275

Winwife. Away, I'll not be seen by him.

Quarlous. No, you were not best, he'd tell his mother, the
widow.

Winwife. Heart, what do you mean?

Quarlous. Cry you mercy, is the wind there? Must not the 280
widow be named?   [*Exeunt Grace, Winwife, Quarlous.*]

---

255 DISPARAGEMENT *N.*
259 PROFFERING *making advances.*

Act III Scene vi

[*Enter from back part of Ursula's booth Littlewit, Win.*]

Littlewit. Do you hear, Win, Win?

Win. What say you, John?

Littlewit. While they are paying the reckoning, Win, I'll tell you a thing, Win: we shall never see any sights i' the Fair, Win,
5 except you long still, Win. Good Win, sweet Win, long to see some hobbyhorses and some drums and rattles and dogs and fine devices, Win. The bull with the five legs, Win, and the great hog. Now you ha' begun with pig, you may long for anything, Win, and so for my motion, Win.

10 *Win.* But we sha' not eat o' the bull and the hog, John; how shall I long then?

Littlewit. O yes, Win! you may long to see as well as to taste, Win. How did the 'pothecary's wife, Win, that longed to see the anatomy, Win? Or the lady, Win, that desired to spit i' the great
15 lawyer's mouth after an eloquent pleading? I assure you they longed, Win; good Win, go in, and long.

[*Exeunt Littlewit, Win.*]

Trash. I think we are rid of our new cus-   *They*
tomer, Brother Leatherhead; we shall hear no   *plot*
more of him.   *to be*
20 *Leatherhead.* All the better; let's pack up all   *gone.*
and be gone before he find us.

Trash. Stay a little, yonder comes a company; it may be we may take some more money.

[*Enter Knockem, Busy.*]

14 ANATOMY *skeleton.*

Knockem. Sir, I will take your counsel and cut my hair and leave vapors. I see that tobacco and bottle-ale and pig and Whit 25 and very Urs'la herself is all vanity.

Busy. Only pig was not comprehended in my admonition; the rest were. For long hair, it is an ensign of pride, a banner, and the world is full of those banners, very full of banners. And bottle-ale is a drink of Satan's, a diet-drink of Satan's, devised to puff us up 30 and make us swell in this latter age of vanity, as the smoke of tobacco to keep us in mist and error; but the fleshy woman, which you call Urs'la, is above all to be avoided, having the marks upon her of the three enemies of man: the world, as being in the Fair; the devil, as being in the fire; and the flesh, as being herself. 35

[*Enter Purecraft.*]

Purecraft. Brother Zeal-of-the-land! what shall we do? My daughter, Win-the-fight, is fall'n into her fit of longing again.

Busy. For more pig? There is no more, is there?

Purecraft. To see some sights i' the Fair.

Busy. Sister, let her fly the impurity of the place swiftly, lest she 40 partake of the pitch thereof. Thou art the seat of the Beast, o Smithfield, and I will leave thee. Idolatry peepeth out on every side of thee.

Knockem. [*Aside.*] An excellent right hypocrite! Now his belly is full, he falls a-railing and kicking, the jade. A very good vapor! 45 I'll in and joy Urs'la with telling how her pig works; two and a half he eat to his share. And he has drunk a pailfull. He eats with his eyes as well as his teeth.   [*Exit.*]

Leatherhead. What do you lack, gentlemen? What is't you buy? Rattles, drums, babies— 50

---

30 DIET-DRINK *medicine.*
46–7 TWO AND A HALF *i.e. portions.*
47 EAT *variant form of* ate; *pronounced* et.

Busy. Peace with thy apocryphal wares, thou profane publican—thy bells, thy dragons, and thy Toby's dogs. Thy hobbyhorse is an idol, a very idol, a fierce and rank idol; and thou the Nebuchadnezzar, the proud Nebuchadnezzar of the Fair, that sett'st it up for
55 children to fall down to and worship.

Leatherhead. Cry you mercy, sir, will you buy a fiddle to fill up your noise?

[*Re-enter Littlewit, Win.*]

Littlewit. Look, Win; do look o' God's name, and save your longing. Here be fine sights.

60 *Purecraft.* Aye, child, so you hate 'em, as our brother Zeal does, you may look on 'em.

Leatherhead. Or what do you say to a drum, sir?

Busy. It is the broken belly of the Beast, and thy bellows there are his lungs, and these pipes are his throat, those feathers are of his
65 tail, and thy rattles the gnashing of his teeth.

Trash. And what's my gingerbread, I pray you?

Busy. The provender that pricks him up. Hence with thy basket of popery, thy nest of images, and whole legend of ginger-work.

Leatherhead. Sir, if you be not quiet the quicklier, I'll ha' you
70 clapped fairly by the heels for disturbing the Fair.

Busy. The sin of the Fair provokes me; I cannot be silent.

Purecraft. Good Brother Zeal!

Leatherhead. Sir, I'll make you silent, believe it.

51 APOCRYPHAL *spurious; alluding to the* Apocrypha, *which the Puritans rejected.*
51 PUBLICAN " *one cut off from the Church, an excommunicated person*" (OED).
52 BELLS, DRAGONS *punning allusion to* Bel and the Dragon *in the* Apocrypha.
52 TOBY'S DOGS *toy dogs presumably representing the faithful dog which goes with*
   Tobias (Toby) in the apocryphal book of Tobit.
54 NEBUCHADNEZZAR *a promulgator of idol worship.*
67 PRICKS HIM UP *stimulates him.*
68 IMAGES *gingerbread in the shape of St. Bartholomew.*
68 LEGEND *i.e. saint's legend.*
70 CLAPPED . . . HEELS *put in the stocks.*

Littlewit. [*Aside to Leatherhead.*] I'd give a shilling you could, i' faith, friend. 75

Leatherhead. Sir, give me your shilling; I'll give you my shop if I do not, and I'll leave it in pawn with you i' the meantime.

Littlewit. A match i' faith, but do it quickly, then.

[*Exit Leatherhead.*]

Busy. (*He speaks to the widow.*) Hinder me not, woman. I was moved in spirit to be here this day in this Fair, this wicked and 80 foul Fair—and fitter may it be called a foul than a Fair—to protest against the abuses of it, the foul abuses of it, in regard of the afflicted saints, that are troubled, very much troubled, exceedingly troubled, with the opening of the merchandise of Babylon again, and the peeping of popery upon the stalls, here, here, in the high 85 places. See you not Goldylocks, the purple strumpet, there, in her yellow gown and green sleeves? the profane pipes, the tinkling timbrels? A shop of relics!

Littlewit. Pray you forbear, I am put in trust with 'em.

Busy. And this idolatrous grove of images, this flasket of idols! 90 which I will pull down— *Overthrows the gingerbread.*

Trash. O my ware, my ware, God bless it.

Busy.—in my zeal, and glory to be thus exercised.

Leatherhead enters with officers.

Leatherhead. Here he is. Pray you lay hold on his zeal; we cannot sell a whistle, for him, in tune. Stop his noise first! 95

Busy. Thou canst not; 'tis a sanctified noise. I will make a loud and most strong noise, till I have daunted the profane enemy. And for this cause—

Leatherhead. Sir, here's no man afraid of you or your cause. You shall swear it i' the stocks, sir. 100

83 SAINTS *i.e. the Puritans.*
90 FLASKET *long shallow basket.*

    Busy. I will thrust myself into the stocks, upon the pikes of the land.

    Leatherhead. Carry him away.

    Purecraft. What do you mean, wicked men?

105   *Busy.* Let them alone; I fear them not.

                       [Exeunt officers with Busy, followed by Purecraft.]

    Littlewit. Was not this shilling well ventured, Win, for our liberty? Now we may go play, and see over the Fair, where we list, ourselves; my mother is gone after him, and let her e'en go and loose us.

110   *Win.* Yes, John, but I know not what to do.

    Littlewit. For what, Win?

    Win. For a thing I am ashamed to tell you, i' faith, and 'tis too far to go home.

    Littlewit. I pray thee be not ashamed, Win. Come, i' faith thou
115 shall not be ashamed; is it anything about the hobbyhorse-man? An't be, speak freely.

    Win. Hang him, base bobchin, I scorn him; no, I have very great what sha' call 'um, John.

    Littlewit. O! is that all, Win, we'll go back to Captain Jordan;
120 to the pig-woman's, Win. He'll help us, or she with a dripping pan, or an old kettle, or something. The poor greasy soul loves you, Win, and after we'll visit the Fair all over, Win, and see my puppet play, Win; you know it's a fine matter, Win.

                    [Exeunt Littlewit, Win into Ursula's booth.]

    Leatherhead. Let's away; I counselled you to pack up afore, Joan.

125   *Trash.* A pox of his Bedlam purity. He has spoiled half my ware; but the best is, we lose nothing if we miss our first merchant.

---

101 PIKES *predecessors of bayonets; Busy momentarily sees himself as a martyr.*
126 MERCHANT *customer.*

Leatherhead. It shall be hard for him to find or know us when we are translated, Joan.

    [*They pack up their wares, take down their stands, and exeunt.*]

128 ARE TRANSLATED *have removed (and transformed) ourselves.*
    SD *N.*

Act IV Scene i

[*Enter Trouble-all, Bristle, Haggis, Cokes, Overdo.*]

Trouble-all. My Masters, I do make no doubt but you are officers.

Bristle. What then, sir?

Trouble-all. And the King's loving and obedient subjects.

5   *Bristle.* Obedient, friend? Take heed what you speak, I advise you; Oliver Bristle advises you. His loving subjects, we grant you; but not his obedient, at this time, by your leave; we know ourselves a little better than so; we are to command, sir, and such as you are to be obedient. Here's one of his obedient subjects going

10 to the stocks, and we'll make you such another, if you talk.

Trouble-all. You are all wise enough i' your places, I know.

Bristle. If you know it, sir, why do you bring it in question?

Trouble-all. I question nothing, pardon me. I do only hope you have warrant for what you do, and so, quit you, and so, multiply

15 you.   *He goes away again.*

Haggis. What's he? Bring him up to the stocks there. Why bring you him not up?

[*Trouble-all*] *comes again.*

6   OLIVER *Haggis calls him Davy at* III.I.7.
14 QUIT YOU *God quit you; see Induction. l.135.*
14–5 MULTIPLY YOU *God increase your family.*

Trouble-all. If you have Justice Overdo's warrant, 'tis well; you are safe. This is the warrant of warrants. I'll not give this button for any man's warrant else. 20

Bristle. Like enough, sir; but let me tell you, an' you play away your buttons thus, you will want 'em ere night, for any store I see about you. You might keep 'em, and save pins, I wusse.

[Trouble-all] goes away.

Overdo. [*Aside.*] What should he be, that doth so esteem and advance my warrant? He seems a sober and discreet person! It is a 25 comfort to a good conscience to be followed with a good fame in his sufferings. The world will have a pretty taste by this, how I can bear adversity; and it will beget a kind of reverence toward me hereafter, even from mine enemies, when they shall see I carry my calamity nobly, and that it doth neither break me nor bend me. 30

Haggis. Come, sir, here's a place for you to preach in. Will you put in your leg? *They put him in the stocks.*

Overdo. That I will, cheerfully.

Bristle. O' my conscience, a seminary! He kisses the stocks.

Cokes. Well, my masters, I'll leave him with you; now I see him 35 bestowed, I'll go look for my goods and Numps.

Haggis. You may, sir, I warrant you; where's the tother bawler? Fetch him too, you shall find 'em both fast enough. [*Exit Cokes.*]

Overdo. [*Aside.*] In the midst of this tumult I will yet be the author of mine own rest, and, not minding their fury, sit in the 40 stocks in that calm as shall be able to trouble a triumph.

[Trouble-all] comes again.

Trouble-all. Do you assure me upon your words? May I undertake for you, if I be asked the question, that you have this warrant?

Haggis. What's this fellow, for God's sake? 45

22 STORE *supply.*
32 LEG *N.*

123

Trouble-all. Do but show me Adam Overdo, and I am satisfied.

Goes out.

Bristle. He is a fellow that is distracted, they say—one Trouble-all. He was an officer in the court of Pie-powders here last year, and put out on his place by Justice Overdo.

50 *Overdo.* Ha!

Bristle. Upon which he took an idle conceit, and's run mad upon't. So that ever since, he will do nothing but by Justice Overdo's warrant; he will not eat a crust, nor drink a little, nor make him in his apparel ready. His wife, sir-reverence, cannot get

55 him make his water or shift his shirt without his warrant.

Overdo. [*Aside.*] If this be true, this is my greatest disaster! How am I bound to satisfy this poor man, that is of so good a nature to me, out of his wits, where there is no room left for dissembling!

[*Trouble-all*] *comes in.*

Trouble-all. If you cannot show me Adam Overdo, I am in

60 doubt of you. I am afraid you cannot answer it.   *Goes again.*

Haggis. Before me, neighbor Bristle, (and now I think on't better) Justice Overdo is a very peremptory person.

Bristle. O! are you advised of that? And a severe justicer, by your leave.

65 *Overdo.* [*Aside.*] Do I hear ill o' that side, too?

Bristle. He will sit as upright o' the bench, an' you mark him, as a candle i' the socket, and give light to the whole court in every business.

Haggis. But he will burn blue and swell like a boil (God bless us!)

70 an' he be angry.

49 ON *of.*
51 IDLE *foolish.*
54 MAKE . . . READY *get dressed.*
60 ANSWER IT *i.e. answer for it.*
63 ADVISED *aware.*

Bristle. Aye, and he will be angry too, when him list, that's more; and when he is angry, be it right or wrong, he has the law on's side ever. I mark that too.

Overdo. [*Aside.*] I will be more tender hereafter. I see compassion may become a justice, though it be a weakness, I confess, 75 and nearer a vice than a virtue.

Haggis. Well, take him out o' the stocks again. We'll go a sure way to work; we'll ha' the ace of hearts of our side, if we can.

They take the Justice out. [*Enter Poacher, Busy, Purecraft.*]

Poacher. Come, bring him away to his fellow, there. Master Busy, we shall rule your legs, I hope, though we cannot rule your 80 tongue.

Busy. No, minister of darkness, no, thou canst not rule my tongue; my tongue it is mine own, and with it I will both knock and mock down your Barthol'mew-abominations, till you be made a hissing to the neighbor parishes round about. 85

Haggis. Let him alone; we have devised better upon't.

Purecraft. And shall he not into the stocks then?

Bristle. No, mistress, we'll have 'em both to Justice Overdo, and let him do over 'em as is fitting. Then I and my gossip Haggis and my beadle Poacher are discharged. 90

Purecraft. O, I thank you, blessed, honest men!

Bristle. Nay, never thank us, but thank this madman that comes here. He put it in our heads.

[Trouble-all] comes again.

Purecraft. Is he mad? Now heaven increase his madness, and bless it, and thank it; sir, your poor handmaid thanks you. 95

Trouble-all. Have you a warrant? An' you have a warrant, show it.

---

71 HIM LIST *he wants to be* (F. *reads* "his list").
90 DISCHARGED *freed from responsibility.*

Purecraft. Yes, I have a warrant out of the Word, to give thanks for removing any scorn intended to the brethren.

100   *Trouble-all.* It is Justice Overdo's warrant that I look for. If you have not that, keep your word, I'll keep mine. Quit ye, and multiply ye.   [*Exeunt all but Trouble-all.*]

98   WORD *Bible.*

Act IV Scene ii

[*Enter Edgworth, Nightingale.*]

Edgworth. Come away, Nightingale, I pray thee.

Trouble-all. Whither go you? Where's your warrant?

Edgworth. Warrant, for what, sir?

Trouble-all. For what you go about; you know how fit it is; an'

5 you have no warrant, bless you, I'll pray for you, that's all I can do.

Goes out.

Edgworth. What means he?

Nightingale. A madman that haunts the Fair; do you not know him? It's marvel he has not more followers after his ragged heels.

Edgworth. Beshrew him, he startled me. I thought he had known

10 of our plot. Guilt's a terrible thing! Ha' you prepared the coster-monger?

Nightingale. Yes, and agreed for his basket of pears. He is at the corner here, ready. [*Enter Costermonger.*] And your prize, he comes down, sailing that way, all alone, without his protector; he is rid

15 of him, it seems.

Edgworth. Aye, I know; I should ha' followed his protectorship for a feat I am to do upon him; but this offered itself so i' the way, I could not let it 'scape. Here he comes; whistle. Be this sport called "Dorring the Dottrel."

[*Enter Cokes.*]

Nightingale.(*Whistles.*) Wh, wh, wh, wh, etc.   20

Cokes. By this light, I cannot find my gingerbread-wife nor my
hobbyhorse-man in all the Fair, now, to ha' my money again.
And I do not know the way out on't, to go home for more, do you
hear, friend, you that whistle? what tune is that you whistle?

Nightingale. A new tune I am practising, sir.   25

Cokes. Dost thou know where I dwell, I pray thee? Nay, on with
thy tune, I ha' no such haste for an answer. I'll practise with thee.

Costermonger. Buy any pears, very fine pears, pears fine.

Nightingale sets his foot afore him, and he falls with his basket.

Cokes. Godso! a muss, a muss, a muss, a muss.

[*He starts picking up the pears.*]

Costermonger. Good gentleman, my ware, my ware! I am a poor   30
man. Good sir, my ware.

Nightingale. [*To Cokes.*] Let me hold your sword, sir, it
troubles you.

Cokes. Do, and my cloak, an' thou wilt; and my hat too.

Cokes falls a-scrambling whilst they run away with his things.

Edgworth. A delicate great boy! methinks he out-scrambles 'em   35
all. I cannot persuade myself but he goes to grammar-school yet,
and plays the truant today.

Nightingale. Would he had another purse to cut, 'Zekiel.

Edgworth. Purse? a man might cut out his kidneys, I think, and
he never feel 'em, he is so earnest at the sport.   40

Nightingale. His soul is half-way out on's body at the game.

Edgworth. Away, Nightingale; that way.

[*Exit Nightingale with sword, cloak, and hat.*]

19 DORRING THE DOTTREL *hoaxing a simpleton; a dottrel is a plover which can be
captured easily.*

29 MUSS *scramble.*

Cokes. I think I am furnished for Cather'ne pears for one undermeal. Gi' me my cloak.

45   *Costermonger.* Good gentleman, give me my ware.

Cokes. Where's the fellow I ga' my cloak to? My cloak? and my hat? Ha! God's lid, is he gone? Thieves, thieves! Help me to cry, gentlemen.   *He runs out.*

Edgworth. Away, costermonger, come to us to Urs'la's. [*Exit*
50   *Costermonger.*] Talk of him to have a soul? 'Heart, if he have any more than a thing given him instead of salt, only to keep him from stinking, I'll be hanged afore my time, presently. Where should it be, trow? In his blood? He has not so much toward it in his whole body as will maintain a good flea. And if he take this
55   course, he will not ha' so much land left as to rear a calf within this twelvemonth. Was there ever green plover so pulled! That his little overseer had been here now, and been but tall enough, to see him steal pears in exchange for his beaver-hat and his cloak thus! I must go find him out next, for his black box and his
60   patent (it seems) he has of his place; which I think the gentleman would have a reversion of, that spoke to me for it so earnestly.

                                                                  [*Exit.*]

He [Cokes] comes again.

Cokes. Would I might lose my doublet, and hose too, as I am an honest man, and never stir, if I think there be anything but thieving and coz'ning i' this whole Fair. Barthol'mew Fair, quoth
65   he; an' ever any Barthol'mew had that luck in't that I have had, I'll be martyred for him, and in Smithfield too. I ha' paid for my pears, a rot on 'em, I'll keep 'em no longer. (*Throws away his pears.*)

---

44 UNDERMEAL *afternoon meal.*

56 PULLED *plucked (as this simpleton has been stripped).*

60 PATENT . . . PLACE *document he apparently has, entitling him to his position. Edgworth supposes that Quarlous wants Wasp's job.*

61 REVERSION *"the right of succeeding to, or next occupying an estate, etc." (OED).*

You were choke-pears to me; I had better ha' gone to mum-
chance for you, I wusse. Methinks the Fair should not have used
me thus, an' 'twere but for my name's sake; I would not ha' used   70
a dog o 'the name so. O, Numps will triumph now! (*Trouble-all
comes again.*) Friend, do you know who I am? Or where I lie? I do
not myself, I'll be sworn. Do but carry me home, and I'll please
thee; I ha' money enough there. I ha' lost myself, and my cloak
and my hat; and my fine sword and my sister and Numps and   75
Mistress Grace (a gentlewoman that I should ha' married) and
a cut-work handkercher she ga' me and two purses, today. And
my bargain o' hobbyhorses and gingerbread, which grieves me
worst of all.

    Trouble-all. By whose warrant, sir, have you done all this?   80

    Cokes. Warrant? thou art a wise fellow, indeed—as if a man need
a warrant to lose anything with.

    Trouble-all. Yes, Justice Overdo's warrant, a man may get and
lose with, I'll stand to't.

    Cokes. Justice Overdo? Dost thou know him? I lie there, he is   85
my brother-in-law, he married my sister. Pray thee show me the
way, dost thou know the house?

    Trouble-all. Sir, show me your warrant; I know nothing with-
out a warrant, pardon me.

    Cokes. Why, I warrant thee, come along. Thou shalt see I have   90
wrought pillows there, and cambric sheets, and sweet bags too.
Pray thee guide me to the house.

    Trouble-all. Sir, I'll tell you: go you thither yourself, first, alone;
tell your worshipful brother your mind; and but bring me three

---

68 CHOKE-PEARS *coarse variety of pears.*
68–9 MUM-CHANCE *a game with dice.*
73 CARRY *take.*
85 LIE *lodge.*
91 SWEET BAGS *bags of fragrant herbs, comparable to the modern sachet.*

95 lines of his hand, or his clerk's, with "Adam Overdo" underneath. Here I'll stay you; I'll obey you, and I'll guide you
presently.

Cokes. [*Aside.*] 'Slid, this is an ass; I ha' found him. Pox upon me,
what do I talking to such a dull fool?—Farewell. You are a very
100 coxcomb, do you hear?

Trouble-all. I think I am; if Justice Overdo sign to it, I am, and
so we are all; he'll quit us all, multiply us all.   [*Exeunt.*]

98 FOUND *found out, detected.*

Act IV Scene iii

[*Enter Grace, Quarlous, Winwife.*] *They* [*the latter*] *enter with
their swords drawn.*

Grace. Gentlemen, this is no way that you take. You do but
breed one another trouble and offence, and give me no content-
ment at all. I am no she that affects to be quarrelled for, or have
my name or fortune made the question of men's swords.

5   *Quarlous.* 'Slood, we love you.

Grace. If you both love me, as you pretend, your own reason
will tell you but one can enjoy me; and to that point there leads
a directer line than by my infamy, which must follow if you fight.
'Tis true, I have professed it to you ingenuously, that rather than
10 to be yoked with this bridegroom is appointed me, I would take
up any husband, almost upon any trust. Though subtlety would
say to me (I know) he is a fool, and has an estate, and I might govern
him and enjoy a friend beside. But these are not my aims. I must

3 AFFECTS *likes.*
6 PRETEND *claim.*
11 SUBTLETY *cunning.*

have a husband I must love, or I cannot live with him. I shall ill
make one of these politic wives!   15

Winwife. Why, if you can like either of us, lady, say which is he,
and the other shall swear instantly to desist.

Quarlous. Content; I accord to that willingly.

Grace. Sure you think me a woman of an extreme levity, gentlemen, or a strange fancy, that (meeting you by chance in such a   20
place as this, both at one instant, and not yet of two hours' acquaintance, neither of you deserving afore the other of me) I should
so forsake my modesty (though I might affect one more
particularly) as to say, "This is he," and name him.

Quarlous. Why, wherefore should you not? What should   25
hinder you?

Grace. If you would not give it to my modesty, allow it yet to
my wit; give me so much of woman and cunning as not to
betray myself impertinently. How can I judge of you so far as to
a choice without knowing you more? You are both equal and alike   30
to me yet; and so indifferently affected by me as each of you might
be the man if the other were away. For you are reasonable
creatures; you have understanding and discourse. And if fate send
me an understanding husband, I have no fear at all but mine own
manners shall make him a good one.   35

Quarlous. Would I were put forth to making for you, then.

Grace. It may be you are; you know not what's toward you.
Will you consent to a motion of mine, gentlemen?

Winwife. Whatever it be, we'll presume reasonableness, coming
from you.   40

Quarlous. And fitness too.

31 INDIFFERENTLY *without distinction.*
33 DISCOURSE *rationality.*
36 PUT FORTH *sent out.*
36 TO MAKING *to be trained, to be made a good husband.*
37 TOWARD *in store for.*

Grace. I saw one of you buy a pair of tables, e'en now.

Winwife. Yes, here they be, and maiden ones too, unwritten in.

Grace. The fitter for what they may be employed in. You shall
45 write, either of you, here, a word or a name—what you like
best—but of two or three syllables at most; and the next person
that comes this way (because destiny has a high hand in business of
this nature) I'll demand which of the two words he or she doth
approve; and according to that sentence fix my resolution and
50 affection without change.

Quarlous. Agreed. My word is conceived already.

Winwife. And mine shall not be long creating after.

Grace. But you shall promise, gentlemen, not to be curious to
know which of you it is, taken; but give me leave to conceal that
55 till you have brought me either home, or where I may safely tender
myself.

Winwife. Why, that's but equal.

Quarlous. We are pleased.

Grace. Because I will bind both your endeavors to work
60 together, friendly and jointly, each to the other's fortune, and have
myself fitted with some means to make him that is forsaken a part
of amends.

Quarlous. These conditions are very courteous. Well, my word
is out of the *Arcadia*, then: "Argalus."

65 *Winwife.* And mine out of the play, "Palamon."

Trouble-all comes again.

42 TABLES *pads of paper,*
45 EITHER *both.*
54 TAKEN *i.e. who has been taken.*
55 TENDER *present, entrust.*
57 EQUAL *fair.*
64 ARGALUS *character in Sir Philip Sidney's pastoral romance.*
65 THE PLAY *probably* The Two Noble Kinsmen, *a dramatization of Chaucer's*
Knight's Tale (*of Palamon and Arcite*), *ascribed to Shakespeare and Fletcher.*
Argalus and Palamon are typical romance lovers.

Trouble-all. Have you any warrant for this gentlemen?

Quarlous. Winwife. Ha!

Trouble-all. There must be a warrant had, believe it.

Winwife. For what?

Trouble-all. For whatsoever it is, anything indeed, no matter   70
what.

    Quarlous. 'Slight, here's a fine ragged prophet, dropped down i'
the nick!

Trouble-all. Heaven quit you, gentlemen.

Quarlous. Nay, stay a little. Good lady, put him to the question.   75

Grace. You are content, then?

Winwife. Quarlous. Yes, yes.

Grace. Sir, here are two names written—

Trouble-all. Is Justice Overdo one?

    Grace. How, sir? I pray you read 'em to yourself—it is for a   80
wager between these gentlemen—and with a stroke or any
difference, mark which you approve best.

    Trouble-all. They may be both worshipful names for ought I
know, mistress, but Adam Overdo had been worth three of 'em, I
assure you, in this place; that's in plain English.   85

Grace. This man amazes me! I pray you, like one of 'em, sir.

    Trouble-all. I do like him there, that has the best warrant. Mis-
tress, to save your longing (and multiply him), it may be this.
[*Marks the book.*] But I am aye still for Justice Overdo, that's my
conscience. And quit you.   [*Exit.*]   90

Winwife. Is't done, lady?

    Grace. Aye, and strangely as ever I saw! What fellow is this,
trow?

    Quarlous. No matter what, a fortune-teller we ha' made him.
Which is't, which is't?   95

    Grace. Nay, did you not promise not to inquire?

82 DIFFERENCE *differentiating mark.*

[Enter Edgworth.]

Quarlous. 'Slid, I forgot that, pray you pardon me. Look, here's our Mercury come. The licence arrives i' the finest time, too! 'Tis but scraping out Cokes his name, and 'tis done.

100   *Winwife.* How now, lime-twig? Hast thou touched?

Edgworth. Not yet, sir; except you would go with me and see't, it's not worth speaking on. The act is nothing without a witness. Yonder he is, your man with the box, fall'n into the finest company, and so transported with vapors; they ha' got in a north-
105 ern clothier and one Puppy, a western man, that's come to wrestle before my Lord Mayor anon, and Captain Whit, and one Val Cutting, that helps Captain Jordan to roar, a circling boy; with whom your Numps is so taken that you may strip him of his clothes, if you will. I'll undertake to geld him for you, if you had
110 but a surgeon, ready, to sear him. And Mistress Justice, there, is the goodest woman! She does so love 'em all over, in terms of justice and the style of authority, with her hood upright—that I beseech you come away, gentlemen, and see't.

Quarlous. 'Slight, I would not lose it for the Fair; what'll you do,
115 Ned?

Winwife. Why, stay here about for you; Mistress Wellborn must not be seen.

Quarlous. Do so, and find out a priest i' the meantime; I'll bring the licence. [*To Edgworth.*] Lead, which way is't?

[Exeunt Winwife, Grace.]

120   *Edgworth.* Here, sir, you are o' the backside o' the booth already; you may hear the noise.

98 MERCURY *who was swift-footed and a thief.*
100 LIME-TWIG *twig smeared with bird-lime.*
101 EXCEPT *unless.*
105-6 WRESTLE . . . MAYOR *a regular feature of the Fair.*
107 CIRCLING BOY *explained, presumably, by* IV.4.128.
120 BACKSIDE *N.*

Act IV Scene iv

[*Knockem, Northern, Puppy, Cutting, Whit, Wasp, Mistress Overdo
revealed in Ursula's booth.*]

Knockem. Whit, bid Val Cutting continue the vapors for a lift,
Whit, for a lift.

Northern. I'll ne mare, I'll ne mare, the eale's too meeghty.

Knockem. How now! my Galloway Nag, the staggers? Ha!
Whit, gi' him a slit i' the forehead. Cheer up, man; a needle and   5
thread to stitch his ears. I'd cure him now, an' I had it, with a
little butter and garlic, long-pepper, and grains. Where's my horn?
I'll gi' him a mash, presently, shall take away this dizziness.

Puppy. Why, where are you, zurs? Do you vlinch and leave us
i' the zuds, now?   10

Northern. I'll ne mare, I is e'en as vull as a paiper's bag, by my
troth, I.

Puppy. Do my northern cloth zhrink i' the wetting, ha?

Knockem. Why, well said, old flea-bitten, thou'lt never tire, I
see.   15

> *They fall to their vapors again.*

Cutting. No, sir, but he may tire, if it please him.

---

1 LIFT *trick, theft* N.

3 NE MARE *no more; Northern and Puppy speak in regional dialects which are
not hard to understand.*

4 GALLOWAY NAG *Scottish breed of horses.*

4 STAGGERS *dizziness in horses; Knockem proposes various treatments for it.*

7 LONG-PEPPER *especially strong variety of pepper.*

7 HORN *horn-shaped vessel used in administering medicine to horses.*

10 I' THE ZUDS *literally (since they are drinking ale) and figuratively: "in
difficulties."*

Whit. Who told dee sho? that he vuld never teer, man?

Cutting. No matter who told him so, so long as he knows.

Knockem. Nay, I know nothing, sir, pardon me there.

20 *Edgworth* [*To Quarlous.*] They are at it still, sir; this they call vapors.

Whit. He shall not pardon dee, Captain, dou shalt not be pardoned. Pre'de shweetheart, do not pardon him.

Cutting. 'Slight, I'll pardon him, an' I list, whosoever says nay

25 to't.

Quarlous. Where's Numps? I miss him.

Wasp. Why, I say nay to't.

Quarlous. O there he is!

Knockem. To what do you say nay, sir?

Here they continue their game of vapors, which is nonsense:
every man to oppose the last man that spoke, whether it concerned
him or no.

30 *Wasp.* To anything, whatsoever it is, so long as I do not like it.

Whit. Pardon me, little man, dou musht like it a little.

Cutting. No, he must not like it at all, sir; there you are i' the wrong.

Whit. I tink I be; he musht not like it, indeed.

35 *Cutting.* Nay, then he both must and will like it, sir, for all you.

Knockem. If he have reason, he may like it, sir.

Whit. By no meansh, Captain, upon reason; he may like nothing upon reason.

Wasp. I have no reason, nor I will hear of no reason, nor I will

40 look for no reason, and he is an ass that either knows any or looks for't from me.

Cutting. Yes, in some sense you may have reason, sir.

Wasp. Aye, in some sense, I care not if I grant you.

Whit. Pardon me, thou ougsht to grant him nothing, in no

45 shensh, if dou do love dyshelf, angry man.

Wasp. Why then, I do grant him nothing; and I have no sense.

Cutting. 'Tis true, thou hast no sense indeed.

Wasp. 'Slid, but I have sense, now I think on't better, and I will grant him anything, do you see?

Knockem. He is i' the right, and does utter a sufficient vapor.   50

Cutting. Nay, it is no sufficient vapor, neither; I deny that.

Knockem. Then it is a sweet vapor.

Cutting. It may be a sweet vapor.

Wasp. Nay, it is no sweet vapor, **neither, sir; it stinks, and** I'll stand to't.   55

Whit. Yes, I tink it doesh shtink, Captain. All vapor doesh shtink.

Wasp. Nay, then it does not stink, sir, and it shall not stink.

Cutting. By your leave, it may, sir.

Wasp. Aye, by my leave, it may stink; I know that.   60

Whit. Pardon me, thou knowesht nothing; it cannot by thy leave, angry man.

Wasp. How can it not?

Knockem. Nay, never question him, for he is i' the right.

Whit. Yesh, I am i' de right, I confesh it; so ish de little man too.   65

Wasp. I'll have nothing confessed that concerns me. I am not i' the right, nor never was i' the right, nor never will be i' the right, while I am in my right mind.

Cutting. Mind? Why, here's no man minds you, sir, nor anything else.   70

They drink again.

Puppy. Vriend, will you mind this that we do?

Quarlous. [*To Edgworth.*] Call you this vapors? This is such belching of quarrel as I never heard. Will you mind your business, sir?

Edgworth. You shall see, sir.   75

74 BUSINESS *i.e. the job he is to do.*

137

Northern. I'll ne mair, my waimb warks too mickle with this auready.

Edgworth. Will you take that, Master Wasp, that nobody should mind you?

80   *Wasp.* Why? What ha' you to do? Is't any matter to you?

Edgworth. No, but methinks you should not be unminded, though.

Wasp. Nor I wu' not be, now I think on't; do you hear, new acquaintance, does no man mind me, say you?

85   *Cutting.* Yes, sir, every man here minds you, but how?

Wasp. Nay, I care as little how as you do; that was not my question.

Whit. No, noting was ty question; tou art a learned man, and I am a valiant man; i' faith la, tou shalt speak for me, and I vill 90 fight for tee.

Knockem. Fight for him, Whit? A gross vapor; he can fight for himself.

Wasp. It may be I can, but it may be I wu' not, how then?

Cutting. Why, then you may choose.

95   *Wasp.* Why, and I'll choose whether I'll choose or no.

Knockem. I think you may, and 'tis true; and I allow it for a resolute vapor.

Wasp. Nay, then, I do think you do not think and it is no resolute vapor.

100   *Cutting.* Yes, in some sort he may allow you.

Knockem. In no sort, sir, pardon me, I can allow him nothing. You mistake the vapor.

Wasp. He mistakes nothing, sir, in no sort.

Whit. Yes, I pre dee now, let him mistake.

105   *Wasp.* A turd i' your teeth, never pre dee me, for I will have nothing mistaken.

76 WAIMB *womb, i.e. stomach.*

138

Knockem. Turd, ha, turd? A noisome vapor; strike, Whit.

They fall by the ears. [As they are fighting, Edgworth
steals the licence out of the box and exits.]

Mistress Overdo. Why gentlemen, why gentlemen, I charge
you upon my authority, conserve the peace. In the King's name,
and my husband's, put up your weapons; I shall be driven to   110
commit you myself, else.

Quarlous. Ha, ha, ha.

Wasp. Why do you laugh, sir?

Quarlous. Sir, you'll allow me my Christian liberty. I may
laugh, I hope.   115

Cutting. In some sort you may, and in some sort you may not,
sir.

Knockem. Nay, in some sort, sir, he may neither laugh nor
hope in this company.

Wasp. Yes, then he may both laugh and hope in any sort, an't   120
please him.

Quarlous. Faith, and I will then, for it doth please me exceedingly.

Wasp. No exceeding neither, sir.

Knockem. No, that vapor is too lofty.   125

Quarlous. Gentlemen, I do not play well at your game of vapors;
I am not very good at it, but—

Cutting. Do you hear, sir? I would speak with you in circle!

He draws a circle on the ground.

Quarlous. In circle, sir? What would you with me in circle?

Cutting. Can you lend me a piece, a jacobus, in circle?   130

Quarlous. 'Slid, your circle will prove more costly than your
vapors, then. Sir, no, I lend you none.

111 COMMIT *consign to custody.*
116 IN SOME SORT *to some extent.*
124 EXCEEDING *going too far, being presumptuous.*
130 JACOBUS *gold coin issued in the reign of James I.*

Cutting. Your beard's not well turned up, sir.

[*Handles Quarlous' beard.*]

Quarlous. How, rascal? Are you playing with my beard? I'll
135 break circle with you.

They draw all, and fight.

Puppy. Northern. Gentlemen, gentlemen!

Knockem. Gather up, Whit, gather up, Whit, Good vapors!

[*Exit.*]

[*Whit gathers up cloaks and conceals them.*]

Mistress Overdo. What mean you? are you rebels, gentlemen?
Shall I send out a sergeant-at-arms or a writ o' rebellion against
140 you? I'll commit you, upon my womanhood, for a riot, upon my
justice-hood, if you persist. [*Exeunt Quarlous, Cutting.*]

Wasp. Upon your justice-hood? Marry, shit o' your hood;
you'll commit? Spoke like a true justice of peace's wife, indeed,
and a fine female lawyer! Turd i' your teeth for a fee, now.

145 *Mistress Overdo.* Why, Numps, in Master Overdo's name, I
charge you.

Wasp. Good Mistress Underdo, hold your tongue.

Mistress Overdo. Alas! poor Numps.

Wasp. Alas! And why alas from you, I beseech you? Or why
150 poor Numps, Goody Rich? Am I come to be pitied by your tuft
taffeta now? Why mistress, I knew Adam, the clerk, your
husband, when he was Adam scrivener, and writ for twopence a
sheet, as high as he bears his head now, or you your hood, dame.
(*The watch comes in.*) What are you, sir?

155 *Bristle.* We be men, and no infidels. What is the matter here, and
the noises? Can you tell?

143 COMMIT *with a play on the meaning, "fornicate."*
150–1 TUFT TAFFETA *a fashionable fabric.*
152 ADAM SCRIVENER *probably an allusion to Chaucer's scribe (see "To his
Scribe Adam").*
154 THE WATCH *N.*

Wasp. Heart, what ha' you to do? Cannot a man quarrel in quietness, but he must be put out on't by you? What are you?

Bristle. Why, we be His Majesty's Watch, sir.

Wasp. Watch? 'Sblood, you are a sweet watch, indeed. A body 160
would think, an' you watched well a-nights, you should be contented to sleep at this time a-day. Get you to your fleas and your flock-beds, you rogues, your kennels, and lie down close.

Bristle. Down? Yes, we will down, I warrant you; down with him in His Majesty's name, down, down with him, and carry him 165
away to the pigeon-holes.   [*Bristle and Poacher seize Wasp.*]

Mistress Overdo. I thank you, honest friends, in the behalf o' the Crown and the peace, and in Master Overdo's name, for suppressing enormities.

Whit. Stay, Bristle, here ish a noder brash o' drunkards, but 170
very quiet, special drunkards, will pay dee five shillings very well. Take 'em to dee, in de graish o' God. One of 'em does change cloth for ale in the Fair here, te toder ish a strong man, a mighty man, my Lord Mayor's man, and a wrestler. He has wreshled so long with the bottle, here, that the man with the beard hash 175
almost streek up hish heelsh.

Bristle. 'Slid, the Clerk o' the Market has been to cry him all the Fair over, here, for my Lord's service.

Whit. Tere he ish, pre de taik him hensh and make ty best on him. [*Exit watch with Wasp, Northern, Puppy.*] How now, woman 180
o' shilk, vat ailsh ty shweet faish? Art tou melancholy?

Mistress Overdo. A little distempered with these enormities; shall I entreat a courtesy of you, Captain?

161 WATCHED *both "stayed awake" and "acted as watchmen."*
163 FLOCK *wool used for stuffing mattresses, etc.*
166 PIGEON-HOLES *stocks.*
170 BRASH *brace.*
175 MAN WITH THE BEARD *jug with a face on it.*
177 CRY *page.*

Whit. Entreat a hundred, velvet voman, I vill do it; shpeak out.

185   *Mistress Overdo.* I cannot with modesty speak it out, but—

Whit. I vill do it, and more, and more, for dee. What, Urs'la, an't be bitch, an't be bawd, an't be!

[*Enter Ursula.*]

Ursula. How now, rascal? What roar you for, old pimp?

Whit. [*To Ursula.*] Here, put up de cloaks, Ursh; de purchase;

190   pre dee now, shweet Ursh, help dis good brave voman to a jordan, an't be.

Ursula. 'Slid, call your Captain Jordan to her, can you not?

Whit. Nay, pre dee leave dy consheits, and bring the velvet woman to de—

195   *Ursula.* I bring her! Hang her! Heart, must I find a common pot for every punk i' your purlieus?

Whit. O good voordsh, Ursh; it ish a guest o' velvet, i' fait la.

Ursula. Let her sell her hood and buy a sponge, with a pox to her. My vessel is employed, sir. I have but one, and 'tis the bottom

200   of an old bottle. An honest proctor and his wife are at it, within; if she'll stay her time, so.

Whit. As soon ash tou cansht, shweet Ursh. Of a valiant man I tink I am the patientsh man i' the world, or in all Smithfield.

[*Re-enter Knockem.*]

Knockem. How now, Whit? Close vapors, stealing your leaps?

205   Covering in corners, ha?

Whit. No, fait, Captain, dough tou beesht a vishe man, dy vit is a mile hence, now. I vas procuring a shmall courtesy for a woman of fashion here.

Mistress Overdo. Yes, Captain, though I am justice of peace's

210   wife, I do love men of war and the sons of the sword, when they come before my husband.

---

196 PURLIEUS *neighborhood; specifically suburbs; see* II.5.78.
205 COVERING *copulating (of horses).*

Knockem. Say'st thou so, filly? Thou shalt have a leap presently; I'll horse thee myself, else.

Ursula. Come, will you bring her in now? and let her take her turn?   215

Whit. Gramercy, good Ursh, I tank dee.

Mistress Overdo. Master Overdo shall thank her.   [*Exit.*]

Act IV Scene v

[*Enter Littlewit, Win.*]

Littlewit. Good Gammer Urs, Win and I are exceedingly beholden to you, and to Captain Jordan and Captain Whit. Win, I'll be bold to leave you i' this good company, Win, for half an hour or so, Win, while I go and see how my matter goes forward, and if the puppets be perfect; and then I'll come and fetch you,   5
Win.

Win. Will you leave me alone with two men, John?

Littlewit. Aye, they are honest gentlemen, Win, Captain Jordan and Captain Whit; they'll use you very civilly, Win; God b' w' you, Win.   [*Exit.*]   10

Ursula. [*To Knockem and Whit.*] What's her husband gone?

Knockem. On his false gallop, Urs, away.

Ursula. An' you be right Barthol'mew-birds, now show yourselves so; we are undone for want of fowl i' the Fair, here. Here will be 'Zekiel Edgworth and three or four gallants with him at   15
night, and I ha' neither plover nor quail for 'em. Persuade this between you two to become a bird o' the game, while I work the velvet woman within (as you call her).

11 WHAT *what for.*
16 PLOVER, QUAIL *loose women.*

Knockem. I conceive thee, Urs! go thy ways. [*Exit Ursula.*]
20 Dost thou hear, Whit? is't not pity my delicate dark chestnut here
—with the fine lean head, large forehead, round eyes, even mouth,
sharp ears, long neck, thin crest, close withers, plain back, deep
sides, short fillets, and full flanks; with a round belly, a plump buttock, large thighs, knit knees, straight legs, short pasterns, smooth
25 hoofs, and short heels—should lead a dull honest woman's life,
that might live the life of a lady?

Whit. Yes, by my fait and trot it is, Captain. De honesht
woman's life is a scurvy dull life, indeed la.

Win. How, sir? Is an honest woman's life a scurvy life?

30 *Whit.* Yes, fait, shweetheart, believe him, de leef of a bond-
woman! But if dou vilt harken to me, I vill make tee a free-
woman and a lady. Dou shalt live like a lady, as te captain saish.

Knockem. Aye, and be honest too, sometimes; have her wires
and her tires, her green gowns and velvet petticoats.

35 *Whit.* Aye, and ride to Ware and Rumford i' dy coash, shee de
players, be in love vit 'em; sup vit gallantsh, be drunk, and cost
de noting.

Knockem. Brave vapors!

Whit. And lie by twenty on 'em, if dóu pleash, shweetheart.

40 *Win.* What, and be honest still? That were fine sport.

Whit. Tish common, shweetheart; tou may'st do it, by my
hand. It shall be justified to ty husband's faish, now; tou shalt be
as honesht as the skin between his hornsh, la!

---

20 CHESTNUT *Knockem as usual relies on the terminology for horses.*

33 WIRES *used to stiffen ruffs.*

34 TIRES *dresses.*

34 GREEN GOWNS *"to give a green gown" meant to seduce (on the grass); hence
green was associated with loose women.*

35 WARE AND RUMFORD *known as places for assignations.*

43 SKIN BETWEEN HIS HORNSH *"skin between his brows" was proverbial; the
change to "horns" introduces the old joke about cuckolds.*

Knockem. Yes, and wear a dressing, top and top-gallant, to compare with e'er a husband on 'em all, for a fore-top. It is the vapor 45
of spirit in the wife to cuckold, nowadays, as it is the vapor of
fashion in the husband not to suspect. Your prying cat-eyed-
citizen is an abominable vapor.

Win. Lord, what a fool have I been!

Whit. Mend, then, and do everyting like a lady hereafter; never 50
know ty husband from another man.

Knockem. Nor any one man from another, but i' the dark.

Whit. Aye, and then it ish no dishgrash to know any man.

[*Re-enter Ursula.*]

Ursula. Help, help here.

Knockem. How now? What vapor's there? 55

Ursula. O, you are a sweet ranger! and look well to your walks!
Yonder is your punk of Turnbull, Ramping Alice, has fall'n upon
the poor gentlewoman within, and pulled her hood over her
ears, and her hair through it.

Alice enters, beating the Justice's wife.

Mistress Overdo. Help, help, i' the King's name. 60

Alice. A mischief on you, they are such as you are that undo us,
and take our trade from us, with your tuft taffeta haunches.

Knockem. How now, Alice!

Alice. The poor common whores can ha' no traffic for the privy
rich ones; your caps and hoods of velvet call away our customers 65
and lick the fat from us.

Ursula. Peace, you foul ramping jade, you—

Alice. Od's foot, you bawd in grease, are you talking?

44–5 DRESSING . . . HUSBAND *high coiffure to match her husband's horns.*
44 TOP AND TOP-GALLANT *sails.*
45 FORE-TOP *top of a mast or of the head.*
64 PRIVY *private, exclusive.*
68 IN GREASE *fat like an animal ready for killing.*

    Knockem. Why, Alice, I say.

70   *Alice.* Thou sow of Smithfield, thou.

    Ursula. Thou tripe of Turnbull.

    Knockem. Catamountain vapors! ha!

    Ursula. You know where you were tawed lately, both lashed and slashed you were in Bridewell.

75   *Alice.* Aye, by the same token, you rid that week, and broke out the bottom o' the cart, night-tub.

    Knockem. Why, lion face! ha! do you know who I am? Shall I tear ruff, slit waistcoat, make rags of petticoat? Ha! go to, vanish, for fear of vapors. Whit, a kick, Whit, in the parting vapor.

80   [*They kick Alice out.*] Come, brave woman, take a good heart, thou shalt be a lady, too.

    Whit. Yes, fait, dey shall all both be ladies and write Madam. I vill do't myself for dem. Do is the vord, and D is the middle letter of Madam. DD, put 'em together and make deeds, without

85   which all words are alike, la.

    Knockem. 'Tis true. Urs'la, take 'em in, open thy wardrobe, and fit 'em to their calling. Green gowns, crimson petticoats, green women! My Lord Mayor's green women! guests o' the game, true bred. I'll provide you a coach to take the air in.

90   *Win.* But do you think you can get one?

    Knockem. O, they are as common as wheelbarrows where there are great dunghills. Every pettifogger's wife has 'em; for first he buys a coach, that he may marry, and then he marries that he may

---

73 TAWED *beaten.*

74 BRIDEWELL *a prison.*

75 RID *a punishment for whores was to cart them.*

76 NIGHT-TUB *tub for "night soil"—excrement.*

78 WAISTCOAT *ordinarily worn under a woman's gown at this time, but when not so covered the sign of a prostitute or "waistcoateer."*

82 WRITE *i.e. sign or style themselves.*

be made cuckold in't. For if their wives ride not to their cuckold-
ing, they do 'em no credit. Hide and be hidden; ride and be   95
ridden, says the vapor of experience.

[*Exeunt Ursula, Win, Mistress Overdo.*]

Act IV Scene vi

[*Enter Trouble-all.*]

Trouble-all. By what warrant does it say so?

Knockem. Ha! mad child o' the Pie-powders, art thou there?
Fill us a fresh can, Urs; we may drink together.

Trouble-all. I may not drink without a warrant, Captain.

Knockem. 'Slood, thou'll not stale without a warrant, shortly.   5
Whit, give me pen, ink, and paper. I'll draw him a warrant
presently.

Trouble-all. It must be Justice Overdo's.

Knockem. I know, man. Fetch the drink, Whit.

Whit. I pre dee now, be very brief, Captain; for de new ladies   10
stay for dee.

Knockem. O, as brief as can be; here 'tis already. "Adam Overdo."

Trouble-all. Why, now I'll pledge you, Captain.

Knockem. Drink it off. I'll come to thee, anon, again.

[*Exit Knockem into back part of Ursula's booth.*
Immediately afterward exit Trouble-all at one door.
At the other enter Quarlous, Edgworth.]

Quarlous. (*To the cutpurse.*) Well, sir, you are now discharged;   15
beware of being spied, hereafter.

7 PRESENTLY *at once.*
SD [EXIT KNOCKEM, ETC.] *for stage action in this scene see Appendix* II, *pp.*
214–15.

Edgworth. Sir, will it please you enter in here at Urs'la's and take part of a silken gown, a velvet petticoat, or a wrought smock? I am promised such, and I can spare any gentleman a moiety.

20 *Quarlous.* Keep it for your companions in beastliness; I am none of 'em, sir. If I had not already forgiven you a greater trespass, or thought you yet worth my beating, I would instruct your manners, to whom you made your offers. But go your ways, talk not to me, the hangman is only fit to discourse with

25 you; the hand of beadle is too merciful a punishment for your trade of life. [*Exit Edgworth.*] I am sorry I employed this fellow; for he thinks me such: *Facinus quos inquinat, aequat.* But it was for sport. And would I make it serious, the getting of this licence is nothing to me, without other circumstances concur. I do think

30 how impertinently I labor, if the word be not mine that the ragged fellow marked; and what advantage I have given Ned Winwife in this time now, of working her, though it be mine. He'll go near to form to her what a debauched rascal I am, and fright her out of all good conceit of me. I should do so by him, I

35 am sure, if I had the opportunity. But my hope is in her temper, yet; and it must needs be next to despair, that is grounded on any part of a woman's discretion. I would give, by my troth, now, all I could spare (to my clothes and my sword) to meet my tattered soothsayer again, who was my judge i' the question, to know

40 certainly whose word he has damned or saved. For till then I live but under a reprieve. I must seek him. Who be these?

Enter Wasp with the officers, [Bristle and Poacher.]

19 MOIETY *share (literally half).*
27 FACINUS . . . AEQUAT *Lucan,* The Civil War, v, *290: "crime levels those whom it pollutes"(J. D. Duff).*
30 IMPERTINENTLY *uselessly.*
33 FORM *depict, set forth.*
34 CONCEIT *idea, opinion.*
    SD [BRISTLE AND POACHER] *see* IV.4.154. N.

Wasp. Sir, you are a Welsh cuckold, and a prating runt, and no constable.

Bristle. You say very well. Come put in his leg in the middle roundel, and let him hole there. 45

Wasp. You stink of leeks, metheglin, and cheese, you rogue.

Bristle. Why, what is that to you, if you sit sweetly in the stocks in the meantime? If you have a mind to stink too, your breeches sit close enough to your bum. Sit you merry, sir.

Quarlous. How now, Numps? 50

Wasp. It is no matter how; pray you look off.

Quarlous. Nay, I'll not offend you, Numps. I thought you had sat there to be seen.

Wasp. And to be sold, did you not? Pray you mind your business, an' you have any. 55

Quarlous. Cry you mercy, Numps. Does your leg lie high enough?

[*Enter Haggis with Overdo and Busy.*]

Bristle. How now, neighbor Haggis, what says Justice Overdo's worship to the other offenders?

Haggis. Why, he says just nothing; what should he say? Or 60 where should he say? He is not to be found, man. He ha' not been seen i' the Fair, here, all this live-long day, never since seven o'clock i' the morning. His clerks know not what to think on't. There is no court of Pie-powders yet. Here they be returned.

Bristle. What shall be done with 'em, then, in your discretion? 65

Haggis. I think we were best put 'em in the stocks, in discretion (there they will be safe in discretion) for the valor of an hour or such a thing, till his worship come.

---

42 RUNT *uncouth, ignorant person.*
46 METHEGLIN *Welsh mead.*
65 DISCRETION *in three senses: judgment, prudence, and separation, respectively.*
67 VALOR *amount.*

Bristle. It is but a hole matter if we do, neighbor Haggis. [*To*
70 *Wasp*.] Come, sir, here is company for you. Heave up the stocks.

Wasp. [*Aside*.] I shall put a trick upon your Welsh diligence,
perhaps.

> *As they open the stocks, Wasp puts his shoe on his hand and*
> *slips it in for his leg. They bring Busy and put him in.*

Bristle. Put in your leg, sir.

Quarlous. What, Rabbi Busy! Is he come?

75 *Busy*. I do obey thee; the lion may roar, but he cannot bite. I am
glad to be thus separated from the heathen of the land, and put
apart in the stocks for the holy cause.

Wasp. What are you, sir?

Busy. One that rejoiceth in his affliction and sitteth here to
80 prophesy the destruction of fairs and May-games, wakes and
Whitsun-ales, and doth sigh and groan for the reformation of these
abuses.

> [*They put Overdo in and walk to one side with their backs to the stocks.*]

Wasp. [*To Overdo*.] And do you sigh and groan too, or rejoice
in your affliction?

85 *Overdo*. I do not feel it, I do not think of it, it is a thing without
me. Adam, thou art above these batt'ries, these contumelies. *In te*
manca ruit fortuna, as thy friend Horace says; thou art one, *Quem*
neque pauperies, neque mors, neque vincula terrent. And therefore, as
another friend of thine says (I think it be thy friend Persius), *Non*
90 *te quaesiveris extra*.

80–1 FAIRS . . . WHITSUN-ALES *customs considered licentious by the Puritans; the*
last named were parish festivals held at Whitsuntide (Pentecost).

85 WITHOUT *outside of*.

86–8 IN TE . . . FORTUNA . . . QUEM . . . TERRENT *adapted from Horace*, Satires,
II, *vii, 88, 84: "Against thee Fortune in her onset is ever maimed"; "whom*
neither poverty nor death nor bonds affright" (based on H. R. Fairclough).

89–90 NON . . . EXTRA *Persius*, Satires, *i, 7: "Look to no one outside yourself"*
(G. G. Ramsay).

Quarlous. What's here? A stoic i' the stocks? The fool is turned philosopher.

Busy. Friend, I will leave to communicate my spirit with you if I hear any more of those superstitious relics, those lists of Latin, the very rags of Rome and patches of Popery. 95

Wasp. Nay, an' you begin to quarrel, gentlemen, I'll leave you. I ha' paid for quarrelling too lately. Look you, a device, but shifting in a hand for a foot. God b' w' you. *He gets out.*

Busy. Wilt thou then leave thy brethren in tribulation?

Wasp. For this once, sir. [*Exit.*] 100

Busy. Thou art a halting neutral—[*Shouts.*] stay him there, stop him—that will not endure the heat of persecution.

Bristle. How, now, what's the matter?

Busy. He is fled, he is fled, and dares not sit it out.

Bristle. What, has he made an escape? Which way? Follow, 105 neighbor Haggis. [*Exeunt Bristle, Haggis.*]

[*Enter Purecraft.*]

Purecraft. O me! In the stocks! Have the wicked prevailed?

Busy. Peace, religious sister; it is my calling, comfort yourself, an extraordinary calling, and done for my better standing, my surer standing hereafter. 110

The madman enters.

Trouble-all. By whose warrant, by whose warrant, this?

Quarlous. O, here's my man dropped in, I looked for.

Overdo. Ha!

Purecraft. O good sir, they have set the faithful here to be wondered at; and provided holes for the holy of the land. 115

Trouble-all. Had they warrant for it? Showed they Justice Overdo's hand? If they had no warrant, they shall answer it.

[*Re-enter Bristle, Haggis.*]

93 LEAVE *cease.*
94 LISTS *strips of cloth.*

Bristle. Sure you did not lock the stocks sufficiently, neighbor Toby!

120 *Haggis.* No? See if you can lock 'em better.

Bristle. [*Tries the lock.*] They are very sufficiently locked, and truly, yet something is in the matter.

Trouble-all. True, your warrant is the matter that is in question; by what warrant?

125 *Bristle.* Madman, hold your peace; I will put you in his room else, in the very same hole, do you see?

Quarlous. How? Is he a madman?

Trouble-all. Show me Justice Overdo's warrant, I obey you.

Haggis.. You are a mad fool; hold your tongue.

130 *Trouble-all.* In Justice Overdo's name I drink to you, and here's my warrant.   *Shows his can.*

[*Exeunt Bristle and Haggis looking for Wasp.*]

Overdo. [*Aside.*] Alas, poor wretch! How it earns my heart for him!

Quarlous. [*Aside.*] If he be mad, it is in vain to question him. I'll 135 try, though. [*To him.*] Friend, there was a gentlewoman showed you two names, some hour since, Argalus and Palamon, to mark in a book. Which of 'em was it you marked?

Trouble-all. I mark no name but Adam Overdo; that is the name of names; he only is the sufficient magistrate; and that name I rever- 140 ence; show it me.

Quarlous. [*Aside.*] This fellow's mad indeed. I am further off now than afore.

Overdo. [*Aside.*] I shall not breathe in peace till I have made him some amends.

145 *Quarlous.* [*Aside.*] Well, I will make another use of him, is come

132 EARNS *grieves.*
145 ANOTHER USE *N.*

in my head: I have a nest of beards in my trunk, one something
like his.   [*Exit.*]
           The watchmen come back again.
  Bristle. This mad fool has made me that I know not whether I
have locked the stocks or no; I think I locked 'em.
  Trouble-all. Take Adam Overdo in your mind and fear   150
nothing.
  Bristle. 'Slid, madness itself, hold thy peace, and take that.
                                     [*Strikes him.*]
  Trouble-all. Strikest thou without a warrant? Take thou that.
    The madman fights with 'em, and they leave open the stocks.
  Busy. We are delivered by miracle; fellow in fetters, let us not
refuse the means; this madness was of the spirit. The malice of the   155
enemy hath mocked itself.   [*Exeunt Busy and Overdo.*]
  Purecraft. Mad, do they call him! The world is mad in error, but
he is mad in truth. I love him o' the sudden (the cunning man said
all true), and shall love him more and more. How well it becomes
a man to be mad in truth! O, that I might be his yoke-fellow and   160
be mad with him! What a many should we draw to madness in
truth with us!   [*Exit.*]
      The watch, missing them, are affrighted.
  Bristle. How now? All 'scaped? Where's the woman? It is witch-
craft! Her velvet hat is a witch, o' my conscience, or my key,
t'one! The madman was a devil and I am an ass; so bless me, my   165
place, and mine office.   [*Exeunt.*]

165 T'ONE *one or the other.*

Act V Scene i

[*Enter Leatherhead, Filcher, Sharkwell.*]
Leatherhead. Well, luck and Saint Barthol'mew! Out with the
sign of our invention, in the name of wit, and do you beat the
drum, the while. All the fowl i' the Fair, I mean all the dirt in
Smithfield (that's one of Master Littlewit's carwitchets now), will
5 be thrown at our banner today if the matter does not please the
people. O the motions that I, Lantern Leatherhead, have given
light to i' my time, since my Master Pod died! *Jerusalem* was a
stately thing; and so was *Nineveh*, and *The City of Norwich;* and
Sodom and Gomorrah, with the rising o' the prentices and pulling
10 down the bawdy houses there, upon Shrove Tuesday; but *The
Gunpowder Plot*, there was a get-penny! I have presented that to an

SD *N.*

2 SIGN *probably the "bill" which Cokes reads in Scene iii; such signs were
usually illustrated with a painting to attract attention.*

4 CARWITCHETS *plays on words.*

7 POD *"Pod was a Master of motions before him" (Jonson's marginal note here);
apparently an actual producer of puppet shows in Jonson's time.*

7–9 JERUSALEM . . . GOMORRAH *N.*

10 SHROVE TUESDAY *Mardi Gras, when apprentices traditionally rioted, destroying
brothels and playhouses.*

11 GUNPOWDER PLOT *the unsuccessful attempt of Guy Fawkes and his fellow
Catholic conspirators to blow up Parliament November 5, 1605.*

eighteen- or twenty-pence audience nine times in an afternoon. Your home-born projects prove ever the best, they are so easy and familiar. They put too much learning i' their things nowadays, and that I fear will be the spoil o' this. Littlewit? I say Micklewit! if not too mickle! Look to your gathering there, goodman Filcher. 15

Filcher. I warrant you, sir.

Leatherhead. An' there come any gentlefolks, take twopence a piece, Sharkwell.

Sharkwell. I warrant you, sir, three pence an' we can. 20

16 GATHERING *collecting the entrance fee.*

Act V Scene ii

The Justice comes in like a porter.

Overdo. This later disguise, I have borrowed of a porter, shall carry me out to all my great and good ends; which, however interrupted, were never destroyed in me. Neither is the hour of my severity yet come, to reveal myself, wherein, cloud-like, I will break out in rain and hail, lightning and thunder, upon the head 5 of enormity. Two main works I have to prosecute: first, one is to invent some satisfaction for the poor kind wretch who is out of his wits for my sake; and yonder I see him coming. I will walk aside and project for it.

[*Enter Winwife, Grace.*]

Winwife. I wonder where Tom Quarlous is, that he returns not; 10 it may be he is struck in here to seek us.

Grace. See, here's our madman again.

6 ONE *i.e. one of them*
9 PROJECT *plan.*
11 STRUCK *gone.*

Act V Scene ii

[*Enter Quarlous, Purecraft.*] *Quarlous in the habit of the madman*
is mistaken by Mistress Purecraft.

Quarlous. [*Aside.*] I have made myself as like him as his gown and
cap will give me leave.

15 *Purecraft.* Sir, I love you and would be glad to be mad with
you in truth.

Winwife. How? my widow in love with a madman?

Purecraft. Verily, I can be as mad in spirit as you.

Quarlous. By whose warrant? Leave your canting. [*To Grace.*]

20 Gentlewoman, have I found you? (Save ye, quit ye, and multiply
ye.) Where's your book? 'Twas a sufficient name I marked, let me
see't, be not afraid to show't me.

> *He desires to see the book of Mistress Grace.*

Grace. What would you with it, sir?

Quarlous. Mark it again, and again, at your service.

25 *Grace.* Here it is, sir; this was it you marked.

Quarlous. Palamon? Fare you well, fare you well.

Winwife. How, Palamon!

Grace. Yes, faith, he has discovered it to you now, and therefore 'twere vain to disguise it longer; I am yours, sir, by the bene-

30 fit of your fortune.

Winwife. And you have him, Mistress, believe it, that shall never
give you cause to repent her benefit, but make you rather to
think that, in this choice, she had both her eyes.

Grace. I desire to put it to no danger of protestation.

> [*Exeunt Winwife, Grace.*]

35 *Quarlous.* Palamon the word and Winwife the man?

Purecraft. Good sir, vouchsafe a yoke-fellow in your madness;
shun not one of the sanctified sisters, that would draw with you
in truth.

Quarlous. Away! You are a herd of hypocritical proud

19 CANTING *Puritan jargon.*

ignorants, rather wild than mad. Fitter for woods and the society 40
of beasts than houses and the congregation of men. You are the
second part of the society of canters, outlaws to order and
discipline, and the only privileged church-robbers of Christen-
dom. Let me alone. Palamon the word and Winwife the man?

Purecraft. [*Aside.*] I must uncover myself unto him or I shall never 45
enjoy him, for all the cunning men's promises.—Good sir, hear
me, I am worth six thousand pound; my love to you is become
my rack; I'll tell you all, and the truth, since you hate the hypocrisy of the party-colored brotherhood. These seven years I have
been a wilful holy widow only to draw feasts and gifts from my 50
entangled suitors. I am also by office an assisting sister of the
deacons and a devourer, instead of a distributor, of the alms. I am
a special maker of marriages for our decayed brethren with our
rich widows, for a third part of their wealth, when they are
married, for the relief of the poor elect; as also our poor handsome 55
young virgins with our wealthy bachelors or widowers, to make
them steal from their husbands when I have confirmed them in the
faith and got all put into their custodies. And if I ha' not my
bargain, they may sooner turn a scolding drab into a silent minister
than make me leave pronouncing reprobation and damnation 60
unto them. Our elder, Zeal-of-the-land, would have had me, but
I know him to be the capital knave of the land, making himself
rich by being made feoffee in trust to deceased brethren, and coz'n-
ing their heirs by swearing the absolute gift of their inheritance.
And thus, having eased my conscience and uttered my heart with 65
the tongue of my love, enjoy all my deceits together, I beseech

49 PARTY-COLORED BROTHERHOOD N.
59 SILENT MINISTER *a Puritan excommunicated ("silenced") for noncompliance
with the laws.*
63 FEOFFEE IN TRUST *"a trustee invested with a freehold estate in land"* (OED).

you. I should not have revealed this to you but that in time I think
you are mad; and I hope you'll think me so too, sir?

Quarlous. Stand aside, I'll answer you presently. (*He considers*
70 *with himself of it.*) Why should not I marry this six thousand
pound, now I think on't? And a good trade too, that she has
beside, ha? The tother wench Winwife is sure of; there's no expectation for me there! Here I may make myself some saver yet,
if she continue mad—there's the question. It is money that I want;
75 why should I not marry the money, when 'tis offered me? I have
a licence and all; it is but razing out one name and putting in
another. There's no playing with a man's fortune. I am resolved!
I were truly mad an' I would not! [*To her.*] Well, come your ways,
follow me an' you will be mad, I'll show you a warrant!

He takes her along with him.

80 *Purecraft.* Most zealously; it is that I zealously desire.

The Justice calls him.

Overdo. Sir, let me speak with you.

Quarlous. By whose warrant?

Overdo. The warrant that you tender and respect so: Justice
Overdo's! I am the man, friend Trouble-all, though thus disguised
85 (as the careful magistrate ought) for the good of the republic, in
the Fair, and the weeding out of enormity. Do you want a house
or meat or drink or clothes? Speak whatsoever it is, it shall be
supplied you. What want you?

Quarlous. Nothing but your warrant.

90 *Overdo.* My warrant? For what?

Quarlous. To be gone, sir.

Overdo. Nay, I pray thee stay. I am serious, and have not many

---

67 IN TIME (?) *seasonably, at a suitable time (for her); perhaps has the sense of*
"*happily.*"

71 TRADE *i.e. the practices she has just described.*

73 MAKE . . . SAVER *compensate for my loss—a gambler's phrase.*

words nor much time to exchange with thee; think what may do thee good.

Quarlous. Your hand and seal will do me a great deal of good; nothing else in the whole Fair, that I know.   95

Overdo. If it were to any end, thou should'st have it willingly.

Quarlous. Why, it will satisfy me; that's end enough to look on. An' you will not gi' it me, let me go.

Overdo. Alas! thou shalt ha' it presently. I'll but step into the scrivener's hereby and bring it. Do not go away.   100
                                                                 The Justice goes out.

Quarlous. [*Aside.*] Why, this madman's shape will prove a very fortunate one, I think! Can a ragged robe produce these effects? If this be the wise Justice, and he bring me his hand, I shall go near to make some use on't. [*Overdo*] *returns.* He is come already!   105

Overdo. Look thee! here is my hand and seal, Adam Overdo; if there be anything to be written above in the paper, that thou want'st now or at any time hereafter, think on't; it is my deed, I deliver it so; can your friend write?

Quarlous. Her hand for a witness, and all is well.   110

Overdo. With all my heart.   *He urgeth Mistress Purecraft.*

Quarlous. [*Aside.*] Why should not I ha' the conscience to make this a bond of a thousand pound, now? or what I would else?

Overdo. Look you, there it is; and I deliver it as my deed again.

Quarlous. Let us now proceed in madness.   115
                                                                 He takes her in with him.

Overdo. Well, my conscience is much eased; I ha' done my part; though it doth him no good, yet Adam hath offered satisfaction! The sting is removed from hence. Poor man, he is much altered with his affliction; it has brought him low! Now, for my other work, reducing the young man I have followed so long in love   120

112 CONSCIENCE *good sense.*
     SD *"in" means "within"—in the tiring-house, offstage.*
120 REDUCING *leading back (a latinism).*

159

from the brink of his bane to the center of safety. Here, or in some such like vain place, I shall be sure to find him. I will wait the good time.

Act V Scene iii

[*Enter Cokes, followed by boys.*]

Cokes. How now? What's here to do? Friend, art thou the master of the monuments?

Sharkwell. 'Tis a motion, an't please your worship.

Overdo. [*Aside.*] My fantastical brother-in-law, Master
5 Barthol'mew Cokes!

Cokes. A motion? What's that? (*He reads the bill.*) "The ancient modern history of *Hero and Leander*, otherwise called *The Touchstone of True Love*, with as true a trial of friendship between Damon and Pythias, two faithful friends o' the Bankside."
10 Pretty i' faith; what's the meaning on't? Is't an interlude? or what is't?

Filcher. Yes, sir; please you come near, we'll take your money within.

Cokes. Back with these children; they do so   *The boys o' the*
15 follow me up and down.   *Fair follow him.*

[*Enter Littlewit.*]

Littlewit. By your leave, friend.

Filcher. You must pay, sir, an' you go in.

---

2 MASTER OF THE MONUMENTS *in charge of this exhibition.*

4 FANTASTICAL *fanciful, capricious.*

6–9 "THE ANCIENT . . . BANKSIDE" N.

10 INTERLUDE *dramatic entertainment.*

Littlewit. Who, I? I perceive thou know'st not me. Call the master o' the motion.

Sharkwell. What, do you not know the author, fellow Filcher? 20
You must take no money of him; he must come in *gratis*. Master Littlewit is a voluntary; he is the author.

Littlewit. Peace, speak not too loud; I would not have any notice taken that I am the author till we see how it passes.

Cokes. Master Littlewit, how dost thou? 25

Littlewit. Master Cokes! you are exceeding well met; what, in your doublet and hose, without a cloak or a hat?

Cokes. I would I might never stir, as I am an honest man, and by that fire; I have lost all i' the Fair, and all my acquaintance too. Didst thou meet anybody that I know, Master Littlewit? my man 30
Numps, or my sister Overdo, or Mistress Grace? Pray thee, Master Littlewit, lend me some money to see the interlude, here. I'll pay thee again, as I am a gentleman. If thou'lt but carry me home, I have money enough there.

Littlewit. O, sir, you shall command it; what, will a crown serve 35
you?

Cokes. I think it will. What do we pay for coming in, fellows?

Filcher. Twopence, sir.

Cokes. Twopence? there's twelvepence, friend. Nay, I am a gallant, as simple as I look now, if you see me with my man about 40
me and my artillery again.

Littlewit. Your man was i' the stocks e'en now, sir.

Cokes. Who, Numps?

Littlewit. Yes, faith.

Cokes. For what, i' faith? I am glad o' that; remember to tell 45

---

22 VOLUNTARY *volunteer (who has given them his show and must be given privileges in return).*
29 FIRE *"in Ursula's booth" (H & S).*
35 CROWN *five shillings.*
41 ARTILLERY *munitions, in the widest sense; trappings, equipment.*

me on't anon; I have enough now! What manner of matter is this, Master Littlewit? What kind of actors ha' you? Are they good actors?

Littlewit. Pretty youths, sir, all children, both old and young;
50 here's the master of 'em—

[*Enter Leatherhead.*]

Leatherhead. (*Whispers to Littlewit.*) Call me not Leatherhead, but Lantern.

Littlewit.—Master Lantern, that gives light to the business.

Cokes. In good time, sir, I would fain see 'em; I would be glad
55 drink with the young company. Which is the tiring-house?

Leatherhead. Troth sir, our tiring-house is somewhat little; we are but beginners, yet, pray pardon us; you cannot go upright in't.

Cokes. No? Not now my hat is off? What would you have done with me if you had had me, feather and all, as I was once today?
60 Ha' you none of your pretty impudent boys, now, to bring stools, fill tobacco, fetch ale, and beg money, as they have at other houses? Let me see some o' your actors.

Littlewit. Show him 'em, show him 'em. Master Lantern, this is a gentleman that is a favorer of the quality.

[*Leatherhead goes behind puppet-booth.*]

65 *Overdo.* [*Aside.*] Aye, the favoring of this licentious quality is the consumption of many a young gentleman; a pernicious enormity.

He [*Leatherhead*] *brings them out in a basket.*

Cokes. What, do they live in baskets?

Leatherhead. They do lie in a basket, sir; they are o' the small
70 players.

Cokes. These be players minors, indeed. Do you call these players?

51–2 CALL . . . LANTERN *N.*
56 TIRING-HOUSE . . . LITTLE *N.*
64 THE QUALITY *the* (*acting*) *profession.*

Leatherhead. They are actors, sir, and as good as any, none displraised, for dumb shows; indeed I am the mouth of 'em all!

Cokes. Thy mouth will hold 'em all. I think one Taylor would   75
go near to beat all this company, with a hand bound behind him.

Littlewit. Aye, and eat 'em all, too, an' they were in cake-bread.

Cokes. I thank you for that, Master Littlewit, a good jest! Which
is your Burbage now?

Leatherhead. What mean you by that, sir?   80

Cokes. Your best actor, your Field?

Littlewit. Good, i' faith! You are even with me, sir.

Leatherhead. This is he that acts young Leander, sir. He is
extremely beloved of the womenkind, they do so affect his action,
the green gamesters that come here; and this is lovely Hero; this   85
with the beard, Damon; and this, pretty Pythias. This is the
ghost of King Dionysius in the habit of a scrivener, as you shall
see anon, at large.

Cokes. Well, they are a civil company. I like 'em for that; they
offer not to fleer nor jeer nor break jests, as the great players do.   90
And then there goes not so much charge to the feasting of 'em or
making 'em drunk, as to the other, by reason of their littleness.
Do they use to play perfect? Are they never flustered?

Leatherhead. No, sir, I thank my industry and policy for it; they
are as well-governed a company, though I say it—And here is   95
young Leander, is as proper an actor of his inches; and shakes his
head like an ostler.

75 ONE TAYLOR *N.*

77 EAT 'EM ALL *tailors were supposed to be great eaters of bread.*

79 BURBAGE *Richard Burbage, one of the most distinguished of the King's Men,
the company which acted most of Shakespeare's plays and many of Jonson's.*

81 FIELD *Nathan Field, a former scholar of Jonson's and an outstanding actor in the
Lady Elizabeth's Men, the company which was performing* Bartholomew Fair.

88 AT LARGE *at length, fully.*

97 OSTLER *possibly an allusion to another actor, William Ostler.*

Cokes. But do you play it according to the printed book? I have read that.

100 *Leatherhead.* By no means, sir.

Cokes. No? How then?

Leatherhead. A better way, sir; that is too learned and poetical for our audience. What do they know what Hellespont is? "Guilty of true love's blood"? Or what Abydos is? Or "the other 105 Sestos hight"?

Cokes. Th' art i' the right. I do not know myself.

Leatherhead. No, I have entreated Master Littlewit to take a little pains to reduce it to a more familiar strain for our people.

Cokes. How, I pray thee, good Master Littlewit?

110 *Littlewit.* It pleases him to make a matter of it, sir. But there is no such matter I assure you. I have only made it a little easy and modern for the times, sir, that's all; as, for the Hellespont, I imagine our Thames here; and then Leander I make a dyer's son, about Puddle Wharf; and Hero a wench o' the Bankside, who 115 going over one morning to Old Fish Street, Leander spies her land at Trig Stairs, and falls in love with her. Now do I introduce Cupid, having metamorphosed himself into a drawer, and he strikes Hero in love with a pint of sherry; and other pretty passages there are o' the friendship, that will delight you, sir, and 120 please you of judgment.

Cokes. I'll be sworn they shall. I am in love with the actors already, and I'll be allied to them presently. (They respect gentlemen, these fellows.) Hero shall be my fairing; but which of my fairings? Le'me see— i' faith, my fiddle! and Leander my fiddle-

---

98 PRINTED BOOK *Marlowe's unfinished poem,* Hero and Leander *(1598), from which Leatherhead quotes below.*

116 STAIRS *steps down to the water at the landing.*

118 WITH *by means of.*

122 ALLIED *by associating each one with one of his purchases.*

stick; then Damon my drum, and Pythias my pipe, and the ghost 125
of Dionysius my hobbyhorse. All fitted.

Act V Scene iv

[*Enter Winwife, Grace.*]

Winwife. Look, yonder's your Cokes gotten in among his
playfellows; I thought we could not miss him at such a spectacle.

Grace. Let him alone. He is so busy, he will never spy us.

Leatherhead. Nay, good sir.   *Cokes is*

Cokes. I warrant thee, I will not hurt her,   *handling the* 5
fellow; what, dost think me uncivil? I pray   *puppets.*
thee be not jealous; I am toward a wife.

Littlewit. Well, good Master Lantern, make ready to begin, that
I may fetch my wife, and look you be perfect; you undo me else
i' my reputation.   10

Leatherhead. I warrant you, sir. Do not you breed too great an
expectation of it among your friends. That's the only hurter of
these things.

Littlewit. No, no, no.   [*Exit.*]

Cokes. I'll stay here and see; pray thee let me see.   15

Winwife. How diligent and troublesome he is!

Grace. The place becomes him, methinks.

Overdo. [*Aside.*] My ward, Mistress Grace, in the company of a
stranger? I doubt I shall be compelled to discover myself before
my time!   20

[*Enter Knockem, Edgworth, Win, Whit, Mistress Overdo,*
the ladies masked.]

7 TOWARD *about to have.*
19 DOUBT *suspect, fear.*

Act V Scene iv

Filcher. Twopence apiece, gentlemen, an ex-   *The door-*
cellent motion.   *keepers speak.*

Knockem. Shall we have fine fireworks and
good vapors?

25   *Sharkwell.* Yes, Captain, and waterworks too.

Whit. I pree dee, take a care o' dy shmall lady, there, Edgworth;
I will look to dish tall lady myself.

Leatherhead. Welcome, gentlemen; welcome, gentlemen.

Whit. Predee, mashter o' de monshtersh, help a very sick lady
30 here to a chair to shit in.

Leatherhead. Presently, sir.   *They bring Mistress Overdo a chair.*

Whit. Good fait now, Urs'la's ale and *aqua vitae* ish to blame
for't; shit down, shweetheart, shit down and shleep a little.

[*She sits down and goes to sleep.*]

Edgworth. [*To Win.*] Madam, you are very welcome hither.

35   *Knockem.* Yes, and you shall see very good vapors.

Overdo. [*Aside.*] Here is my care come! I like   *By Edgworth.*
to see him in so good company; and yet I
wonder that persons of such fashion should resort hither!

Edgworth. This is a very private house,   *The cutpurse*
40 madam.   *courts Mistress*

Leatherhead. Will it please your ladyship sit,   *Littlewit.*
madam?

Win. Yes, good-man. They do so all-to-be-madam me, I think
they think me a very lady!

45   *Edgworth.* What else, madam?

Win. Must I put off my mask to him?

Edgworth. O, by no means.

---

25 WATERWORKS *tears, presumably, though the reply need not be any more specific
that Knockem's question.*

36 BY *referring to.*

39 PRIVATE HOUSE *term used for the roofed-in small theaters, which were more
exclusive and more expensive than the open public theaters.*

Win. How should my husband know me, then?

Knockem. Husband? an idle vapor; he must not know you, nor
you him; there's the true vapor.   50

Overdo. [*Aside.*] Yea, I will observe more of this. [*To Whit.*] Is
this a lady, friend?

Whit. Aye, and dat is anoder lady, shweetheart; if dou hasht a
mind to 'em, give me twelvepence from tee, and dou shalt have
eder-oder on 'em!   55

Overdo. [*Aside.*] Aye? This will prove my chiefest enormity. I
will follow this.

Edgworth. Is not this a finer life, lady, than to be clogged with a
husband?

Win. Yes, a great deal. When will they begin, trow, in the name   60
o' the motion?

Edgworth. By and by, madam; they stay but for company.

Knockem. Do you hear, puppet-master, these are tedious
vapors; when begin you?

Leatherhead. We stay but for Master Littlewit, the author, who   65
is gone for his wife; and we begin presently.

Win. That's I, that's I.

Edgworth. That was you, lady; but now you are no such poor
thing.

Knockem. Hang the author's wife, a running vapor! Here be   70
ladies will stay for ne'er a Delia o' em all.

Whit. But hear me now, here ish one o' de ladish ashleep; stay
till she but vake, man.

[Enter Wasp.]

Wasp. How now, friends? What's here to do?   *The door-*

Filcher. Twopence apiece, sir, the best motion   *keepers*   75
in the Fair.   *again.*

---

71 DELIA *the lady of Samuel Daniel's sonnets* (1592).

Wasp. I believe you lie; if you do, I'll have my money again and beat you.

Winwife. Numps is come!

80   *Wasp.* Did you see a master of mine come in here, a tall young squire of Harrow o' the Hill, Master Barthol'mew Cokes?

Filcher. I think there be such a one within.

Wasp. Look he be, you were best; but it is very likely; I wonder I found him not at all the rest. I ha' been at the eagle, and

85   the black wolf, and the bull with the five legs and two pizzles (he was a calf at Uxbridge Fair, two years agone), and at the dogs that dance the morris, and the hare o' the tabor, and missed him at all these! Sure this must needs be some fine sight that holds him so, if it have him.

90   *Cokes.* Come, come, are you ready now?

Leatherhead. Presently, sir.

Wasp. Hoyday, he's at work in his doublet and hose. Do you hear, sir? are you employed, that you are bare-headed and so busy?

95   *Cokes.* Hold your peace, Numps; you ha' been i' the stocks, I hear.

Wasp. Does he know that? Nay, then the date of my authority is out; I must think no longer to reign, my government is at an end. He that will correct another must want fault in himself.

100 *Winwife.* Sententious Numps! I never heard so much from him before.

Leatherhead. Sure, Master Littlewit will not come; please you take your place, sir, we'll begin.

Cokes. I pray thee do; mine ears long to be at it, and my eyes

105 too. O Numps, i' the stocks, Numps? Where's your sword, Numps?

Wasp. I pray you intend your game, sir; let me alone.

---

87 HARE O' THE TABOR *hare which played on the tabor, a small drum.*

Cokes. Well then, we are quit for all. Come, sit down, Numps;
I'll interpret to thee. Did you see Mistress Grace? It's no matter,
neither, now I think on't, tell me anon. 110

Winwife. A great deal of love and care he expresses.

Grace. Alas! would you have him to express more than he has?
That were tyranny.

[*The curtain of the puppet booth is drawn.*]

Cokes. Peace, ho; now, now.

Leatherhead. *Gentles, that no longer your expectations may wander,* 115
Behold our chief actor, amorous Leander,
With a great deal of cloth lapped about him like a scarf,
For he yet serves his father, a dyer at Puddle Wharf,
Which place we'll make bold with, to call it our Abydos,
As the Bankside is our Sestos, and let it not be denied us. 120
Now, as he is beating, to make the dye take the fuller,
Who chances to come by but fair Hero in a sculler?
And seeing Leander's naked leg and goodly calf,
Cast at him, from the boat, a sheep's eye and a half.
Now she is landed, and the sculler come back; 125
By and by you shall see what Leander doth lack.

Pup. Leander. *Cole, Cole, old Cole.*

Leatherhead.   *That is the sculler's name*
    without control.

Pup. Leander. *Cole, Cole, I say, Cole.*

Leatherhead.   *We do hear you.*

Pup. Leander.   *Old Cole.*

Leatherhead. *Old Cole? Is the dyer turned collier? How do you*
    sell?

115 GENTLES, ETC. *N.*
121 FULLER *more thoroughly.*
127 OLD COLE *slang for a pander.*
129 COLLIER *derogatory term, since colliers were reputed to be cheaters.*

Act V Scene iv

130 Pup.Leander. *A pox o' your manners, kiss my hole here and smell.*
Leatherhead. *Kiss your hole and smell? There's manners indeed.*
Pup. Leander. *Why, Cole, I say, Cole.*
Leatherhead.   *It's the sculler you need!*
Pup. Leander. *Aye, and be hanged.*
Leatherhead.   *Be hanged! Look you yonder,*
Old Cole, you must go hang with Master Leander.
135 Pup. Cole. *Where is he?*
    Pup. Leander.   *Here, Cole. What fairest of fairs*
Was that fare that thou landedst but now a' Trig Stairs?

    Cokes. What was that, fellow? Pray thee tell me; I scarce understand 'em.
    Leatherhead. *Leander does ask, sir, what fairest of fairs*
140 *Was the fare that he landed but now at Trig Stairs.*
    Pup. Cole. *It is lovely Hero.*
    Pup. Leander. *Nero?*
    Pup. Cole. *No, Hero.*
    Leatherhead. *It is Hero*
145 *Of the Bankside, he saith, to tell you truth without erring,*
Is come over into Fish Street to eat some fresh herring.
Leander says no more, but as fast as he can,
Gets on all his best clothes, and will after to the Swan.

    Cokes. Most admirable good, is't not?

150 Leatherhead. *Stay, sculler.*
    Pup. Cole.   *What say you?*
    Leatherhead.   *You must stay for Leander,*
And carry him to the wench.
    Pup. Cole.   *You rogue, I am no pander.*

137–8 UNDERSTAND *N.*
148 SWAN *name of an inn.*

Cokes. He says he is no pander. 'Tis a fine language; I understand it now.

Leatherhead. *Are you no pander, Goodman Cole? Here's no man
     says you are.*
You'll grow a hot Cole, it seems; pray you stay for your fare.   155
     Pup. Cole. *Will he come away?*
     Leatherhead.   *What do you say?*
     Pup. Cole.   *I'd ha' him come
          away.*
     Leatherhead. *Would you ha' Leander come away? Why pray,
          sir, stay.*
You are angry, Goodman Cole; I believe the fair maid
Came over w' you o' trust. Tell us, sculler, are you paid?
     Pup. Cole. *Yes, Goodman Hogrubber o' Pickt-hatch.*   160
     Leatherhead. *How, Hogrubber o' Pickt-hatch?*
     Pup. Cole.   *Aye, Hogrubber o'
          Pickt-hatch.*
Take you that.   The puppet
     Leatherhead. *O, my head!*   strikes him over
     Pup. Cole.   *Harm watch, harm catch.*   the pate.

Cokes. Harm watch, harm catch, he says. Very good i' faith;
the sculler had like to ha' knocked you, sirrah.
     Leatherhead. Yes, but that his fare called him away.   165

     Pup. Leander. *Row apace, row apace, row, row, row, row, row.*
     Leatherhead. *You are knavishly loaden, sculler, take heed where
          you go.*
     Pup. Cole. *Knave i' your face, Goodman rogue.*
     Pup. Leander.   *Row, row, row, row, row, row.*

160 HOGRUBBER *swineherd.*
160 PICKT-HATCH *section noted for prostitutes.*
162 HARM WATCH, HARM CATCH *If you look for trouble you'll get it.*

Cokes. He said knave i' your face, friend.

170   *Leatherhead.* Aye, sir, I heard him. But there's no talking to these watermen; they will ha' the last word.

Cokes. God's my life! I am not allied to the sculler yet; he shall be Dauphin my boy. But my fiddle-stick does fiddle in and out too much; I pray you speak to him on't; tell him, I would have
175   him tarry in my sight more.

Leatherhead. I pray you be content; you'll have enough on him, sir.

Now gentles, I take it, here is none of you so stupid,
But that you have heard of a little god of love, called Cupid.
180   *Who out of kindness to Leander, hearing he but saw her*
This present day and hour, doth turn himself to a drawer.
And because he would have their first meeting to be merry,
He strikes Hero in love to him with a pint of sherry.

Which he tells her from amorous Leander is sent her,	Puppet Leander goes into
185 *Who after him into the room of Hero doth venter.*	Mistress Hero's
Pup. Jonas. *A pint of sack, score a pint of sack*	room.
i' the Coney.	

Cokes. Sack? You said but e'en now it should be sherry.

Pup. Jonas. *Why so it is: sherry, sherry, sherry.*

Cokes. Sherry, sherry, sherry. By my troth he makes me
190   merry. I must have a name for Cupid too. Let me see, thou mightst help me now, an' thou wouldst, Numps, at a dead lift, thou art dreaming o' the stocks still! Do not think on't, I have

---

173 DAUPHIN MY BOY *reference to a ballad quoted in* King Lear, III.4.103–04.

173 FIDDLE-STICK *Leander.*

186 SACK (*from sec, "dry"*), *a general term for sherry and similar wines; Cokes again shows his ignorance.*

186 CONEY *the rooms of taverns were often given such names.*

191 AT A DEAD LIFT *in an emergency.*

forgot it. 'Tis but a nine days' wonder, man; let it not trouble thee

Wasp. I would the stocks were about your neck, sir; condition
I hung by the heels in them till the wonder were off from you, 195
with all my heart.

Cokes. Well said, resolute Numps. But hark you, friend, where
is the friendship, all this while, between my drum, Damon, and
my pipe, Pythias?

Leatherhead. You shall see by and by, sir. 200

Cokes. You think my hobbyhorse is forgotten, too. No, I'll see
'em all enact before I go; I shall not know which to love best, else.

Knockem. This gallant has interrupting vapors, troublesome
vapors, Whit; puff with him.

Whit. No, I pre dee, Captain, let him alone. He is a child i' 205
faith, la.

Leatherhead. *Now, gentles, to the friends, who in number are two,*
And lodged in that ale-house in which fair Hero does do.
Damon (for some kindness done him the last week)
Is come fair Hero in Fish Street this morning to seek. 210
Pythias does smell the knavery of the meeting,
And now you shall see their true friendly greeting.

Pup. Pythias. *You whoremasterly slave, you.*

Cokes. Whoremasterly slave you? Very friendly and familiar,
that! 215

Pup. Damon. *Whoremaster i' thy face,*
Thou hast lien with her thyself, I'll prove't i' this place.

Cokes. Damon says Pythias has lien with her himself; he'll
prove't in this place.

Leatherhead. *They are whoremasters both, sir, that's a plain case.* 220

---

194 CONDITION *on condition that.*
201 HOBBYHORSE IS FORGOTTEN *another reference to a popular ballad.*

Pup. Pythias. *You lie like a rogue.*
Leatherhead.   *Do I lie like a rogue?*
Pup. Pythias. *A pimp and a scab.*
Leatherhead.   *A pimp and a scab?*
I say between you, you have both but one drab.
Pup. Damon. *You lie again.*
225   Leatherhead. *Do I lie again?*
Pup. Damon. *Like a rogue again.*
Leatherhead. *Like a rogue again?*
Pup. Pythias. *And you are a pimp again.*

Cokes. And you are a pimp again, he says.

230   Pup. Damon. *And a scab again.*

Cokes. And a scab again, he says.

Leatherhead. *And I say again you are both whoremasters again,*
And you have both but one drab again.   They fight.
Pup. Damon and Pythias. *Dost thou, dost thou, dost thou?*
235   Leatherhead. *What, both at once?*
Pup. Pythias. *Down with him Damon.*
Pup. Damon. *Pink his guts, Pythias.*
Leatherhead. *What, so malicious?*
Will ye murder me, masters both, i' mine own house?

240   *Cokes.* Ho! well acted, my drum, well acted, my pipe, well
acted still.

Wasp. Well acted, with all my heart.

Leatherhead. *Hold, hold your hands.*

Cokes. Aye, both your hands, for my sake! for you ha' both
245 done well.

Pup. Damon. *Gramercy, pure Pythias.*

222 SCAB *rascal.*

Pup. Pythias. *Gramercy, dear Damon.*

Cokes. Gramercy to you both, my pipe and my drum.

Pup. Damon and Pythias. *Come now we'll together to breakfast to Hero.*
Leatherhead. *'Tis well, you can now go to breakfast to Hero,*   250
You have given me my breakfast, with a 'hone and 'honero.

Cokes. How is't, friend, ha' they hurt thee?
Leatherhead.   O no!
Between you and I, sir, we do but make show.

Thus, gentles, you perceive, without any denial,
'Twixt Damon and Pythias here, friendship's true trial.   255
Though hourly they quarrel thus and roar each with other,
They fight you no more than does brother with brother.
But friendly together, at the next man they meet,
They let fly their anger, as here you might see't.

Cokes. Well, we have seen't, and thou hast felt it, whatsoever   260
thou sayest. What's next? What's next?

Leatherhead. *This while young Leander with fair Hero is drinking,*
And Hero grown drunk, to any man's thinking!
Yet was it not three pints of sherry could flaw her,
Till Cupid, distinguished like Jonas the drawer,   265
From under his apron, where his lechery lurks,
Put love in her sack. Now mark how it works.
Pup. Hero. *O Leander, Leander, my dear, my dear Leander,*
I'll forever be thy goose, so thou'lt be my gander.

Cokes. Excellently well said, fiddle! She'll ever be his goose, so   270
he'll be her gander: was't not so?
Leatherhead. Yes, sir, but mark his answer, now.

Pup. Leander. *And sweetest of geese, before I go to bed,*

251 'HONE AND 'HONERO alas (Scots: ochone, ochonarie).

I'll swim o'er the Thames, my goose, thee to tread.

275   *Cokes.* Brave! he will swim o'er the Thames and tread his goose tonight, he says.

   Leatherhead. Aye, peace, sir, they'll be angry if they hear you eavesdropping, now they are setting their match.

     Pup. Leander. *But lest the Thames should be dark, my goose, my dear friend,*

280 *Let thy window be provided of a candle's end.*

     Pup. Hero. *Fear not, my gander, I protest I should handle*
My matters very ill, if I had not a whole candle.

     Pup. Leander. *Well then, look to 't, and kiss me to boot.*

     Leatherhead. *Now here come the friends again,*   Damon and
        Pythias and Damon,   Pythias enter.

285 *And under their cloaks they have of bacon a gammon.*

     Pup. Pythias. *Drawer, fill some wine here.*

     Leatherhead.   *How, some wine there?*
There's company already, sir, pray forbear!

     Pup. Damon. *'Tis Hero.*

     Leatherhead.   *Yes, but she will not be taken,*
After sack and fresh herring, with your Dunmow-bacon.

290   Pup. Pythias. *You lie, it's Westfabian.*

     Leatherhead.   *Westphalian, you should say.*

     Pup. Damon. *If you hold not your peace,*   Leander and
        you are a coxcomb, I would say.   Hero are kissing.

     Pup. Pythias. *What's here? What's here? Kiss, kiss upon kiss.*

     Leatherhead. *Aye, wherefore should they not? What harm is in this?*
'Tis Mistress Hero.

     Pup. Damon. *Mistress Hero's a whore.*

295   Leatherhead. *Is she a whore? Keep you quiet, or sir knave out of door.*

---

274 TREAD *copulate with (of birds).*
289 DUNMOW-BACON *N.*

Pup. Damon. *Knave out of door?* Here the puppets

Pup. Hero. *Yes, knave* quarrel and fall

out of door. together by the

Pup. Damon. *Whore out of door.* ears.

Pup. Hero. *I say knave out of door.*

Pup. Damon. *I say whore out of door.*

Pup. Pythias. *Yea, so say I too.*

Pup. Hero. *Kiss the whore o' the arse.*

Leatherhead. *Now you ha' something to do:*

You must kiss her o' the arse, she says.

Pup. Damon and Pythias. *So we will, so we will.* [They kick her.] 300

Pup. Hero. *O my haunches, o my haunches, hold, hold,*

Leatherhead. *Stand'st thou still?*

Leander, where art thou? Stand'st thou still like a sot,

And not offer'st to break both their heads with a pot?

See who's at thine elbow there! Puppet Jonas and Cupid.

Pup. Jonas. *Upon' em, Leander, be not so stupid.* They fight. 305

Pup. Leander. *You goat-bearded slave!*

Pup. Damon. *You whoremaster knave!*

Pup. Leander. *Thou art a whoremaster.*

Pup. Jonas. *Whoremasters all.*

Leatherhead. *See, Cupid with a word has ta'en up the brawl.*

Knockem. These be fine vapors!

Cokes. By this good day they fight bravely, do they not, 310
Numps?

Wasp. Yes, they lacked but you to be their second, all this
while.

Leatherhead. *This tragical encounter, falling out thus to busy us,*

It raises up the ghost of their friend Dionysius, 315

Not like a monarch, but the master of a school,

316 MASTER OF A SCHOOL *Dionysius the younger, tyrant of Syracuse 367–43 B.C.,*
was said to have taught school after his expulsion from Syracuse.

In a scrivener's furred gown, which shows he is no fool.
For therein he hath wit enough to keep himself warm.
"O Damon," he cries, "and Pythias, what harm
320 *Hath poor Dionysius done you in his grave,*
That after his death you should fall out thus, and rave,
And call amorous Leander whoremaster knave?"

Pup. Dionysius. *I cannot, I will not, I promise you, endure it.*

323 PUP. DIONYSIUS N.

Act V Scene v

[*Enter Busy.*]

Busy. Down with Dagon, down with Dagon! 'Tis I will no longer endure your profanations.

Leatherhead. What mean you, sir?

Busy. I will remove Dagon there, I say, that idol, that heathen-
5 ish idol, that remains, as I may say, a beam, a very beam, not a beam of the sun, nor a beam of the moon, nor a beam of a balance, neither a house-beam nor a weaver's beam, but a beam in the eye, in the eye of the brethren; a very great beam, an exceeding great beam; such as are your stage-players, rhymers, and morris-dancers,
10 who have walked hand in hand in contempt of the brethren and the cause, and been borne out by instruments of no mean countenance.

1 DAGON *Philistine god of whom idols were made.*

6 BALANCE *scale.*

7 WEAVER'S BEAM *part of a loom.*

11 INSTRUMENTS *agents.*

11–2 COUNTENANCE *repute; doubtless an allusion to the nobility, who always showed favor to the players, to the great annoyance of the Puritans.*

Leatherhead. Sir, I present nothing but what is licensed by authority.

Busy. Thou art all licence, even licentiousness itself, Shimei! 15

Leatherhead. I have the Master of the Revels' hand for it, sir.

Busy. The master of rebels' hand thou hast—Satan's! Hold thy peace; thy scurrility shut up thy mouth; thy profession is damnable, and in pleading for it thou dost plead for Baal. I have long opened my mouth wide and gaped, I have gaped as the oyster for 20 the tide, after thy destruction; but cannot compass it by suit or dispute; so that I look for a bickering ere long, and then a battle.

Knockem. Good Banbury-vapors.

Cokes. Friend, you'd have an ill match on't if you bicker with him here; though he be no man o' the fist, he has friends that will 25 go to cuffs for him. Numps, will not you take our side?

Edgworth. Sir, it shall not need; in my mind, he offers him a fairer course, to end it by disputation! Hast thou nothing to say for thyself, in defence of thy quality?

Leatherhead. Faith, sir, I am not well studied in these controver- 30 sies between the hypocrites and us. But here's one of my motion, Puppet Dionysius, shall undertake him, and I'll venture the cause on't.

Cokes. Who? My hobbyhorse? Will he dispute with him?

Leatherhead. Yes, sir, and make a hobby-ass of him, I hope. 35

Cokes. That's excellent! Indeed he looks like the best scholar of 'em all. Come, sir, you must be as good as your word, now.

Busy. I will not fear to make my spirit and gifts known! Assist me, zeal; fill me, fill me, that is, make me full.

Winwife. What a desperate, profane wretch is this! Is there any 40

---

15 SHIMEI *a man of the house of Saul who cursed King David* (2 Samuel *16: 5–13*).

16 MASTER OF THE REVELS *a Court officer who licensed plays.*

19 BAAL *another "heathen" god associated with idolatry.*

28 DISPUTATION *N.*

ignorance or impudence like his? To call his zeal to fill him
against a puppet?

    Grace. I know no fitter match than a puppet to commit with
an hypocrite!

45   *Busy.* First, I say unto thee, idol, thou hast no calling.

    Pup. Dionysius. You lie; I am called Dionysius.

    Leatherhead. The motion says you lie, he is called Dionysius i'
the matter, and to that calling he answers.

    Busy. I mean no vocation, idol, no present lawful calling.

50   *Pup. Dionysius.* Is yours a lawful calling?

    Leatherhead. The motion asketh if yours be a lawful calling.

    Busy. Yes, mine is of the spirit.

    Pup. Dionysius. Then idol is a lawful calling.

    Leatherhead. He says, then idol is a lawful calling! For you called
55   him idol, and your calling is of the spirit.

    Cokes. Well disputed, hobbyhorse!

    Busy. Take not part with the wicked, young gallant. He neigheth
and hinnyeth; all is but hinnying sophistry. I call him idol again.
Yet, I say, his calling, his profession is profane, it is profane, idol.

60   *Pup. Dionysius.* It is not profane!

    Leatherhead. It is not profane, he says.

    Busy. It is profane.

    Pup. Dionysius. It is not profane.

    Busy. It is profane.

65   *Pup. Dionysius.* It is not profane.

    Leatherhead. Well said, confute him with "not," still. You
cannot bear him down with your base noise, sir.

    Busy. Nor he me with his treble creaking, though he creak like
the chariot wheels of Satan. I am zealous for the cause—

43 GRACE *N.*

43 COMMIT *engage.*

45 NO CALLING *N.*

57–8 NEIGHETH AND HINNYETH *alluding to the high nasal voice.*

Leatherhead. As a dog for a bone.   70

Busy. And I say it is profane, as being the page of pride and the waiting-woman of vanity.

Pup. Dionysius. Yea? What say you to your tire-woman, then? *Leatherhead.* Good.

Pup. Dionysius. Or feather-makers i' the Friars, that are o' your   75 faction of faith? Are not they with their perukes and their puffs, their fans and their huffs, as much pages of pride and waiters upon vanity? What say you? What say you? What say you?

Busy. I will not answer for them.

Pup. Dionysius. Because you cannot, because you cannot. Is a   80 bugle-maker a lawful calling? or the confect-maker's? such you have there; or your French fashioner? You'd have all the sin within yourselves, would you not? would you not?

Busy. No, Dagon.

Pup. Dionysius. What then, Dagonet? Is a puppet worse than   85 these?

Busy. Yes, and my main argument against you is that you are an abomination; for the male among you putteth on the apparel of the female, and the female of the male.

Pup. Dionysius. You lie, you lie, you lie abominably.

Cokes. Good, by my troth, he has given him the lie thrice.   90

73 TIRE-WOMEN *dressmakers.*

75 FEATHER-MAKERS *dealers in feathers.*

76 PUFFS *protuberant masses of cloth, ribbons, etc.*

77 HUFFS *similar to puffs, for raising shoulders, etc.*

81 BUGLE *black tubular glass bead.*

81 CONFECT *confectionery, candy.*

82 FASHIONER *tailor.*

85 DAGONET *King Arthur's fool.*

86–8 MAIN ARGUMENT . . . MALE *a constantly recurring argument in Puritan attacks on the stage.*

Pup. Dionysius. It is your old stale argument against the players, but it will not hold against the puppets; for we have neither male nor female amongst us. And that thou may'st see, if thou wilt, like a malicious purblind zeal as thou art!

The puppet takes up his garment.

95 *Edgworth.* By my faith, there he has answered you, friend; by plain demonstration.

Pup. Dionysius. Nay, I'll prove, against e'er a rabbin of 'em all, that my standing is as lawful as his; that I speak by inspiration as well as he; that I have as little to do with learning as he; and do 100 scorn her helps as much as he.

Busy. I am confuted; the cause hath failed me.

Pup. Dionysius. Then be converted, be converted.

Leatherhead. Be converted, I pray you, and let the play go on!

Busy. Let it go on. For I am changed, and will become a 105 beholder with you!

Cokes. That's brave i' faith. Thou hast carried it away, hobby-horse; on with the play!

The Justice discovers himself.

Overdo. Stay, now do I forbid, I, Adam Overdo! Sit still, I charge you.

110 *Cokes.* What, my brother-i'-law!

Grace. My wise guardian!

Edgworth. Justice Overdo!

Overdo. It is time to take enormity by the forehead, and brand it; for I have discovered enough.

98 STANDING *profession.*
106 CARRIED IT AWAY *won the contest.*

Act V Scene vi

[*Enter Quarlous (like the madman) with Purecraft.*]

Quarlous. Nay, come, Mistress bride. You must do as I do, now. You must be mad with me in truth. I have here Justice Overdo for it.

Overdo. [*To Quarlous.*] Peace, good Trouble-all; come hither, and you shall trouble none. I will take the charge of you and your   5
friend too. (*To the cutpurse and Mistress Littlewit.*) You also, young man, shall be my care; stand there.

Edgworth. Now, mercy upon me.

Knockem. Would we were away, Whit;   *The rest are*
these are dangerous vapors; best fall off with   *stealing away.*   10
our birds, for fear o' the cage.

Overdo. Stay, is not my name your terror?

Whit. Yesh, faith, man, and it ish for tat we would be gone, man.

[*Enter Littlewit.*]

Littlewit. O gentlemen, did you not see a wife of mine? I ha'   15
lost my little wife, as I shall be trusted, my little pretty Win; I left her at the great woman's house in trust yonder, the pig-woman's, with Captain Jordan and Captain Whit, very good men, and I cannot hear of her. Poor fool, I fear she's stepped aside. Mother, did you not see Win?   20

Overdo. If this grave matron be your mother, sir, stand by her, *et digito compesce labellum;* I may perhaps spring a wife for you

11 CAGE *prison.*

19 STEPPED ASIDE *gone astray.*

22 ET . . . LABELLUM *Juvenal,* Satires, *i, 160:* "'restrain your lips with your finger' (*lest you be an informer*)" (*Horsman*).

183

anon. Brother Barthol'mew, I am sadly sorry to see you so
lightly given, and such a disciple of enormity, with your grave
25 governor Humphrey; but stand you both there in the middle-
place; I will reprehend you in your course. Mistress Grace, let me
rescue you out of the hands of the stranger.

Winwife. Pardon me, sir, I am a kinsman of hers.

Overdo. Are you so? Of what name, sir?

30 *Winwife.* Winwife, sir.

Overdo. Master Winwife? I hope you have won no wife of her,
sir. If you have, I will examine the possibility of it at fit leisure.
Now to my enormities: look upon me, o London! and see me,
o Smithfield! the example of justice and mirror of magistrates,
35 the true top of formality and scourge of enormity. Hearken unto
my labors and but observe my discoveries, and compare Hercules
with me, if thou dar'st, of old; or Columbus, Magellan, or our
countryman Drake of later times. Stand forth you weeds of
enormity, and spread. (*To Busy.*) First, Rabbi Busy, thou super-
40 lunatical hypocrite. (*To Lantern.*) Next, thou other extremity, thou
profane professor of puppetry, little better than poetry. (*To the
horse-courser and cutpurse.*) Then thou strong debaucher and
seducer of youth; witness this easy and honest young man. (*Then
Captain Whit and Mistress Littlewit.*) Now thou esquire of dames,
45 madams, and twelvepenny ladies. Now my green madam herself, of the price. Let me unmask your ladyship.

Littlewit. O my wife, my wife, my wife!

Overdo. Is she your wife? *Redde te Harpocratem!*

    Enter Trouble-all, [followed by Ursula and Nightingale.]

Trouble-all. By your leave, stand by, my masters; be uncovered.
50 *Ursula.* O stay him, stay him, help to cry, Nightingale; my pan,
my pan.

---

48 REDDE TE HARPOCRATEM "*make yourself a Harpocrates*" (*the god of silence*).
49 BE UNCOVERED *take off your hats* (*as if some dignitary were coming*).

Overdo. What's the matter?

Nightingale. He has stol'n Gammer Urs'la's pan.

Trouble-all. Yes, and I fear no man but Justice Overdo.

Overdo. Urs'la? Where is she? O the sow of enormity, this! (*To*   55
Ursula and Nightingale.) Welcome, stand you there; you songster,
there.

Ursula. An' please your worship, I am in no fault. A gentleman
stripped him in my booth, and borrowed his gown and his hat;
and he ran away with my goods, here, for it.   60

Overdo. (*To Quarlous.*) Then this is the true madman, and you
are the enormity!

Quarlous. You are i' the right, I am mad but from the gown out-
ward.

Overdo. Stand you there.   65

Quarlous. Where you please, sir.

Mistress Overdo [*waking up*,] *is sick, and her husband is silenced.*

Mistress Overdo. O lend me a basin, I am sick, I am sick. Where's
Master Overdo? Bridget, call hither my Adam.

Overdo. How?

Whit. Dy very own wife, i' fait, worshipful Adam.   70

Mistress Overdo. Will not my Adam come at me? Shall I see him
no more then?

Quarlous. Sir, why do you not go on with the enormity? Are
you oppressed with it? I'll help you, sir, i' your ear: your
"innocent young man," you have ta'en such care of all this day,   75
is a cutpurse, that hath got all your brother Cokes his things, and
helped you to your beating and the stocks; if you have a mind to
hang him now and show him your magistrate's wit, you may; but
I should think it were better recovering the goods, and to save

58 GENTLEMAN *i.e. Quarlous.*
60 HE *i.e. Trouble-all.*
68 BRIDGET *N.*

80 your estimation in him. I thank you, sir, for the gift of your ward,
Mistress Grace; look you, here is your hand and seal, by the way.
Master Winwife, give you joy, you are Palamon; you are
possessed of the gentlewoman, but she must pay me value, here's
warrant for it. And honest madman, there's thy gown and cap

85 again; I thank thee for my wife. (*To the widow.*) Nay, I can be mad,
sweetheart, when I please, still; never fear me. And careful
.Numps, where's he? I thank him for my licence.

    Wasp. How!

    Quarlous. 'Tis true, Numps.

90   *Wasp.* I'll be hanged then.

    Quarlous. Look i' your box, Numps. (*Wasp misseth the
licence.*) [*To Overdo.*] Nay, sir, stand not you fixed here, like a stake
in Finsbury to be shot at, or the whipping post i' the Fair, but get
your wife out o' the air; it will make her worse else; and remember

95 you are but Adam, flesh and blood! You have your frailty; forget
your other name of Overdo and invite us all to supper. There you
and I will compare our discoveries, and drown the memory of all
enormity in your bigg'st bowl at home.

    Cokes. How now, Numps, ha' you lost it? I warrant 'twas when

100 thou wert i' the stocks. Why dost not speak?

    Wasp. I will never speak while I live, again, for aught I know.

    Overdo. Nay, Humphrey, if I be patient, you must be so too; this
pleasant conceited gentleman hath wrought upon my judgment,
and prevailed. I pray you take care of your sick friend, Mistress

105 Alice, and my good friends all—

    Quarlous. And no enormities.

    Overdo. I invite you home with me to my house, to supper. I will

---

80 ESTIMATION IN *good opinion of; it might be saved by not treating him as a
criminal.*

81 HAND AND SEAL *on the blank* "*warrant*"; *see* IV.6.145 N.

92–3 STAKE IN FINSBURY *for archery contests.*

have none fear to go along, for my intents are *ad correctionem, non ad destructionem; ad aedificandum, non ad diruendum*. So lead on.

Cokes. Yes, and bring the actors along, we'll ha' the rest o' the   110
play at home.   [*Exeunt.*]

108–9 AD . . . DIRUENDUM *"for correction, not destruction; for building, not ruining."*

THE END.

THE
EPILOGUE

Your Majesty hath seen the play, and you
   Can best allow it from your ear and view.
You know the scope of writers, and what store
   Of leave is given them, if they take not more,
And turn it into licence. You can tell   5
   If we have used that leave you gave us well;
Or whether we to rage or licence break,
   Or be profane, or make profane men speak.
This is your power to judge, great sir, and not
   The envy of a few. Which if we have got,   10
We value less what their dislike can bring,
   If it so happy be, t' have pleased the King.

Notes

8 PARTICULAR WRONG *It is a standard charge against satirists that they maliciously attack individuals. Very largely because of the appearance of a number of thinly disguised personal lampoons, the publication of satires and epigrams had been forbidden in 1599, and the accusation continued to be leveled at dramatists who introduced satire into their plays. Jonson had frequently been charged with lampooning his enemies (such as rival dramatists) but maintained that his satirical portraits were generalized types. See O. J. Campbell,* Comicall Satyre and Shakespeare's Troilus and Cressida *(San Marino, Calif., 1938), pp. 1–14.*

THE PERSONS OF THE PLAY

[TINDERBOX-MAN] *The Folio has "Mousetrap-man" here, and the Induction refers to "the seller of mousetraps," but at the one appearance of this character (II.4) he is called the Tinderbox-man. Since contemporary drawings of these peddlers show mousetraps which were small boxes, it seems likely that the same man sold both mousetraps and tinderboxes.*

THE INDUCTION

INDUCTION *There are inductions to a number of Elizabethan plays. They normally consist, as Richard Hosley points out ("Was there a 'Dramatic Epilogue' to* The Taming of the Shrew?" Studies in English Literature 1 [1961], 21–22), *of a short action performed by two or more actors, "creating a fictional situation different from that of the play itself." Jonson uses such dramatic introductions in several other plays as means of dramatizing*

189

possible objections to his work, answers to the objections, and theories of drama.

[STAGE-KEEPER.] *Jonson does not provide a speech heading for the first speech in a scene. He lists the characters who are to take part in the scene, beginning with the one who is to speak first. In this edition the lists of characters are deleted and the necessary speech headings added. In the remaining scenes brackets are omitted.*

79 SIX PEN'ORTH *It usually cost a penny to stand in the pit of a public theater, more to sit in the galleries surrounding the open court, and still more (often sixpence) for seats in "rooms" somewhat like modern boxes. The scale of prices given here is much higher than usual, possibly because* Bartholomew Fair *was a new play in a new house. See E. K. Chambers,* The Eliza- . bethan Stage *(Oxford, 1923), 2, 532–34.*

95 JERONIMO OR ANDRONICUS *Both plays were very popular and both contained a kind of extravagant rhetoric of which Jonson liked to make fun. To admire them was to have an old-fashioned and uneducated taste.*

97 FIVE AND TWENTY, OR THIRTY YEARS *Jonson probably did not intend these figures to be taken literally. First performances of the two plays were very likely in the late eighties and early nineties respectively.*

117 JIGS AND DANCES *Dances were often introduced into plays, as in* The Winter's Tale *and* The Tempest, *and jigs were frequently performed at the conclusion of a play or even between the acts.*

126–7 MIRROR OF MAGISTRATES "Mirror" *often had the meaning of pattern or paragon, which fits here, but the phrase means more than this. It recalls* A Mirror for Magistrates, *a famous 16th-century collection of cautionary tales in verse presenting the downfalls of rulers. A more precise allusion is probably intended to Whetstone's lesser known* A Mirror for Magistrates of Cities *which advises magistrates to go about in disguise to find out what is happening—advice which Justice Overdo seems to follow in this play.*

146 COMMODITY *An allusion to the "commodity" swindle, well known in this period. A borrower was induced to take part of his loan in merchandise of inferior quality—a miscellaneous collection, or "commodity," which the lender then bought back through an agent at a much lower figure. The implication is that if the spectators have no laughter to pay for Jonson's wares, they may be obliged to accept inferior ones elsewhere.*

Act I, Scene i

11 PAUL'S *The middle aisle of St. Paul's in London was at this time the meeting place for courtiers, lawyers, and men of various occupations, who transacted business or passed the time of day here.*

21–2 SPANISH LADY *From Spain came the fashion for shoes with high cork soles. In* The Devil is an Ass *Jonson makes fun of an Englishwoman who is called "the Spaniard" because she affects Spanish fashions.*

36 BECAUSE . . . GOSSIPS *An elliptical clause, the meaning of which seems to be that the poets at the Mermaid, etc, pride themselves on their friendship with the players, whereas other men, like Littlewit, who "have wives as fine as the players," can outshine these poets.*

Act I, Scene iii

71 INHERIT . . . INCHES *Cf. Juvenal's first satire, where the lovers of an old woman inherit, "each according to the dimensions of his parts" (ll. 40–1).*

130–2 (HE HAS UNDONE . . . WAY) *What Jonas Barish calls the "spasmodic quality" of this entire passage—the bursts of loosely related phrases and clauses—makes this parenthesis initially puzzling. The grocer, as zealous as Busy, trusted him with currants, then broke with him and was ruined by Busy, but it is not in this order that Quarlous describes these events. Jonson's prose here conveys the manner in which a person often thinks and speaks rather than the logical arrangement of literary composition. See Barish,* Ben Jonson and the Language of Prose Comedy *(Cambridge, Mass., 1960), pp. 190–93.*

Act I, Scene iv

6 SAVED . . . BOOK *An old law, still on the books in Jonson's time, exempted a man from the death penalty if he pled the benefit of clergy by proving in court his ability to read a latin verse, usually the opening of the 51st Psalm. In this way Jonson himself escaped hanging after he had killed another actor in a duel (H & S, 1, 18–19).*

33 CLOISTER *Christ Church Cloisters, formerly part of a monastery and very close to Smithfield, had been given over to shops where various wares, including gingerbread, were sold at the time of the Fair.*

101 DRAWN . . . POND *A practical joke in which a bet is made that a cat will pull a person through a pond. A rope is tied around him and the other end is*

> *thrown across the pond, where it is fastened to a cat. Then those who are to
> "lead the cat" pull the victim through the pond.*

Act II, Scene i

11–2 A WORTHY . . . MAN *An allusion, as C. S. Alden poi nted out, to the Lord
Mayor of London, Sir Thomas Hayes, who tells in a letter written in 1614
how he visited ale houses and other establishments in disguise to check on
their illegal practices; see H & S, 10, 185.*

Act II, Scene ii

ACT II SCENE II *I have preserved Jonson's scene division in accordance with the
principles of this edition, although, as I explain in Appendix II, it is
probable that Leatherhead and Trash enter during Overdo's soliloquy and
set up their stands. Jonson normally (but by no means always) begins a
scene when new speakers appear, and therefore begins Scene ii when
Leatherhead and Trash begin to speak. It will be noticed, however, that the
arrival of even so important a character as Ursula at l.40 does not mark the
beginning of another scene.*

103 SD ONE KNOCKS *Overdo must approach Ursula's booth from one side in such
a way that she does not see him from where she is sitting. If the booth is
constructed in the manner described in Appendix II he may knock on one of
the front posts.*

Act II, Scene iii

22 VAPORS *One of Knockem's favorite words and one of the key words of the
play. He uses vapor so obsessively that in some of his speeches it becomes
almost meaningless—a kind of verbal tic, but ordinarily it carries the suggestion of two related meanings. The more specific, seen in the game of
vapors in IV, 4, is a senseless urge to contradict, to quarrel, to be touchy.
More generally, a "vapor" is similar to what Jonson meant by a "humor"
in* Every Man in his Humor—*a bent of character, a predisposition, or
merely a whim, but in any event an aberrant form of behavior due to some
sort of imbalance. Taken together, the two meanings of vapor make it
applicable not only to Knockem and the foolish game which he encourages
but also to the waspishness of Wasp, the more detached cynicism of Quarlous,
and the censoriousness of Overdo and Zeal-of-the-land Busy. The absurd
quarreling of the puppets is the ultimate image of vapors. See the excellent
discussion in Barish,* Ben Jonson, *pp. 217–19, 230–31, 233–34.*

50 FOUND'RING *Knockem's application of veterinary terms to human beings not only reminds us of his profession but also contributes to the strong emphasis on animality conspicuous in many parts of the play.*

54 HERE'S EZEKIEL EDGWORTH *The characters whose entrance into the dialogue marks the beginning of a new scene necessarily come onstage a moment before their first lines, and often their appearance is hailed, as it is here, by one of the characters already onstage. Thus the actual entrance often occurs slightly before the indication of it in the stage direction.*

Act II, Scene vi

25 ALLIGARTA *Seventeenth-century descriptions of the materials used in the preparation, preservation (and adulteration) of tobacco make Overdo's suggestion seem a little less fantastic. See* The Alchemist, *I.3. 24 ff.*

44 HOLE IN THE NOSE *Parts of the nose are sometimes destroyed by syphilis; Overdo claims that smoking has the same effect.*

Act III, Scene i

1–6 *Jonson is not consistent in his representation of this dialect, but it is not hard to understand. A "translation" of this first speech will illustrate the main consonantal changes: "Nay, 'tis all gone, now! This 'tis, when thou wilt not be within call, Master Officer! What is a man the better to listen out noises for thee an' thou art in another world—being very sufficient noises and gallants too, one o' their brabbles would have fed us all this fortnight; but thou art so busy about beggars still, thou hast no leisure to intend gentlemen, an't be."*

2–3 PHAT . . . TEE *Whit evidently has an arrangement with the watch, whereby he informs them where they may make arrests and splits with them the money they take in.*

Act III, Scene ii

65 JUNIPER *Juniper was sometimes burned to purify the air, but Ursula may use it along with rosemary and bay-leaf (l.60) to season the pig with its aromatic smoke.*

92 WAIT *Whit is supposed to find women for Ursula's friends. Presumably Knockem is telling him here to keep an eye on Win, whom he later persuades to go in disguise with Edgworth and him to the puppet show.*

SD HE FOLLOWS . . . URSULA *Since Jonson does not indicate exits, it is difficult to tell what the stage business is here. Knockem obviously speaks through the curtain to Mooncalf, who is in the rear of the booth. It is possible that the Puritans have already gone into this part of the booth and that Busy's orders are delivered "within," as Gifford thought. It is more likely, however, that they start going in after Knockem's speech and that Busy follows the procession, "driving" his flock, as Winwife has said. Whit's movements are also mysterious. The fact that Knockem speaks to him after speaking to Mooncalf might indicate that Whit was also "within" at this point, but there is no good reason for him to have left. He probably follows Littlewit and Win after Knockem's speech. It should be understood that stage directions here are more speculative than usual.*

Act III, Scene iv

85 MASQUE *The masque was a fashionable dramatic entertainment in which dancing, music, and spectacle were important components. At court Queen Anne was fond of taking part along with her ladies in waiting and other members of the court. Technically such amateur participants, disguised as they were in gorgeous costumes, were the "masquers," but they were often assisted by professional players. When Jonson began writing masques at the invitation of the King, his dramatic imagination and mastery of language made them into something much more than disguisings which ended in a dance: they became highly sophisticated works of art in which the many diverse elements were made to contribute to a single effect. Jonson was aided and in fact rivalled in his efforts by the great designer, Inigo Jones, whose scenery for these court masques introduced into England the elaborate movable sets already known to Italy and France, where stage illusion was achieved by the art of perspective. What Cokes has in mind is, of course, rather simpler than a Jonson-Jones masque, but his wanting a masque is a testimony to its popularity at this period.*

Act III, Scene v

255 DISPARAGEMENT *Grace would not have to forfeit her land if she could show that marriage to Cokes would be a "disparagement," i.e. an unequal or unsuitable match.*

Act III, Scene vi

SD *Curtains are probably pulled around the front of Ursula's booth at this time (see Appendix II, p. 213). When Leatherhead and Trash leave, the stage is cleared for the first time since the opening of Act II.*

Act IV, Scene i

32 LEG *Here and in IV, vi the offender is told to put in his leg, not his legs. Wasp in Scene vi puts his leg "in the middle roundel," as if in a single hole, and when he escapes he does so by putting "his shoe on his hand" and slipping it in "for his leg." It would seem that the stocks used here had only three holes (note the "middle roundel") and that those sitting in them were fastened by one leg only. Though it was much more common to fasten criminals by both legs, illustrations of stocks from the middle ages to the 17th century occasionally show people held by one leg only (see Wm. Andrews, Old Time Punishments [London, 1890], pp. 121, 125). Hudibras and Ralph are apparently so fastened in Part II, Canto I of Samuel Butler's Hudibras.*

Act IV, Scene iii

120 BACKSIDE *Quarlous and Edgworth have walked from the vicinity of the stocks to the back part of Ursula's booth. As they go on to the front, the curtains around that part of the booth are drawn, revealing Knockem and his friends. Quarlous and Edgworth at first stand looking at them and then join them (see Appendix II, pp. 210–11).*

Act IV, Scene iv

1 LIFT *Knockem and Whit are preparing to steal whatever they can get away with if there is a brawl; their preparations bear fruit later in the scene. It is possible that Edgworth has asked Knockem to help him in his plan to rob Wasp and that Knockem is also laying the ground for this theft; for he later gives Whit the order to start the fight in which Wasp is robbed.*

154 THE WATCH *Jonson does not specify which members of the watch, but from what happens later it appears that Haggis has been left with Overdo and Busy and therefore that Bristle and Poacher come to pick up Wasp. Presumably, then, they are the "officers" who enter with Wasp in Scene vi. Shortly after their entrance in that scene Bristle asks Haggis, who seems to have Overdo and Busy with him, what the justice has ruled in their case.*

Act IV, Scene vi

145 ANOTHER USE *It becomes clear in V, ii, that Quarlous decides to disguise himself as Trouble-all in order to get a look at Grace's book. This sudden decision and Dame Purecraft's equally sudden decision to set her cap for Trouble-all are vital links in the intricate construction of the denouement of the play. It is characteristic of Jonson's plotting that although both moves are prepared for, they are so unemphatically introduced that the spectator has very little idea what is afoot until later. A somewhat breathless sense of being always one step behind the author is increased by his habit of building one trick upon another. In this instance Quarlous makes use of his impersonation of Trouble-all not only to find out from Grace's book that Winwife has won, but also to get a blank warrant from Overdo, which he makes into a conveyance of the guardianship of Grace and uses at the end to get money from Grace and Winwife. Still further, he takes advantage of Purecraft's desire to marry the madman, and, using the license stolen from Wasp (on which Quarlous changes the names), makes the rich widow his wife. None of these maneuvers are fully revealed until the end of the play, and even then they are no more than mentioned. One result of this technique is that although Jonson's plots are logical to a fault, they are capable of producing continual surprises as in this play or* The Alchemist.

Act V, Scene i

SD *Leatherhead and his doorkeepers set up their puppet theater during this scene and remain onstage during the next, possibly completing their arrangements (see Appendix II, pp. 215–16).*

7–9 JERUSALEM . . . GOMORRAH *There are many references to puppet shows of the stories of Nineveh and Sodom and Gomorrah from the Bible, the destruction of Jerusalem, and the building of the city of Norwich, as well as the Gunpowder Plot mentioned below.*

Act V, Scene ii

49 PARTY-COLORED BROTHERHOOD *The epithet is appropriate in that it suggests the inconsistency with which the Puritans were constantly charged. There is also a play on party in the sense of "faction": their minds are colored by their factiousness. Cf. Marvell's jibe at the Scots in* An Horation Ode *(ll. 105–6):*

> *The Pict no shelter now shall find*
> *Within his party-colour'd Mind . . .*

Act V, Scene iii

6–9 "THE ANCIENT . . . BANKSIDE" *This title, like that of the play performed by Bottom and his friends in* A Midsummer Night's Dream, *is a take-off of the titles given to many plays of the period just before Shakespeare and Jonson. See also V.4.115 N.*

51–2 CALL . . . LANTERN *Leatherhead does not want to be recognized by Cokes who would ask for his money back. Though Trash has told him (III. 4. 129–31) that he will see Leatherhead in a velvet jerkin, interpreting Littlewit's "motion," Cokes does not show any glimmer of recognition. It is somewhat surprising that Jonson has made Trash so specific, but Cokes is rattle-brained enough to forget the most definite warning.*

56 TIRING-HOUSE . . . LITTLE *In the public theater one could go backstage to the tiring-house to make the acquaintance of the actors in their dressing rooms. Cokes and Leatherhead are standing in front of the puppet booth, where the stage is about shoulder height, and the puppeteers beneath, in what could in fun be called the tiring-house, have to sit down. It is clear from this reference and from some of the action in the puppet play that Jonson wrote it for glove puppets, not marionettes on wires.*

75 ONE TAYLOR *A triple play on words referring to the proverbial timidity of the tailor, to the actor, Joseph Taylor, of the company which was giving* Bartholomew Fair, *and to John Taylor, the water poet, who challenged a man to a combat of wit at the Hope Theater and won by default.*

Act V, Scene iv

115 GENTLES, ETC. *The puppet play which begins here is not only a farcical vulgarization of Marlowe's* Hero and Leander, *of which there are occasional verbal echoes, but also a burlesque of Richard Edwards'* Damon and Pythias, *a play performed at court in 1564. The incongruous combination of the two stories is in itself a satirical commentary on some Elizabethan drama. The loose, four-beat verse of the puppet play is very similar to one of the meters used by Edwards, as the following lines from the first speech of his play will show:*

> *I am wise for myself, then tell me of troth,*
> *Is not that great wisdom as the world go'th?*
> *Some philosophers in the street go ragged and torn,*
> *And feeds on vile roots, whom boys laugh to scorn,*

> But I in fine silks haunt Dionysius' palace,
> Wherein with dainty fare myself I do solace.

In Thomas Dekker's Satiromastix (1601), in which Jonson is satirized in the guise of a character named Horace, there are tantalizing allusions which suggest that Jonson may have written the puppet play before that time. Horace is called a "puppet-teacher" (IV.3.174) and is addressed as "old Cole" in a passage which also refers to Damon and Pythias (I.2.330–32).

137–8 UNDERSTAND Cokes has difficulty understanding because Leatherhead, who speaks for all the puppets ("I am the mouth of 'em all"), uses the high-pitched, nasal voice cultivated by puppet showmen; see George Speaght, The History of the English Puppet Theatre (New York, n.d.), p. 67.

289 DUNMOW-BACON A flitch of Bacon was presented to any couple who could convince a jury of bachelors and maidens in Little Dunmow, Essex, that they had spent the first year of married life in perfect harmony and had never regretted marrying.

323 PUP. DIONYSIUS The Folio has Pup. D., the abbreviation used for both Damon and Dionysius. Gifford and Horsman give the line to Damon, but Levin, correctly I think, gives it to Dionysius, for whom it is much more appropriate. It is a continuation of the speech Leatherhead has been narrating.

Act V, Scene v

28 DISPUTATION John Selden reported in his Table Talk (1689) under Religion: "Ben Johnson Satyrically express'd the vain Disputes of Divines by Inigo Lanthorne, disputing with his puppet in a Bartholomew Fair. It is so; It is not so: It is so, It is not so, crying thus one to another a quarter of an Hour together" (H & S 10, 213). The reference is puzzling in a number of ways, for Lantern Leatherhead is never called Inigo and the disputes he has with the puppets have little bearing on religious controversy, whereas the disputation between Busy and the puppet is clearly satirical of Puritan attacks on the stage. Possibly Selden's statement (if it has come down to us accurately) reflects a confusion of two or more episodes in the play. It may be that Leatherhead was understood by Jonson's contemporaries as in part a satire of his collaborator, Inigo Jones (see III.4.85 N), with whom Jonson later quarreled bitterly; in the "Expostulation with Inigo Jones" (1631) the great stage designer is compared to a puppet showman. Jonson's growing jealousy may have prompted him to make a very oblique attack on Jones in Bartholomew Fair, but Selden's is our only real evidence for thinking so, and

the substance of Selden's observations bears on Busy rather than Leatherhead (*note especially ll. 59–66*).

43 GRACE *The Folio gives this speech to Quarlous, though he has left the stage in Scene ii and does not return until Scene vi. Since his name is abbreviated "Qua." and Grace is abbreviated "Gra." it seems likely that misreading was responsible for the confusion. The speech is similar to others which Grace makes to Winwife, and therefore appropriate for her. For a longer discussion of the matter see my* "A Misprint in Bartholomew Fair," N & Q NS 10 (1963), 103–4.

45 NO CALLING *The Puritans always denied that acting was a legal profession. For many years an actor in England was liable to arrest as a vagabond unless he could prove that he was in the service of some nobleman. At the time of* Bartholomew Fair *each acting company was protected by a patent which gave it the patronage of a member of the royal family; hence the King's Men, the Lady Elizabeth's Men, etc. Puritan opposition to the acting profession was still strong, however, and was responsible for the closing of the theaters in 1642.*

Act V, Scene vi

68 BRIDGET *Simpson suggests that this is a slip for "Grace" (H & S, 10, 214). Perhaps, however, Mistress Overdo thinks she is at home and calls on some servant of hers.*

Appendix I: The Text

The only authoritative text of *Bartholomew Fair* is the one which was printed in 1631 and published in 1640 as part of the second volume of Jonson's *Works*. For the complicated and puzzling history of the publication of this volume the reader is referred to the Herford and Simpson edition of Jonson (*9*, 94–197) and to Walter Greg's *Bibliography of the English Printed Drama to the Restoration* (*3*, 1015–76). The important facts for the student of *Bartholomew Fair* are these: Jonson apparently intended to issue a successor to the first volume of his *Works* in 1631, when this play and two others were printed. A few copies of the separate plays seem to have been distributed at this time (we know that Jonson sent one of *Bartholomew Fair* to his patron, the Earl of Newcastle), but there is no proof that the three plays were officially published before 1640. In that year and the following one several works by Jonson—plays, poems, and prose—were printed and brought out together with the three 1631 plays. Jonson had a great deal of trouble with the printer of *Bartholomew Fair*, John Beale, who did a much less satisfactory job than William Stansby had done on the first volume of the *Works* (the 1616 Folio). As a result, there are errors of many kinds in the text of this play, discussed fully in Herford and Simpson (*6*, 3–8) and more briefly in the edition of E. A. Horsman (London, Methuen, 1960, pp. xxix-xxxi).

In preparing this edition I have made use of three copies at Yale: a separate *Bartholomew Fair* in the Elizabethan Club and two copies of the second volume of the *Works*, one in the Elizabethan Club and one in Sterling Memorial Library. The text is modernized in accordance with the policy of the Yale Ben Jonson. This has meant the elimination of such seventeenth-century variant forms of words in current usage as *then* for *than* and *murther* for *murder*, which were used interchangeably. They have no more significance than spelling variants, and may be due to the printer rather than to Jonson. However, a few distinct variants such as *itch* for *eke* (II.2.88) and *alligarta* for *alligator* (II.6.25) have been preserved. Although there is a danger of giving a distorted impression of the language by retaining a few archaic forms in the midst of a text otherwise modern in appearance, these seem to be in the same category as words which are obsolete, like *carwitchet* (V.1.4) or words used in an obsolete sense like *earns* in the sense of "grieves" (IV.6.132) or the common *and* in the sense of "if." Such words are as much a part of the language of the author or of his character as the seventeenth-century syntax. To alter is to rewrite.

Though a modernized edition cannot represent Elizabethan pronunciation faithfully, it is obvious that an editor must do what he can to preserve one part of the sound of the language, the optional contractions which form so important a part of colloquial speech and are sometimes a distinguishing feature of an author's style. In a play like *Bartholomew Fair*, where the effect of the dialogue depends so often on the patterns of everyday speech, this aspect of seventeenth-century English must be kept even where the spelling is today's. Thus *i'th* for *in the*, *o'th* for *of the*, *ha'* for *have*, etc. are carefully retained wherever they occur. It is quite likely that such contractions were often made in speech even when the words were spelled out, but an editor is not justified in normalizing to either the contracted or uncontracted form. By reproducing contractions where they are found he can best approximate this aspect of the language.

Some problems remain, for it is not always possible to be sure whether a given word represents a contraction of this sort or a variant form. *Again*, a variant form of *against*, is sometimes, but not always, spelled with an apostrophe at the end, as if it were a contraction. In this case I have removed the apostrophe wherever it occurs, since *again* was not in fact a contraction but a distinct form. In the case of *and* in the sense of "if," it seems likely that the frequent spelling, *an'*, though undoubtedly a contraction, had little if any bearing on the sound, particularly in the combination *and't*, also spelt *an't*. If it was difficult or impossible to recognize the contraction in speech, it cannot have indicated the distinctive habit of any speaker. Purely for the sake of clarity, therefore, *and* always appears in this text as *an'* when it is used in the sense of "if."

Contractions of proper names present another kind of problem. There is little doubt that such names as *Bartholomew* and *Ursula* were normally contracted in speech, no matter how they were spelled. The first appears in the Folio text of the play (with one exception) as *Bartholmew;* it is even so printed on one title page (it appears in full on another) and in the running head. *Ursula* appears as *Ursla* when it is not further contracted to *Urs.* The editors of modernized texts have usually given these names in their standard forms, some editors printing *Urs'la* when it occurs in dialogue. I have followed their lead in using the standard forms in the title of the play, the list of characters, and speech headings. In the dialogue it has seemed preferable, for reasons discussed already, to indicate the contractions: *Barthol'mew, Urs'la.*

With the exception of a very few normalizations, then, I have adhered faithfully to the vagaries of speech of Jonson's voluble cast of characters. In this way I hope to have preserved as much of the distinctive character of Jonson's dialogue as possible without sacrificing the readability of modern spelling.

The only other departures from the Folio occur in speech headings, stage directions, and the correction of a few errors. Whereas the Folio uses abbreviations for the names of speakers, they are given here in full. In the indication of entrances I have not followed Jonson's method. In this play he is markedly inconsistent. Though he generally lists at the beginning of the scene the characters who are to speak during the scene, the lists are not always complete. He sometimes indicates in them that one or two characters are to come later on, at other times marks entrances for such characters at the appropriate place, and in one instance (III.2) gives a speech to a character whose presence has not been indicated in any way. Sometimes, but not always, Jonson shows that a character onstage is joined by another by using the words "to him", as in Act I, Scene 1, which has *Littlewit. To him Win.* In the interests of clarity and consistency I have substituted my own indications of entrances in brackets and have omitted Jonson's lists. All stage directions not in

Appendix I

brackets are Jonson's, and in many cases his customary way of placing them in the margin has been approximated by printing them at one side. In other cases the position of the direction has been changed slightly to avoid awkwardness.

Finally, a number of errors in the Folio text have been corrected, many of them of a kind which made the intended reading perfectly obvious. The following list gives the only significant departures from the Folio, the readings of this text appearing in the first column, those of the Folio in the second:

The Persons of the Play	[Tinderbox-man]	Mousetrap-man
,, ,,	Folio includes Porters, who never appear.	
I.2. 40	good do	do good
I.2. 58	Winwife	Win.
I.3. 23	I am drunk	I drunke
I.3. 95	Winwife	Win.
III.5. 28	than	then then
IV.1. 71	him	his
IV.4. 199	vessel is	vessell
V.4. 79	Winwife	Win.
V.4. 140	that he	thhe
V.4. 251	me my	mmy
V.4. 298	Pythias	Folio omits
V.5. 43	Grace	Qua.

Appendix II: The Staging

The Induction to *Bartholomew Fair* treats the play frankly as an artifice—
something worked on by the author and possibly botched, according to
the Stage-keeper—something which the actors will try to perform.
When theatrical contrivance is pointed at in this way rather than concealed, as it is in realistic plays of more recent times, a detailed knowledge
of the staging, always desirable, is especially tempting. Many uncertain-
ties about the exact physical characteristics of stages in the Elizabethan
public theaters usually make the visualization of a performance of
Shakespeare or Jonson a very hazy venture. The moment we try to
conjure up a picture of stage action we are confronted by crucial problems about the acting areas. Was the discovery space a large "inner
stage," recessed in the tiring-house wall, a smaller space behind the
central door, or some sort of booth or pavilion set up on the main stage?
How much of an acting area was there "above"? And was it in the bal-
cony or on top of a structure on the stage? About the staging of Ben
Jonson's *Bartholomew Fair* we have two important facts—not much, one
might think, but taken in rapid succession, rather heady for the student of
the Elizabethan theater, used to surviving for considerable lengths of time
with no facts at all. First, it is known that the play was performed on 31
October 1614 at the Hope, the theater recently constructed with a stage
which could be removed to permit bear baiting. Secondly, the records
show that it was acted at court the following night, on which occasion a
payment was made for "Canvas for the Boothes and other necessaries for
a play called Bartholomewe Faire."[1] Here is enough information to

1. H & S, 9, 245.

explain some of the references to staging in the text of the play, and hence to encourage one to reconstruct from a close examination of the text at least the outlines of the play's appearance when it was first performed. Since our interest today is focused chiefly on the public theater, and since the play was first performed there, I shall concentrate attention on the performance at the Hope. It is a reasonable assumption, however, that the method of staging was not basically different the next evening at court. Our information about the booths there may fairly be used in discussing the earlier showing.

We know from the contract for the Hope Theater that this particular stage was built on trestles, like many a street stage, to make it easy to set up and remove. For the same reason, its canopy overhead was not supported by posts, as in the Swan Theater. The contract provides no other details about the appearance of the stage except that it should be "of suche large compasse, fforme, widenes, and height as the Plaie house called the Swan,"[2] from which we may reasonably infer that there were two doors, left and right, in the tiring-house wall, as in the famous De Witt sketch. The stage-keeper gives us, in the induction, one or two more indications. He refers to the arras (l.8) behind which Master Brome may be hiding, and to the "Canvas-cut i' the night" (l.18) which, properly handled, might lead to a "jig-a-jog i' the booths" (l.22). This last seems like a confirmation of the use at the Hope of canvas-covered booths like those paid for at court, and the arras clearly refers to hangings on the tiring-house wall. All in all, it does not sound like one of the more elegant London stages—an impression which is reinforced by the book-holder's allusion to the dirt and stench from the animals used in the baitings. Yet Jonson uses the very crudity of means as a realistic device, for the theater is said to be "as dirty as Smithfield, and as stinking every whit" (ll.141-42). Thus the stage on which Smithfield is to be presented is also somewhat the kind of stage one might see at Smithfield.[3]

2. E. K. Chambers, *The Elizabethan Stage* (Oxford, 1923), 2, 466.
3. C. Walter Hodges, *The Globe Restored* (London, 1953), p. 65. As will be clear in what follows, I am greatly indebted to Hodges' theories and those of Alois Nagler in his *Shakespeare's Stage* (New Haven, 1958). See also Wm. A. Armstrong, "Ben Jonson and Jacobean Stagecraft," in *Jacobean Theatre, Stratford-upon-Avon Studies, 1* (1960).

Presumably no properties were put on the stage during the induction. There was only the arras, which was there from the beginning. Was anything added for the first act? There is no reason to think so. The stage, backed by the arras, is quite satisfactory for the interior of John Littlewit's house. To visualize the tiring-house wall, however, we must face the problem of where the arras was hung in such a theater. It might have been between the two doors or it might have covered the entire wall, including the doors. The latter arrangement, as described by Nagler (p. 50), would in fact be essential for several scenes if there were no more than two doors at the Hope, for three entrances to the stage are sometimes required (as in IV.6), and access to a central opening in the arras could only be hidden from the audience if the arras also covered at least one of the two doors. If the Hope had three doors, as some theaters probably did, the arras may have covered only the central one. Otherwise—and the little evidence we have points to this alternative—it probably extended the full length of the tiring-house wall and had three slits from which entrances could be made.

At the opening of Act I, then, it is easy to imagine Littlewit coming through the center opening as if from an inner room in his house. Either of the other entrances might serve as the outside door of his house, through which his various visitors would come in the course of the act. Herford and Simpson (*10*, 170) suppose that the entire first act was played "above" on whatever served for an upper stage at the Hope, but it seems unlikely to me that so much action would be relegated to such a relatively confined space upstage (in Scene 5 there are eight people onstage at once). There is no reference in stage-directions or dialogue to "above" or "below" but only to "in" and "within, in my study." Surely the main stage would lend itself more readily to this situation.

The staging of the first act presents no very puzzling problems. The remainder of the play, in which the action is at the Fair, provides more matter for speculation. The text refers specifically to five places on the stage:[4] (1) to Leatherhead's "shop" on the "ground" he has paid for (II.2.4, 14); (2) to the "ground" Joan Trash has paid for (II.2.14) and her

4. In each case I give the first reference, though in some cases there are many more. I reserve for later discussion the problem of variant terminology—"shop," "booth," etc.

"shop" (III.4.90); (3) to Ursula's "booth" (II.2.66); (4) to the "stocks" (IV.1.17); and (5) to the place where Leatherhead runs his puppet-show, attended by the doorkeepers, Filcher and Sharkwell, who take the customers' money and allow them to "go in" (V.3.17). To get any clear idea of the staging of this part of the play, one needs to know how these places were represented, how and when any practicable structures were set up on the stage, and how many of them were visible at any time.

The answer to the first question is made easier by our knowledge that booths were constructed for the court performance. We know from Henslowe's records that various scenic elements, such as rocks, tombs, and cages, were used on the stage of the public theater, so that there is nothing improbable in the use of booths or stocks. Structures of canvas stretched over wooden frames, such as were used for "houses" in many performances at court, may well have been used for the booths in *Bartholomew Fair*, both at court and at the Hope.[5] They would answer well to Zeal-of-the-land's reference to the "tents of the wicked" (I.6.67). However, there is no reason to suppose that all these structures were identical; hints of what they were like must be sought in the text.

At the beginning of II.2, Leatherhead is asking Joan Trash, the gingerbread-woman, to sit farther away so as not to hinder "the prospect" of the "shop" where he sells "hobbyhorses." A few lines later, some of the action takes place in the "booth" where Ursula, as we soon learn, provides "pig and punk" and other conveniences. All three places must be visible at once, Leatherhead's and Trash's obviously close together, and probably somewhat removed from Ursula's, as they have no conversation with her until they go to help her when she falls. Joan Trash has a basket of gingerbread, also called a "hamper" (III.4.133–34), and a "flasket" (III.6.90), probably on some sort of table or stand, which Busy knocks over when he *"overthrows the gingerbread"* (III.6.91). Although there are references to her "shop" (as in the stage-direction at III.4.90), I doubt if the term denotes any special structure. All she needs is a place to sit by her stand. That Leatherhead's shop is a more pretentious establishment is made quite clear when Cokes offers to "buy up his shop, and thy basket" (III.4.98–99). The difference between the prices they ask seems significant even when allowance is made for the different cost of

5. See Nagler's summary of the evidence in *Shakespeare's Stage*, pp. 34–42.

hobbyhorses and gingerbread: Leatherhead asks "six and twenty shillings seven pence halfpenny, besides three shillings for my ground," while Trash asks only "four shillings, and eleven pence, sir, ground and all" (III.4.137-38, 141). However, even Leatherhead's shop need not be elaborate. On the contrary, it must be such that he can take it down and carry it away at the end of the third act, when he and Trash decide to disappear. He refers to "packing up" twice during this scene (III.6.20, 124), and there is nothing to show that they have been there when Cokes returns in the second scene of Act IV. Leatherhead, then, has a larger stall than Trash, very likely with a covered part behind the counter, like many a booth at a fair. The fact that the term "booth" is used only for Ursula's establishment does not mean that hers is the only booth shown on the stage, for we know that more than one booth was built at court. It seems likely that Leatherhead's shop might also have been called a booth.

Ursula's booth must meet several specific requirements. In the first place, it must obviously have both a front and a back part, separated in some way—presumably by a curtain. From the back part she emerges, sweating profusely, when we first see her (II.2.39). There she has her fire for roasting pigs; there the Puritan family goes in to eat and drink; there are taken various stolen goods; there she accommodates the ladies with "the bottom of an old bottle" (IV.4.199-200) and later provides them with fancy clothes. The front part of her booth is shaded with boughs and displays a sign, advertising her roast pig (III.2.50-54). In this front part of the booth Knockem and his pals must be revealed playing their game of vapors at the opening of IV.4. That the booth remains visible to the end of the play is suggested by Littlewit's saying in the last scene, "I left her at the great woman's house in trust yonder, the pig-woman's" (V.6.17-18), presumably pointing to it as he speaks. Cokes may do the same when he swears "by that fire" (V.3.28-29), interpreted by Herford and Simpson (*10*, 209) as the fire in Ursula's booth.

It is also arguable that Ursula's booth is taken down to make way for Leatherhead's puppet theater at the opening of Act V, but if so, it is the one instance in the play where one position on the stage represents successively two places in the Fair. The characters often seem to be aware of returning to a certain part of the Fair when they come onstage, and it is noteworthy that in Act V, Scene 2, after Leatherhead has set up his theater booth, Winwife and Grace come to look for Quarlous, wondering why he does not "return" to the place where they left him in Act IV.

There are at least two ways in which Ursula's booth might be constructed. In front of the central opening on the arras might be set up such a "pavilion" as Hodges and Nagler describe, or the variant form of it recently postulated by Albert Weiner.[6] It must be large enough to contain at least the seven characters revealed there at the opening of Act IV, Scene 4. There should be curtains on three sides, so that when they are drawn, leaving only two posts to mark the front of the booth, the actors seated inside drinking can be seen clearly by all the audience. Once the actors are discovered, however, they might in any case move out into the area in front of the booth for the succeeding action in which three more characters eventually participate. With any form of pavilion in this position, the arras itself would serve as the division between the front and back parts of Ursula's booth, as it divides Littlewit's front room from his "study within".

While this might be a quite satisfactory rendition of the pig-woman's booth, it would also be possible to set up, a few feet downstage from the central entrance, a free-standing structure, divided into two compartments. This would be a pavilion identical with the one just described, except that it would be deeper, and hence would project farther out on the stage. Though no scenes are played in the back part of the booth, this arrangement would have the advantage of bringing the action in the front of the booth closer to most of the audience, and of allowing occasional glimpses of the smoke from Ursula's fire, to which there are several allusions, as in Overdo's oration against tobacco: "the brain smoked like the backside of the pig-woman's booth, here" (II.6.39-40). At the end of Act IV, Scene 3, the text suggests that Quarlous and Edgworth might even be expected to walk in back of the booth; for as Edgworth is leading Quarlous there from the stocks, he says, "Here, sir, you are o' the backside o' the booth already; you may hear the noise" (IV.3.120-21).

6. Hodges, pp. 51-65; see his sketch of the Hope, p. 176; Nagler, pp. 26-32; Albert Weiner, "Elizabethan Interior and Aloft Scenes: A Speculative Essay," *Theatre Survey*, 2 (1961), 15-34.

Immediately afterwards the scene in the booth begins, presumably with the drawing of curtains from the front of the booth. By line 26 Quarlous is at the front of the booth, looking for Wasp. Now the word "back-side" could mean back yard as well as part of the booth, but in either case we are to imagine Quarlous and Edgworth behind the booth and then shortly in front of it. If they could pass between the back of the booth and the arras the sense of their movements would be immediately clear. And if the space were small, it would doubtless be possible for actors to get offstage from the rear of the booth unobserved. There is the further consideration that at court the booth would necessarily have been a free-standing structure. That the booth, however constructed, should have a rectangular look is implied by Ursula's reference to the "corner o' the booth" (II.2.66) and Quarlous's phrase (referring to the rear portion), "a pig-box" (III.2.126).

If the booths of Leatherhead and Ursula were somewhat as we have described them, we can return to the question of how and when they were erected. It is possible that they were on the stage from the beginning, in which case the first act might have to be played on the upper stage. I think it is more likely that they were set up at the beginning of the second act, combining a frank display of theatrical process with a kind of local color, since the setting up of the stage booths would, after all, approximate closely the setting up of the actual booths in the Fair. The process is referred to in Wasp's sarcastic speech to Cokes (II.6.84): "Will you fix here? And set up a booth, sir?" The first scene of Act II is a soliloquy given by Justice Overdo in his disguise as mad Arthur of Bradley. It is clear that he has just arrived at the Fair and in his search for "enormities" is lurking in the neighborhood of some activity. From other indications we know that it is still fairly early in the morning and that not much is going on yet. Since Leatherhead opens the next scene with his complaints to Joan Trash, he may enter with her during the Justice's soliloquy and start setting up the booth which he is later to pack up and take away. At the same time Ursula's booth could be set up with its pig's-head sign, "Here be the best pigs, and she does roast 'em as well as ever she did" (III.2.63-64). These doings would provide an obvious attraction to the zealous eye of Overdo.

One more property, the stocks, could be put in place at the opening of

Appendix II

Act II. Though they are not needed except in Act IV, when Overdo, Busy, and Wasp are put in, they could appropriately be onstage through the last four acts as a part of the Fair, like Ursula's booth. But whereas Ursula's booth is so central to the meaning of the play that it should be in the center of the stage, the stocks might better be at one side, where the "criminals" would be only a few feet from the standees in the pit, and hence in a very similar situation to that of real criminals exposed in a public place. When the stocks were not in use they would not be in the way on this part of the stage.

Let us suppose, then, in order to give our picture more precision, that from the opening of Act II to the close of Act III the spectators had before them, going from stage right to stage left, Leatherhead's booth, Joan Trash's stand, Ursula's booth (stage center), and the stocks. None of them could have been far from the tiring-house wall, because all the action of the play takes place in front of them. Such structures and such an arrangement of the stage were firmly rooted in theatrical tradition. The booths were similar to the houses, of which there were sometimes three or four, in plays based on classical models and acted at the court or the universities.[7] They resembled more closely the mansions of the mystery plays. The *Ludus Coventriae* required mansions fully as large as Ursula's booth must be (e.g. the "council house"), and one (Pilate's house) divided in two sections. Knockem's ironical mention of "Urs'la's mansion" (II.5.39) must certainly have struck some of the audience as an amusing reference to the mysteries. What is most notable is Jonson's use of the principles of simultaneous staging, for although the imagined distances between the several locations strung across the back of his stage are not so great as those between medieval mansions, the flow of the action from one to another is remarkably similar. Supernumeraries stroll from side to side of the stage gaping at what the Fair offers, and the principal characters move freely from one center of interest to another, as Cokes in the third act goes first to Leatherhead's shop, then to the stand of the gingerbread-woman, and is then distracted by the itinerant ballad-singer. A corollary of this kind of staging is that characters who do

7. See T. S. Graves, *The Court and the London Theatre during the Reign of Elizabeth* (Menasha, Wis., 1913), p. 51.

not participate in the action in one locality may nevertheless remain on-stage in their localities, as I suppose Leatherhead and Trash do through most of the second and third acts.[8] Since Jonson merely lists at the beginning of each scene the names of the speakers in that scene, there is often no indication of the presence of these inactive characters, and sometimes there is none even when a character has one speech to make during the scene, as is the case with Leatherhead in Act III, Scene 2.

In Act IV Leatherhead's booth, where so much of the previous action has taken place, is gone, the curtains around the front part of Ursula's booth have presumably been drawn after the retirement of Littlewit and his wife into the back, and the stocks on the other side of the stage come into prominence. Gifford, one of the editors who cared most about the staging of Jonson, divided the act into four scenes: 1, "Booths, stalls, a pair of stocks, etc."; 2, "Another part of the Fair" (where Quarlous and Winwife argue over Grace); 3, "Ursula's Booth, as before" (for the game of vapors); and 4, "The back of Ursula's Booth. Overdo in the stocks." Levin, who built and improved on Gifford's indications of locality, reduced the scenes to three: 1, "The stocks in the Fair," 2, "Between the stocks and Ursula's booth" (including both the episode of Grace and her lovers and the game of vapors), and 3, "The stocks." Both editors were obviously aware that the action of Jonson's Scene 3, ending with the departure of Quarlous and Edgworth from Winwife and Grace, is continuous with that of Scene 4, in which Quarlous and Edgworth arrive at Ursula's booth by way of its "backside." However, the various indications of change of place ("Another part of the Fair," etc.) imply a rather different sort of staging from that which I am describing. Though Levin's indications correspond to the shifts of the action from one focus of interest to another, they do not make it sufficiently clear that the places referred to are all visible at once, or that the action of his Scene 2 is not all, strictly speaking, "between the stocks and Ursula's booth," but partly in the neighborhood of the stocks and partly

8. Trash leaves at II.5.166 to get cream for Ursula's burned leg, but probably returns during II.6; Leatherhead may leave at the end of II.5 to help Ursula off the stage, returning during the following scene. He certainly leaves briefly at III.6.78, when he goes for the watch, but returns less than twenty lines later.

inside the booth, as his later stage direction shows. If one recognizes the nature of the setting, the problem of indicating locality for a scene vanishes; for the action flows from one part of the stage to another regardless of scene divisions—Jonson's or those of later editors.

The example of Act IV is telling. With the departure of Leatherhead and Trash at the end of Act III the stage has been cleared for the first time since the opening of Act II. Then the watch enter left, bringing Overdo to the stocks, and conversing with mad Trouble-all. At the end of the scene only Trouble-all is left, and in Scene 2 he is joined by Edgworth and Nightingale, who have come to play a prank on Cokes. When Cokes enters looking for Leatherhead and Trash (l.19), he is presumably stage right, where their "shops" were, but moves past Ursula's, where no activity can be seen, to Nightingale, who whistles to attract his attention. After the two tricksters have again gulled him, the stage is once more cleared momentarily before the arrival of Grace and her two lovers in Scene 3. No special locality is required for their discussion of who is to have Grace, but the stage direction, "*Trouble-all comes again*" suggests that he is returning to the locality he left a moment before, stage left; and when Edgworth, somewhat later, says that Wasp is with Knockem and others "yonder" (l.103), he is obviously pointing to Ursula's booth. The last line of the scene, referring to the "backside" of the booth, shows that he and Quarlous have by that time moved from near the stocks, where they must have been with Trouble-all, to the rear of Ursula's place. Scenes 4 and 5 are in her booth, beginning with the discovery of the game of vapors, already referred to several times. During the course of Scene 6 the action moves back once again to the stocks. The scene opens with Trouble-all reappearing. Knockem, drinking at Ursula's with Whit, asks him over. After they have persuaded him to have a drink, they leave him to join their ladies in the back part of the booth. Trouble-all apparently wanders out with his drink by one of the stage entrances just as Quarlous enters at another, looking for him. Quarlous is accompanied by Edgworth, who makes their locality onstage clear by saying, "Sir, will it please you enter in here at Urs'la's" (l.17). When Edgworth leaves him, Quarlous, after a few minutes of self-debate, sees some of the watch coming with Wasp. They are followed by more of the watch with Busy and Overdo, and most of the scene concerns their unsuccessful efforts to keep these worthies in the stocks. At the end of the act the stage is clear.

The action of the last act is all in or near the puppet booth. The chief problems about the staging are therefore the appearance and location of this booth, which has not been seen before. To begin with the most essential feature, there must be a puppet theater so situated that both the audience onstage and the audience in the auditorium can see Littlewit's "motion" of *Hero and Leander*. George Speaight, who arranged and performed the puppet play in the Old Vic's production of *Bartholomew Fair* in 1950, argues persuasively that the puppets were glove puppets,[9] in which case there must be a narrow booth, topped, at about the height of a man's shoulders by the stage where the puppets move on the hands of the manipulators as they sit on stools inside. That the booth is low is shown by Leatherhead's statement, "Troth, sir, our tiring-house is somewhat little . . . you cannot go upright in't" (V.3.56-57). There is probably a curtain over the stage, drawn just before Cokes, realizing the "motion" is to begin, says, "Peace, ho; now, now" (V.4.114). Leatherhead, the puppet master, stands in front of the booth, interprets, speaks for the puppets ("I am the mouth of 'em all" [V.3.74]), engages in slanging matches with them, and allows himself to be struck "over the pate." In fact, he does everything but the actual manipulation. But what might be referred to as Leatherhead's booth in this act is not strictly speaking the puppet booth, but a structure which contains the puppet booth; for no one is to see the motion who has not paid his fee; even the author is challenged by the overzealous doorkeeper. We are to imagine a considerable group of characters entering the door of the booth, sitting down, and watching the play which we also see. Hence, we must see outside and inside Leatherhead's booth at once. Outside there is some sort of banner and a sign—probably the bill which Cokes reads in Scene 3. Possibly the simplest way to satisfy these requirements would be to have posts, representing the front of the booth, set some distance in front of the puppet theater. Between the posts and the theater would be benches and chairs, "inside" the booth, though the walls would be purely imaginary.

Act V begins with the arrival of Leatherhead and his doorkeepers on a

9. *The History of the English Puppet Theatre* (New York, n.d.), p. 65.

stage just vacated by the watch and the other characters involved in the action at the stocks. It would be natural for Leatherhead to enter at the opposite side of the stage and to set up his puppet show near where he has his toy booth in the morning. Thus the action, which has been largely at stage left during Act IV, would return to the right. He tells his men to put out the sign and beat the drum, and instructs them about how much to charge. It would not be difficult for the three of them to bring the puppet booth in with them, set it up, and set up the posts on which a flag and playbill could be displayed. Again the action has a certain realism in its reflection of what actual operators of such booths did at Smithfield and elsewhere. By an odd coincidence the site of the Hope Theater was very near (if not identical with) the old Paris Gardens, where puppet shows had been "set up for comic relief . . . after bull- and bear-baiting was over," as far back as 1584, when such a show was described by the German Lupold von Wedel.[10]

Though Leatherhead and the doorkeepers are not heard from in Scene 2, when Quarlous, disguised as Trouble-all, obtains his warrant from Justice Overdo, the action of the scene must not be far from their booth, since the justice remains onstage after Quarlous, Purecraft, and the others have left, and sees Cokes looking at Leatherhead's sign at the opening of Scene 3. Scene 2 might well be played near Ursula's booth, where, as we later learn, Quarlous has been just prior to Scene 2. In Scene 3, while Justice Overdo stands by, Cokes is admitted to Leatherhead's booth and shown the puppets, which are brought out in a basket from behind the puppet stage. In Scene 4 Grace and Winwife return for the second time, also observed by the justice, and place themselves where they can see Cokes, though he does not see them. Since they are never challenged by the doorkeepers, they apparently do not "go in" and take seats, but remain just outside like Overdo. Knockem, Whit, Mistress Overdo, Mistress Littlewit, and Wasp are now given seats inside and soon the puppet play begins. It is not long until, one after another, all the remaining characters come to Leatherhead's booth. The last to arrive is a group headed by Trouble-all, carrying Ursula's pan, and hotly pursued by the pig-woman herself and Nightingale. Presumably they run out from the rear of Ursula's booth, where they

10. Speaight, p. 61.

have certainly been, and after circling around to the front of Leather-head's booth, run in amongst the others. Thus in the last act the puppet booth becomes what the "pig-box" earlier was—the chief locus of the action.

If *Bartholomew Fair* was staged in the manner I have described, it is one of the clearest examples of the survival in the Elizabethan public theater of the essentially medieval tradition of simultaneous staging,[11] and at the same time suggests something of the classical convention. While the "special decorum" of the Fair relates the spectacle to contemporary Smithfield, the booths recall the mansions of the old mysteries and, more dimly, the houses of Plautus and Terence. Only in the change from Littlewit's house to the Fair is the entire stage used to represent first one locality, then another. Thereafter all localities are simultaneously present and the action moves from one to another. Thus theatrical contrivance, accepted here with a frankness typical of the times, makes its own contribution to the dramatic experience by asserting the connection of Jonson's play with long-established forms of theatrical presentation to which the play gives new life and from which it derives an extension of significance.

11. Such a survival has been discussed by many scholars; see Chambers, *Elizabethan Stage*, *3*, 117; G. F. Reynolds, *The Staging of Elizabethan Plays at the Red Bull Theater 1605-1625* (New York, 1940), Chap. VII; Herford and Simpson, *10*, 170; Hodges, p. 65.

Selected Reading List

EDITIONS

Ben Jonson, ed. C. H. Herford and Percy and Evelyn Simpson, 11 vols., Oxford, 1925–52. The standard edition of Jonson's complete works. Volumes 1 and 2 contain a biography of Jonson and introductions to the plays. The text of *Bartholomew Fair* is in Volume 6 and the commentary in Volume 10.

Bartholomew Fair, ed. Carroll S. Alden, Yale Studies in English, 25, New York, 1904.

Bartholomew Fair, ed. E. A. Horsman, The Revels Plays, Cambridge, Mass., 1960.

CRITICISM

Barish, Jonas, *Ben Jonson and the Language of Prose Comedy* (Cambridge, Mass., 1960), pp. 187–239.

Enck, John J., *Jonson and the Comic Truth* (Madison, Wis., 1957), pp. 189–208.

Heffner, Ray L., Jr., "Unifying Symbols in the Comedy of Ben Jonson," in *Elizabethan Drama*, ed. Ralph J. Kaufmann (New York, 1961), pp. 170–86.

Levin, Harry, Introduction to *Ben Jonson, Selected Works*, New York, 1938.

Morley, Henry, *Memoirs of Bartholomew Fair*, London, 1857.

Townsend, Freda L., *Apologie for Bartholomew Fayre: The Art of Jonson's Comedies*, New York, 1947.

Index of Words Glossed

Index of Words Glossed

Index of Words Glossed

except at (vb.), II.v.52
exchange, I.ii.6–7
faction, Prol.4
fain, I.iv.74
fairing, Prol.12
fall in, I.iii.46
famelic, III.ii.77
fantastical, v.iii.4
fashioner, v.v.82
faucet, II.ii.46
feather-makers, v.v.75
feofee in trust, v.ii.63
ferret, II.iv.12
fidge, I.v.58
Field, v.iii.81
fine, II.v.164
fine and, III.iv.52
Finsbury, stake in, v.vi.92–3
fitted, II.i.3
flasket, III.vi.90
fleaing your breech, II.ii.66–7
flock, IV.iv.163
fly . . . to a mark, II.iv.44
for, I.iii.77
for and, III.v.70
fore-right, III.ii.27
fore-top, IV.v.45
form, IV.vi.33
found, IV.ii.98
foundering, II.iii.50
fox, II.vi.55
French-hood, I.v.14
fuller, v.iv.121
Galloway nag, IV.iv.4
Garnester, Pers.
garden-pot, II.ii.50
gathering, v.i.16
gear, II.v.75
gentlemen o' the ground, Ind.43–4

Gib-cat, I.iv.101
gilt, II.ii.31
glisters, I.iv.50
go, I.i.22
God be w' you, I.v.95
God you, I.iv.2
Godso, III.iv.107
Gomorrah, v.i.7–9
goodman, III.iv.105
goody, III.iv.92
goose-green, II.iv.14
gossips, I.i.36
governor, III.v.228
grass, II.iii.53
grease, in, IV.v.68
green gowns, IV.v.34
grounded judgments, Ind.50–1
guarded, II.v.47
Gunpowder Plot, v.i.11
hair o' the same wolf, I.iii.14
half a crown, Ind.80
hand, at any, I.iv.112
handkercher, III.v.169
handle your matters, II.ii.120
handsel, II.ii.132
handy-dandy, III.v.109
hare o' the tabor, v.iv.87
harm watch, harm catch, v.iv.162
Hayes, Sir Thomas, II.i.11–2
heavy hill, II.iii.5
hedge-bird, II.v.111
high places, I.vi.52–3
hinnyeth, v.v.57–8
hobbyhorse is forgotten, v.iv.201
hobbyhorse-seller, Pers.
hogrubber, v.iv.160
hole in the nose, II.vi.44
'hone and 'honero, v.iv.251
hood, I.ii.25

Index of Words Glossed

mallanders, II.v.166-7

malmsey, I.ii.64

malt-horse, II.vi.100

man with the beard, IV.iv.175

mansion, II.v.39

mark, I.iv.21

mar'l, III.v.165

marrow-bone man, I.iii.5

Marry Gip, I.v.14

mart, II.iv.20

maryhinchco, III.ii.57

masque, III.iv.85

massacre, II.vi.138

meditant, Ind.110-2

meet, II.iii.17

melicotton, I.ii.15

merchant, III.vi.126

Mercury, IV.iii.98

meridian, Ind.50

Mermaid, I.i.30

mess, III.v.25

metheglin, IV.vi.46

Michaelmas Term, III.iv.23

Mirror of Magistrates, Ind.126-7

mistaking words, Ind.39

Mistress o' the game, Pers.

Mitre, I.i.30

moderates, I.iii.86

moiety, IV.vi.19

monsters, III.i.11

monuments, master of, V.iii.2

Mooncalf, Pers.

Moorfields, I.ii.6

morrises, I.iii.114

mother, I.v.154

motion, I.vi.14, III.iv.124

——, seditious, I.iii.128

motion-man, I.v.136

multiply you, IV.i.14-5

mum-chance, IV.ii.68-9

muss, IV.ii.29

mustard, I.i.31

nativity-water, I.ii.42

Nebuchadnezzar, III.vi.54

neigheth, V.v.57-8

nephew, II.ii.115

nest, Ind.114

night-tub, IV.v.76

Nineveh, V.i.7-9

noise, III.iv.83

Norwich, V.i.7-9

off, II.v.44

offer at, III.ii.135

on, I.iv.73,IV.i.49

ostler, V.iii.97

overbuy, I.v.74

overparted, III.iv.48

Ovid, *Metamorphoses*, II.iv.66

Paggington's Pound, III.v.54

painful, I.ii.61

—— brethren, I.ii.61

pannier-man, II.v.111,III.iv.64

Pannyer Alley, I.iii.63

parcel-poet, II.ii.15

particular wrong, Prol.8

partizan, II.v.97

party-colored brotherhood, V.i.49

passengers, Pers.

passionate, II.iv.58

patch, II.v.103

patent, IV.ii.60

patience, I.iii.81

patrico, II.vi.136

Paul's, I.i.11

peck, II.vi.89

peel, III.ii.46

pen'orth, Ind.79

perpetuity, I.iii.63

Index of Words Glossed

Index of Words Glossed

wires, IV.v.33
with, V.iii.118
without, IV.vi.85
word, IV.i.98

worship, II.ii.108
wrestle . . . mayor, IV.iii.105–6
wrought, III.i.35
zuds, i' the, IV.iv.10

CPSIA information can be obtained
at www.ICGtesting.com
Printed in the USA
LVHW031437150119
604013LV00001B/26/P